Why Lenin? Why Stalin? Why Gorbachev?

CRITICAL PERIODS OF HISTORY

Robert D. Cross and Paul K. Conkin, GENERAL EDITORS

WHY LENIN? WHY STALIN? WHY GORBACHEV? *The Rise and Fall of the Soviet System, Third Edition*
BY THEODORE H. VON LAUE

THE LONG FUSE *An Interpretation of the Origins of World War I*
BY LAURENCE LAFORE

CRITICAL PERIODS OF HISTORY

Why Lenin?
Why Stalin?
Why Gorbachev?

The Rise and Fall of the Soviet System

Third Edition

Theodore H. Von Laue

Jacob and Frances Hiatt Professor of History Emeritus
Clark University

HarperCollins*CollegePublishers*

Executive Editor: Bruce Borland
Project Editor: Shuli Traub
Design Supervisor/Cover Design: Stacey Agin
Cover Photos: The Bettmann Archive; UPI/Bettmann Newsphotos
Photo Research: Leslie Coopersmith
Production Manager/Assistant: Willie Lane/Sunaina Sehwani
Compositor: Ruttle Graphics, Inc.
Printer and Binder: R. R. Donnelley & Sons Company
Cover Printer: The Lehigh Press, Inc.

Why Lenin? Why Stalin? Why Gorbachev? The Rise and Fall of the Soviet System,
Third Edition

Library of Congress Cataloging-in-Publication Data

Von Laue, Theodore H. (Theodore Hermann)
    Why Lenin? Why Stalin? Why Gorbachev? : the rise and fall of the
Soviet system / Theodore H. Von Laue.—3rd ed.
        p. cm.—(Critical periods of history)
    Rev. ed. of: Why Lenin? Why Stalin? 2nd ed. c1971.
    Includes bibliographical references and index.
    ISBN 0–06–501111–2
    1. Soviet Union—History—20th century. 2. Soviet Union—Politics
and government—1985–1991. I. Von Laue, Theodore H. (Theodore
Hermann). Why Lenin? Why Stalin?. II. Title.
DK246.V58 1993
947.084–dc20

                                                    92–15870
                                                        CIP

97 98 99 9 8 7 6 5 4

To my former students at the University of California, Riverside, at Washington University, St. Louis, Missouri, and at Clark University, Worcester, Massachusetts

C O N T E N T S

Preface to the First Edition

We exist and survive by making judgments. In the big issues that shape the fates of men and nations our judgments are based on simplifications and generalizations, on "images." The present world of baffling complexities therefore demands the reduction of mazes that only experts can follow—and even they imperfectly—to simple patterns comprehensible to ordinary men and women. All people, particularly in a democracy, deal with and judge these issues, one way or the other. The choice before us then is not of simplicity or complexity but of good or bad, penetrating or misleading simplification. Generalizations guide public opinion, public opinion influences and sometimes determines government policy, and government policy holds the fatal trigger of war and peace, particularly when the subject is Russia and communism. Let our generalizations, therefore, be knowledgeable and just.

This essay offers a novel explanation of the rise of Lenin and Stalin. It attempts to view the emergence of Russian communism as an integral part of European and global history, treating it, as it should have been from the start, as a problem of comparative studies, not as an isolated phenomenon to be explained largely from Russian conditions alone. Its bent of argument thus runs counter to the tendency of some cultural anthropologists and their followers in sociology and political science to derive the causes of modern Russian development chiefly, if not exclusively, from internal factors. Without denying the importance of the latter this essay stresses the primacy of the external conditions, of the pressure of global power politics. Russia's leaders before and after 1917, so this story runs, tried to reshape Russian state and society—and human nature to boot—in order to make their country respected in a world where power, and power in many disguises, was trump.

This treatise, however, does not aim at a miniature likeness of modern Russian history (whatever, viewed objectively, that likeness is). It presents an image drawn in the manner of a sketch. A sketch, our experience of modern art shows, is a debatable vision of reality. Yet to the artist it accentuates just those features that are crucial. So with this essay of macrohistory: It is a summary search for the best way of looking at a chain of momentous events in twentieth-century history. It wishes, by a few strokes of analysis, to set the proper perspectives, indicate the chief characteristics, and, above all, establish a sense of proportion that must guide us if we want to judge this all-important subject responsibly. The task requires that while we sketch the Russians we also scan ourselves. Portraying them we must, in one of the profiles of the subject, draw our own likeness to the same scale.

Sketching the Russian revolution is bound to be a controversial enterprise. Russian and Soviet studies are set, in the minds of most experts, into an unexamined and hidden net of basic assumptions about the course of modern Russian history. These assumptions are apt to be charged—and surcharged—with the tensions of past and current politics. The subject is alive with subtle furies; few Western students (the author included) have remained immune to their siren call. Yet whatever the risks of disputation, the hidden assumptions must be brought into the open and tested by rational analysis. We easily spot the Marxist-Leninist doctrines underlying Soviet historiography, but we are purblind to the convictions on which we mount our own individual inquiries into Russian and Soviet affairs. Let this elusive background be examined; and let it be brought up to date with the help of the knowledge we have gained about the dilemmas of the underdeveloped countries.

THEODORE H. VON LAUE

Preface to the Third Edition

The previous editions of this book have been published when the Soviet system was at its height. Now, in the wake of Gorbachev's reforms, the Soviet system has crumbled; new miseries harrass the diverse peoples in the vast spaces of Eurasia. The perennial crisis of state building and modernization in that part of the world has taken yet another tragic turn. Preparing for the twenty-first century, we need to take a careful look at the immense problems confronting the peoples of what once was the largest state in the world, the now-defunct other superpower.

This edition offers an analysis of the Soviet experiment, one of the most harrowing phenomena of the twentieth century, viewing that extraordinary historical phenomenon with an awareness of its eventual collapse. This updated account is addressed to Americans (and Western observers generally) concerned with contemporary affairs. In our tightly interdependent world we need to look more attentively than ever into the political and cultural dynamics at work beneath the surface of the daily news or even our prevailing insights. Our high ideals of human dignity can be realized only if we understand the realities within which we must work.

Such liberating understanding must proceed from a comparative perspective. We cannot judge by American standards (evolved under uniquely favorable conditions) a country that from its historical beginnings has had to cope with extraordinary hardships. Only if we comprehend the full range of differences can we help to promote in the Russian-Eurasian setting the premises for a more humane society. For this reason the emphasis here rests on basic perspectives and constructive reflection rather then on historical detail, with due attention to the character of the people, the human raw material shaping state and society.

Inevitably, the following pages offer a personal interpretation by a detached but compassionate outsider. Analyzing the painful history of twentieth-century Eurasia remains a challenging intellectual task. Taking many shortcuts, this essay concentrates on the political dynamics shaping the course of events in that distant part of the world. It does not offer the ultimate truth; it merely wishes to stimulate discussion by broadening perspectives and refining human sensibilities. Thus guided, readers will have to extend the story here outlined to the end of 1991 into their own time frames. History moves from the past into the future, from the historians to their readers, who must update the story to the ever advancing present.

Acknowledgments

Credit should go first to my son-in-law John Bernard for his suggestion, in September 1990, that the changes in the Soviet Union called for an updated version; and to Bruce Borland of the HarperCollins College Division for readily giving his approval. The new chapters added to the revised and shortened earlier edition have greatly benefited from the comments submitted by Samuel Baron of the University of North Carolina, Chapel Hill; John Bushnell and David Joravsky of Northwestern University; Max Okenfuss of Washington University in St. Louis, Missouri; and Alexander Fursenko, Director of the Institute of History, St. Petersburg, Russia. The new edition as a whole is indebted, in more respects than words can express, to the labors of my wife Angela. Finally, thanks are due also to Lauren Harp, formerly editorial assistant at HarperCollins, for all her work in preparing the manuscript for publication.

THEODORE H. VON LAUE

In praise of Crises we might first say that passion is the mother of great things, real passion that is, bent on something new and not merely the overthrow of the old. Unsuspected forces awaken in individuals and even heaven takes on a different hue. Whoever has got something to him can make himself felt because the barriers have been or are being trampled down.

—Jacob Burckhardt,
Weltgeschichtliche Betrachtungen

INTRODUCTION

More than 75 years have passed since November 1917, when the Bolsheviks overthrew the Provisional Government (which the previous March had supplanted the tsar and his ministers) and declared themselves masters of a new, a Soviet Russia. Their coup was hardly taken seriously by the crowd on the boulevards of Petrograd or by the newspaper readers, editorialists,* or even statesmen in the capitals of the West, all preoccupied with fighting Germany and Austria-Hungary in World War I. Yet the Bolshevik seizure of power has turned into one of the landmarks of the twentieth century. Starting as a revolutionary regime desperately clinging to power, Soviet Russia grew for a time into a political colossus matched only by the United States, before its economic decline, accelerated by Gorbachev's reforms, set off its unexpected descent from a superpower to an international charity case. Our understanding has hardly been able to keep up with the rise and fall of that revolutionary regime started in 1917.

The history of Bolshevik power covers a critical period in modern history. Its significance must be assessed in the largest context, the context that Lenin, the leader of the Bolsheviks, adopted for his justification: world revolution. He envisaged a vast struggle for changing the global balance of power in favor of the poor and exploited masses. Within this framework this essay runs from the turn of the present century to its final decade. It deals with the history of Soviet totalitarianism, devoting its major section to analyzing the historical circumstances creating that system. The insights thus gained help us understand also its collapse, as outlined in the concluding chapters.

The story begins at the turn of the present century, when the world was relatively at peace. It carries the narrative to the first Five Year Plan, the Great Depression, fascism and national socialism, Hitler and Stalin. These 30-odd years revealed in their unprecedented violence the first corollaries of the new globalism of human affairs. Mass politics, an

---

* On November 10, 1917, *The New York Times* observed editorially that the Bolsheviks were "pathetically ignorant and shallow men, political children without the slightest understanding of the vast forces they are playing with, men without a single qualification for prominence but the gift of gab, and if they could be left alone long enough their mere incompetence would destroy them. . . ."

ever-faster tempo of technological change, and the intense interaction between Westerners and non-Westerners, "developed" and "underdeveloped," combined to produce a more explosive instability than had ever arisen in the past millennia of human existence. The Bolshevik Revolution was one of the blast furnaces of terrifying transformation suddenly sprung on the world, and foremost on the unprepared peoples in the vast spaces of Eurasia between eastern Europe and the Sea of Okhotsk.

The ordeal of building a modern state under highly adverse conditions revolved around two parallel long-range trends. First, the anger accumulated over many decades in the past overthrew, in a revolution from below, the tsarist autocracy and its privileged supporters. In this respect the Russian Revolution resembled, however vaguely, the French Revolution; propelled by domestic discontent it aimed at some form of democratic government. Yet that revolution was quickly overtaken by an altogether different one: The revolution of forcible reculturation carried out from above by a small minority, the Communist party, determined to revive the collapsed Russian empire in a superior form. Both society and government had to undergo a drastic process of catching up to the social, economic, and political efficiency of Russia's more powerful rivals, the victors in World War I and ever more prominently the United States. It was a revolution essentially enforced from without, by the relentless pressures of power politics generated by the universal ambition for political survival and global preeminence.

Seen in this larger context, the much dramatized "classic" events of the Russian Revolution and civil war were but surface phenomena. Disguised by Marxist-Leninist ideology, traditional Russian ambition compelled a reorganization of state and society matching the fast progress of Western culture. For that purpose native spontaneity and tradition had to be pressed into a new mold, copying the Western sources of strength by the un-Western method of compulsion. What in Western society was achieved by the hidden discipline of voluntary cooperation had to be matched by the compulsory discipline enforced by the Communist party.

This revolutionary transformation of state and society was set into a revolutionary change in international relations. During the climactic battles of World War I the United States, the decisive contributor to the Allied victory, proclaimed its aim to make the world safe for democracy (its own form of government). In response, Lenin, the heir of the tsarist ambition to be counted in the world, established an emotional and political link between Russia and the backward peoples trying to escape colonial domination. Designing a new order for his own country, he also wanted to introduce a morally and politically superior world order. War-ring against the inferiority of their own country, the Bolsheviks pro-claimed themselves leaders in the mounting anti-Western revolt, adopting at a shriller pitch the messianic presumption of universality so characteristic of the West's own elites. For many decades their message deeply impressed anti-Western intellectuals in Asia, Africa, and Latin America, who wanted to liberate their peoples from humiliating depen-dence on the all-powerful West. Under Lenin's inspiration Soviet Rus-sia, the weakest among the Western Great Powers, became the strongest among the underdeveloped countries. It bridged the gap between the First World and the Third.

Yet even while rebuilding under Stalin's direction their country's strength after its disastrous defeat in World War I, the Communists failed to resolve their most crucial problem: how to infuse the creativity of Western urban-industrial civilization, evolved under highly favorable geographic and historical circumstances, into habits and institutions shaped by relentless adversity.

That failure has now discredited Soviet communism at home and abroad, while enhancing the prestige of Western institutions and ways of life, which have grown into the model of what Gorbachev has called "historical progress." The ideals of freedom and democracy have inspired a new revolution from below. The people—and especially the younger generations—in the major cities of Russia, together with the non-Russian nationalities of the former Soviet Union, have successfully rebelled against the Communist dictatorship. The Soviet system and Gorbachev's vain efforts to reform it have collapsed. But the old prob-lems remain: The civic discipline subliminally hidden in these ideals is not automatically transferred from Western society to the Eurasian vast-ness. Where political and economic unity has been traditionally imposed by force, it cannot be readily replaced, in the face of profound geograph-ical and historical obstacles, by voluntary cooperation. The unresolved challenge of state-building in divided Eurasia tragically continues in a new form.

Thus, roughly, run the arguments of this essay. They prescribe that throughout we view the political history of Russian Eurasia in its global context, beginning our story with the state of the world in the decades before World War I.

The Setting: The West and the World

I

The most conspicuous fact about the global world at the turn of the century was the unquestioned supremacy of Europe, specifically western Europe and, within that select company, Great Britain. The United States also loomed increasingly large in what came to be considered "the West," and for the same reasons that had given Britain its head start, although it did not yet occupy the dominant position which it inherited after World War II. The Western powers jointly were the overlords of the globe.

The early years of the twentieth century marked the climax of a long process of Western expansion. By 1914 all (or practically all) parts of the non-Western world had fallen under the sway of the West. Only the American hemisphere, Westernized earlier than the other continents, was off-limits, except for the restless ambition of the United States. The rest of the non-Western world was fair game. Africa, except for Abyssinia, was carved up. Asia was taken over through outright occupation, the allocation of spheres of influences, or, more indirectly, through the subversion of native authority. In China, for instance, the Manchu dynasty was overthrown by Westernized Chinese because it had not been able to prevent the despoliation of the country by the foreigners. Considerable portions of territory had already been severed from the Chinese Empire, and its sovereignty over what was left was severely limited. Southeast Asia had long been ruled more directly by the French, the Dutch, the Spaniards; in 1898 the Americans took the Philippine islands away from Spain. The English were the masters of India. In Persia, England and Russia vied for ascendancy. In 1907, they divided the country into three parts, Russia taking the north and England the south. In the center, left to the Persians themselves, an American expert, W. Morgan Shuster, vainly tried to reconstruct Persian finance and administration on a Western basis. The Ottoman Empire, long in receivership to its European creditors, survived because its existence was a political convenience to the Great Powers, yet it could not prevent sizable losses of its territory. It lingered on the brink of collapse even after the infusion of new energy by the Young Turk Revolution of 1908. Pacific Oceania, petty spoils indeed, likewise slipped under European or American occupation. The only significant non-Western country capable of resisting subjection was Japan. In 1899 its government succeeded in repealing most privileges of the foreigners that had been imposed earlier; in 1905 it defeated the Russian Empire; and in 1911 it regained full control over its foreign trade. Yet Japan, a unique case, rose to its prominence only because its ruling classes voluntarily undertook Westernization and did so under exceptionally favorable circumstances, such as the great distance from Europe, insularity, smallness, and the persistence of traditional social controls despite the rapid change.

What gave that final spurt of imperialist expansion its frantic character was the intensified competition among the European powers themselves. Their rivalry, held at bay within Europe by the balance of power, was carried into the open territories beyond; the European framework of power politics was being widened out into a global one. The new tools of technology and science and the wealth of the industrial age stimulated the political appetite and thus increased the pressure of power politics to an intensity unheard of in human history. "The future lies with the great empires," so a British statesman proclaimed, and the fear of falling behind haunted men of affairs in even the mightiest countries. The position of the weaker members of the Great Power elite—of Austria-Hungary, Italy, or Russia, for instance—suffered as their governments were threatened with bankruptcy because of their armaments or bold political ventures, or with military and political defeat because of their poverty. The lesser states—Holland, Sweden, and Spain—largely standing outside the competition under the protection of the European equilibrium, counted even less. There began, in short, the brutal recasting of the traditional power structure in Europe and the world which led, within half a century, to the emergence of the "superpowers" in a category above the Great Powers. Needless to say, in this intensified rivalry the price of sovereignty soared ever higher. The demands on the resources of a country that was determined—or compelled—to compete became ever more exorbitant.

Yet more was involved in the expansion of the West than political dominion. Having cleared the way through their superior power, the Europeans—and increasingly Americans as well—poured into the non-Western world the very essence of their civilization. There arrived among the natives conquerors, adventurers, businessmen, missionaries, scholars, administrators, rebels, saints; every kind of character and skill. With them also came machines, money, and technical know-how. At the great crossroads, in Singapore, Hong Kong, Calcutta, Bombay, Cairo, or Johannesburg, the Westerners created their own metropoles, outposts carefully segregated yet dispersing men, methods, and standards like so many seeds into their respective hinterlands.

This outpouring of Western manpower and accomplishments was as elemental and irreversible as the force of gravity. Destiny obviously was on its side. Every white man abroad felt like a missionary civilizing the world—in terms of his own parochial values, to be sure. But even if the Westerners were only writing with chalk on granite, as Kipling put it, they were convinced, with a certitude bordering on arrogance, that they alone had the right for such inscription.

In those days the white man's presumption seemed indeed impregnable. He possessed the weapons, the organization, the ingenuity necessary to make his rule stick. Even his machines exerted authority. They ordered people's lives in a new way and thereby undermined established custom. What excited the native population most deeply, of course, were the technical and organizational instruments of power. It could not so easily perceive the vastly more important but largely invisible wrappings of Western attitudes and habits in which the machines were delivered—and which remained indispensable for their continued efficient operation.

To the more sophisticated native leadership, however, the ascendancy of the West was made manifest not only in the blunt form of superior machines or economic penetration, but in the more insidious form of a universal model. This form of power, the least noticed among the power tools of the imperialists yet the most potent of all, acted as a constant silent subversion. It hollowed out the prestige of native authority and custom and undermined the attachment of a people to their traditions and their government. Never in all history has there been such a vast subversive power as that of the West. By comparison—and invidious comparison became an instinctive reaction of minds constantly confronted with novelty—Western ways stood out as superior not only because of the persuasion of guns but also because they were more "civilized" than, say, the practice of suttee, child marriage, slavery, bound feet, and a host of other nativisms. Almost anything the white man did, down to his passing whims, was imitated, sometimes merely because it was his way. Certain big concepts, such as democracy and freedom, wore such a halo of prestige that they came to serve as key slogans in countries that perverted their meaning into its very opposite. In this vast outpouring one looks in vain among the run of the Westerners for the saving grace of humility or respect for native ways. They were not devoid of kindness—their own variety of kindness—but for the most part they were oblivious to the suffering caused by their impact. They had deprived the indigenous people of their cultural sovereignty, leaving them profoundly disoriented, mentally and spiritually.

II

The replacement of native values by Western ones was sometimes a result of close and frequently profitable association of native leaders with their European masters. An Indian nationalist, Surendranath Banerjea, writing in 1895, has well described the descent of English attitudes into native society:

> We should be unworthy of ourselves and our preceptors . . . if with our souls stirred to their inmost depths, our warm Oriental sensibilities roused to an unwanted pitch of enthusiasm by the contemplation of these great ideals of public duty, we did not seek to transplant into our country the spirit of these free institutions which have made England what she is. . . . Never in the history of the world have the inheritors of an ancient civilization been so profoundly influenced by the influx of modern ideas. . . .

There could hardly have been a better vindication of Macaulay, who had wanted to make the Indians English "in taste, in opinions, in morals, and in intellect."

More often, perhaps, such transfer of values resulted from the embittered realization that continued adherence to one's native ways led to humiliation by the foreigner. As a Chinese intellectual, Liang Qichao, phrased his reaction in 1902:

> If we wish to make our nation strong, we must investigate extensively the methods followed by other nations and races in becoming independent. . . . Selecting their superior points, we can appropriate them to make up our own shortcomings. . . .

In 1915, when the position of China had further deteriorated, another writer, Chen Duxiu, made the same point with greater urgency:

> Considered in the light of the evolution of human affairs, it is plain that those races that cling to antiquated ways are declining or disappearing day by day, and the peoples who seek progress and advancement are just beginning to ascend in power and strength. It is possible to predict which of these will survive and which will not. Now our country still has not awakened from its long dream and isolates itself by going down the old rut. . . . Revering only the history of the twenty-four dynasties and making no plans for progress and improvement, our people will be turned out of this twentieth century world and be lodged in the dark ditches fit only for slaves, cattle, and horses. . . . I would much rather see the past culture of our nation disappear than see our race die out now because of its unfitness for living in the modern world.

And so this writer turned to "Mr. Science and Mr. Democracy" to cure "the dark maladies" of Chinese life.

The reluctant conclusion among Asian intellectuals—the awakening of Africa in these terms occurred only a generation later—was that the conditions of progress and improvement were those of the West. Westernization was the price of survival.

Yet was there not a flaw in the argument? If one wanted to follow the Western model, should one not strive above all to imitate the white man's pride in his own native accomplishments, his belief in himself and his traditions? The Europeans did not imitate. They stood out as paragons of cultural and spiritual independence, of an uninterrupted, autochthonous development. Should Westernization then not mean the affirmation of native tradition? A Young Turk spokesman, Ahmed Riza Bey, writing from Paris in 1895, made that point very clear:

> We wish to advance in the path of civilization, but we declare resolutely that we do not wish to advance otherwise than in fortifying the Ottoman element and respecting its own conditions of existence. We are determined to guard the originality of our oriental civilization.

In India the same pride in native civilization made other men turn against the British influence; as Brahmabandhab Upadhyay wrote in 1899:

> With the spread of English rule India has lost her own ideal of civilization. Our educated classes think as they have been taught by the Firinghi [foreign] masters. Our minds have been conquered. We have become slaves. The faith in our own culture and the love for things Indian are gone. India will reach Swaraj [self-government] the day she will again have faith in herself.

In the mind of Vivekananda, one of Brahmabandhab's contemporaries and a leading figure in the Hindu revival, that faith was already burning bright:

> This is the great ideal before us and everyone must be ready for it—
> the conquest of the whole world by India—nothing less than that, and
> we must all get ready for it, strain every nerve for it. Let foreigners
> come and flood the land with their armies, never mind. Up, India, and
> conquer the world with your spirituality.

The weapon of spirituality was India's own—there were no others—and
spiritual superiority, of course, was the most superior of all.

Yet obviously spirituality alone could not create a modern India. Disillusionment eventually overtook every native leader who tried to convert
any aspect of his country's endowment of backwardness into a creed for
the future. Gandhi was succeeded by Nehru, the struggle for independence by the responsibilities of statehood. The pressure for Westernization was inexorable. This, however, did not prevent constant rearguard
action on behalf of other, seemingly more tenable redoubts of native tradition in dress, art, or language. The Western model of autochthonous
development (and the normal human preference for it) continues to exert
a powerful influence to this day.

While the ideological defense of nativism proved difficult (if not
impossible), the chances were better for plain political assertion. If the
Western model proved anything, it was the glory of political independence and greatness. The Western states enjoyed cultural preeminence
only because they were so powerful. Native originality likewise must be
protected by power. An Indian moderate, G. K. Gokhale, writing the
statutes of the newly founded Servants of Indian Society in 1905, has
well expressed the force of that ambition among his countrymen:

> The idea of a united and renovated India, marching onwards to a place
> among the nations of the world, worthy of her past, is no longer a mere
> idle dream of a few imaginative minds, but is the definitely accepted
> creed of those who form the brain of the community. . . .

Power, Napoleon once observed, is never ridiculous. It covers up
many embarrassments. As native intellectuals became more sensitive to
the incessant humiliations that accompanied backwardness, they began
to appreciate the uses of power. The search for self-assertion, for native
strength (on whatever ideological foundation), was thus a natural corollary of European penetration, whether through admiration or resentment
of the example.

The beginnings of an anti-Western revolt throughout the world were
dimly visible before 1914. They grew from the Westernized native intelligentsia that had been apprenticed in Europe, the United States, or in
the Western schools of their own countries. Sun Yat-sen in China;

Gokhale and Tilak, Ghose and Gandhi in India; and the Young Turks in the Ottoman Empire established a nucleus of native ambition. The Chinese Republic in 1911 and the Guomindang were a first practical manifestation. In India, the Morley-Minto reforms of 1909 were designed to meet the nascent Indian nationalism by giving it a share, however minimal, in the government of the country. Four years later in Egypt—the origins of the revolt are visible in many places—the rising opposition forced the British protectorate to alter the organic law in favor of native representation. While in India the reception of the reforms was favorable for the time being, the first meeting of the new Egyptian legislative assembly resulted in an anti-British riot.

At the time, these events appeared as mere straws in the cross-draft of trends. Only an obscure Russian revolutionary, searching for allies wherever they might be found, was able to perceive the beginnings of the countertide beneath the continuing triumphant outpouring of Western influence. Writing in 1913, Lenin found "the European spirit" rising in Asia. Asia was awakening and contributing to the global revolutionary movement, which heralded a new era of world history. Europe was becoming backward, he wrote, and Asia progressive. In the future, he predicted, the Westernized proletariat and the rising masses of young Asia would combine forces. But how this might be done and how, in general, the Westernized leaders might weld the European tradition to their native heritage, he did not reveal. Maybe the subversion by the Western model would continue even while the anti-Western revolt ran its course.

The opportunity for native assertion, to be sure, did not necessarily arise from the strength of native power alone. It might even more successfully derive from the weakness of Europe. How strong then was the West, especially Europe, at the culmination of its historical career, how capable of coping with the novel challenge of its supremacy?

III

The internal progress of Western Europe and North America demonstrated and justified the West's global preeminence. Western society was an "open society" where those with ability could rise to a commensurate social and economic position. Thanks furthermore to an unprecedented volume of economic productivity (based largely on private enterprise), even the lowliest were improving their condition. The bulk of the population grew prosperous with material goods and physical comforts beyond all expectations of earlier ages. In this benevolent setting the spiritual values inherent in the Judeo-Christian tradition raised people to a higher level of civility and respect for human life than prevailed elsewhere in the world. The advanced standard of living, moreover, made possible a system of government in which every adult male citizen could cast a vote and influence the course of politics.

Whatever the imperfections, it is fair to say that never before in human history had the relationship between the rulers and the ruled been so close and individual freedom so well meshed with governmental authority as under the new institutions of political democracy then being promoted on both sides of the Atlantic. It is important to remember, however, that political liberty is based on a deep-seated individual and collective discipline of voluntary civic cooperation not found in other societies.

The crowning triumph in England, France, the United States, and even Germany up to a point was the combination of political freedom for the citizen under constitutional government with power for the state in the emerging global state system. The amazing ascendancy of these countries, both in terms of power and cultural radiation, was largely the result of the spontaneous enterprise of individuals, not of their governments. In the case of England, which then served as the universal model, it had come about, one writer teased, in "a fit of absentmindedness," as a result of circumstance, not of deliberate effort. Lightly indeed did these countries carry their burden of global power!

Yet despite these tremendous accomplishments that set them above the rest of the world, all was not well in the major states of Europe. Before the outbreak of World War I the advent of "mass politics" caused by the extension of the suffrage tremendously complicated the tasks of government. On the one hand, the demands made on the state were constantly increased. The common voter wanted to better his share of the good life by political means if he could not do so by any other. On the other hand, the ability of the state to provide these services was limited, above all because its citizens could not agree among themselves as to what they desired most. Mass participation in politics threw into bold relief all the existing varieties of regional and social outlook within a country. It even seemed as if, under the tensions of modern life, these differences multiplied and deepened.

On the surface it would appear that parliamentary debate offered the best process of mutual accommodation. Yet parliamentary procedure could operate only under certain conditions. It presupposed a deep-seated, almost instinctive willingness to make it work in all kinds of political weather. Here exactly lay the rub. In states without a long-standing parliamentary tradition and a common past, such willingness did not exist. And while most people in Europe attained universal suffrage before 1914, obviously not all of them knew how to make the best of it.

The most disturbing feature of European mass politics was the undercurrent of dissatisfaction with the most signal accomplishments of contemporary civilization. It was expressed, although moderately, by the socialists, who pointed to the many discrepancies between the steady progress in technology and the material well-being of the ruling class on the one hand and the continuous deprivation of the masses on the other. Poverty, unemployment, disease, denials of human dignity, militarism, inequality, and exploitation still haunted even the most civilized countries. The ideals of liberty, equality, and fraternity were being only imperfectly realized (even though the peoples of Western and Central Europe at least enjoyed more of them than any others). The responsibility for this, according to the socialists, lay with the entire system, with "capitalism."

Most commonly their attack stayed within the mainstream of Western tradition; their socialism was a liberalism carried to its logical—or utopian—conclusion. Yet there was also an extremist, pessimist undercurrent, voiced most clearly perhaps by the French syndicalist Georges Sorel. He found fault not only with the "bourgeoisie" but with the very premises of contemporary thought and life, its trust in democracy and science and its confidence in uninterrupted progress. To him, modern life had lost its savor; it was moving toward degeneracy. The escape, for him, lay in a reaffirmation of—violence:

> Two accidents alone . . . would be able to stop this movement, a great foreign war which might renew lost energies and which, in any case, would doubtless bring into power men with the will to govern; or a great extension of proletarian violence, which would make the revolutionary reality evident to the middle class and would disgust them with their humanitarian platitudes. . . .

A more resounding repudiation of Western humanitarianism and of the rationalism that stood at its core could hardly have been imagined.

What provided a common bond between the different voices of revolt was a vague conviction that life had jumped too rapidly from a slow, loosely meshed, and heroic style of life into the tight and "artificial" social discipline of industrialism and the shallow compromises of parliamentary politics. The "inner man" had been left far behind. The revolt of the irrational was strongest, therefore, where the rate of change had been most precipitous, in the newly industrialized areas and along their peripheries in central, southern, and eastern Europe. Who could foretell the effects of that violence-prone intellectual ferment on domestic politics and international relations in case of a major war?

IV

The relations between the European states gave cause for alarm on grounds of their own. Europe before 1914 has often been likened to a military camp. Each of the major powers was armed to the limits of its capacity (and sometimes beyond); none trusted the others. All talked of the likelihood of war and prepared accordingly. What gave their preparations their modern, limitless character was the fact that the entire population became involved, not only in body but in mind as well; all major decisions of the government now tended to be ratified, formally or informally, by public opinion. As a result, the quality of foreign policy deteriorated. All too frequently its issues were reduced to the lowest level of popular comprehension, thrown open to the prejudices of people too hard-pressed by their daily cares to take an intelligent and continuous interest in foreign affairs, and saturated with the mounting domestic tensions. Internal maladjustments thus spilled over into international relations, to the detriment of the common European heritage.

The period of rising democracy was also the period of rising imperialism. The new mass electorates were instructed in the fundamentals of foreign policy not by the diplomats with their limited objectives but by visionary politicians who preached that the future belonged to the great empires and that only territorial sway, *Lebensraum*, guaranteed the survival of the race in history. Thus were planted the dark, irrational drives in modern international relations which threatened to rip apart the traditional order of Europe and the world at large, stopping at nothing. The age of global ambitions and of apocalyptic ideologies had begun.

It was a frightening paradox that the disintegration of the common European outlook inherited from the past should have occurred at a time when, in fact, the interdependence of Europe attained unprecedented proportions. Their exports and imports, their credit structure, their transportation and communication, their scientific discoveries—all tied them ever more closely together, so closely indeed that, if human action had been prompted by economic and material factors alone, war would have become impossible. The discrepancy between the political and psychological mobilization for war on the one hand and the deepening interdependence on the other—the discrepancy between war and industrial society in general—did not escape attention at the time. Pacifism was a lively cause, and schemes for world peace under one world government were not wanting, particularly among socialist intellectuals who, for other reasons as well, had their doubts about the validity of the existing order.

V

This sketch of Europe on the eve of World War I admittedly differs from any contemporary self-portrait. Hindsight has put the pockmarks of later torments into a face still flushed with success. Never before (or since) had Europe been so satisfied, so powerful, so self-assured. Yet it would be a mistake to assume that World War I suddenly descended on an innocent Europe and drained away its marrow. Violence and destruction were already in its bones; they transformed the traditional power conflict and the domestic crises into a universal catastrophe that marked the end of an epoch. Distanced from the troubles of Europe, the United States meanwhile advanced its industrial mastery and business influence, impressing observers everywhere as a newcomer bound to shape global politics in the twentieth century. In that emerging world order the fate of Russia was intimately involved.

T W O

The Condition of
Russia

I

In May 1896, a few days after the coronation of Nicholas II in the Kremlin, a disaster occurred at the Khodynka Field on the outskirts of
Moscow. As was customary at a coronation, the tsar had set out presents
for the good people of the ancient capital. Instead of waiting for the signal, the crowd, greedy and poorly controlled, suddenly surged forward
toward the trinkets and trampled to death over 1000 people, turning the
joyous intention into an ominous debacle. Thus began a reign beset with
deepening tragedy. As the tsar himself observed, he was born on the day
of Job.

Unlike Job, however, he was never restored to calm and glory. After a
sequence of revolutions that destroyed his reign and much besides,
Nicholas together with his wife and children were foully murdered. The
reason why the tsar could not reap the rewards of his righteousness and
kindliness (no one who observed him in his family circle denied him
these attributes) was that in statecraft these qualities are not sufficient.
They must be matched by political astuteness. If autocracy was to survive, the tsar had to lead, and lead with passion. A tsar worth his title
had to master the condition of Russia.

II

To clear away a common misunderstanding about this condition, Russia
was only in part a European country. In any survey of world civilizations,
to be sure, Russia (whether Tsarist or Soviet) belongs to Europe. To a

visiting foreigner the observable differences, except perhaps for the Cyrillic alphabet, would not transgress the customary European variety. Nicholas's family, the Romanovs, was closely related by family ties to European royalty. The tsar and his wife habitually conversed with each other in English; other educated Russians might prefer French or German. Russian readers were exceedingly well informed by their newspapers and periodicals of European events in any field of human endeavor—better, in fact, than most Europeans. In the late 1890s, moreover, a remarkable economic advance took place. As a result, Russian society more than ever judged (or misjudged) its affairs by the example set by Western Europe. Russia, furthermore, was closely associated with the other Great Powers of Europe. It was a weighty member of the European Concert of Nations, dependent economically on Germany and, after 1894, intimately tied to France by a diplomatic and military alliance; after 1907 it was linked to England as well. As a European power, too, it took its share in the division of the world, penetrating into central Asia and the Far East.

Yet while emphasizing the basic European nature of Russia, one must also consider basic peculiarities that set it apart. By geographic location it was a neighbor of China and Japan, of Persia, Afghanistan, and the Ottoman Empire, as well as of Austria-Hungary, Germany, and Sweden. It was thus far larger than any of the European states. Its hugeness was the occasion of much boasting in patriotic circles—imagine a country one-sixth of the world's land surface, as vast as the face of the moon! Yet its size was also the source of many embarrassments unknown to its more compact European rivals, and much of its territory was as useless as the moon!

Its population likewise was enormous by European standards, about 127 million in 1897 (Germany was edging toward 65 million at the time and Britain toward 45 million). But it could not compare in unity and cohesion, in loyalty or skill, with any European people; it was far more divided than even Austria-Hungary. The ethnic Russians who had created the Russian state (and with whom this essay will be mostly concerned) constituted less than one-half of the total; they did not stand on friendly terms with other Slavic groups, such as the Ukrainians or Poles. The various nationalities, Slav or non-Slav, are too numerous to survey here—they numbered well over one hundred. The ethnic quilting was further mottled by religious diversity. All major religions of the world were represented, and many minor ones as well. The followers of the Russian Orthodox faith formed the largest group among the Christians, but they too were divided among themselves.

An extraordinary variety again prevailed in the levels of civilization descending from the Western urbanity of St. Petersburg or Warsaw to the barbarism of some Siberian tribes. The Russian Empire thus faced among its inhabitants the deep cultural cleavages that the other European states encountered only in their contact with colonial peoples overseas.

Anyone familiar with the tortuous evolution of the modern state in Western Europe can imagine the extraordinary difficulties faced by the long succession of Russian rulers whose task it was to establish secure boundaries, weld together their inchoate territories, and make their subjects into willing and capable citizens. In the vast open plains of Eurasia with their harsh climate and difficult communications, stability sufficient for continuity in government and culture had to be bought at an inhuman price of plain physical power concentrated in the hands of a single ruler. In Eurasia far more than among the infinitely more secure countries of Western Europe raw power was crucial, for the state as well as for the ruler. Thus did their past lay an exceptionally heavy burden on the Russian people, sharply setting them off from their favored neighbors to the west. By 1900, the task was far from completed. Whatever effective unity Nicholas II could summon was imposed by the state, symbolized in the guiding ideology of Orthodoxy, Autocracy, and Nationality: The vast conglomerate of peoples and territories in the empire was to be cemented together, after the Western model, by a common church (Russian orthodoxy), a common subjection to the tsar, and a common ethnic bond (the Great Russian nationality). Needless to say, the forcible imposition of this ideology aroused resentment that again hardened the differences.

How starved of cultural resources was Russia by comparison with her more favored Western neighbors! Feudalism had never flowered here, nor the Renaissance, nor the quiet industry of the middle class. The dearth was reflected in the character of the Russian state. In Western Europe the state could draw freely on the wealth and skills of its subjects and allow them considerable freedom in their various pursuits: What was good for the citizen had, on the whole, proved advantageous for the state, too. In Russia, on the other hand, the government did not find the prerequisite cultural resources among its subjects. It had to organize them by command, by copying Western models, drafting its subjects into compulsory service, and making them into docile patriots by instilling in them a national pride equal to the Western sense of superiority. As a result, autocracy had always contained more than a streak of totalitarianism. In its endeavors to build up Russian strength, it had destroyed or crippled all autonomous institutions and the native common law as useless or even inimical to its purpose. No middle ground of spontaneous nongovernmental public activity was left, alas, to mediate between an extreme absolutism and anarchy.

III

Despite considerable admixtures of Western influence, especially after the Great Reforms of the 1860s, the basic formula of tsarist power continued into the twentieth century. Wherever one looked, one could detect the presence of an omnipotent state; this was another of the abnormalities that set the country apart. While in England and France civic freedom and individual initiative had gradually been harmonized with government authority, in Russia the state had grown fat at the expense of the people. The state was the biggest landowner, employer of labor, investor in capital, promoter of industry—in short, the only effective public force in society. In the minds of the people it was *nachal'stvo*—the sole agency responsible for getting things moving.

The state was personified in the autocrat ruling from his capital at St. Petersburg. No other monarch in Europe claimed such large powers or stood so high above his subjects, and for good reason. As a writer of the early nineteenth century had put it, autocracy was the soul and life of Russia. Despite terrifying obstacles it had raised the country to the position of a Great Power, protected its inhabitants from invasion and foreign rule, and upheld the glory of Russia in the world. Inevitably, the constant strain had affected its character. Autocracy was traditionally impatient and short-tempered. Too much still had to be done, too many hurdles overcome. There was never time for public argument about ways and means, no leisure for debate to convince the people at large. The tsar always knew best. He issued the command and all Russians obeyed (in legal theory at least). Even his most powerful ministers squirmed in the imperial presence. They were merely "servitors," not advisors.

The autocrat wielded his power through the bureaucracy, which, on the whole, contained the ablest and most knowledgeable members of Russian society. Despite all its inherent faults, the bureaucracy was a remarkable institution, carefully graded by rank and conferring nobility on its most deserving and advanced officers; until the end it offered a career open to talent. Like the tsar, the bureaucracy was proud of its progressive role and disdainful of criticism. It too did not trust its slow-witted and wayward subjects, equating spontaneity on their part with stupidity and mismanagement. It rarely judged its charges by their native standards, but rather applied the imported concepts of Western statecraft and citizenship to their activities. Like the tsar, the *chinovniki*, as the bureaucrats were called, stood above the people, and like the tsar they were always in danger of being corrupted by their omnipotence; their authority was apt to degenerate into arbitrariness. Besides, the poverty of the Russian state manifested in their low salaries tended to corrupt them in a material sense as well. This was true particularly of the inferior ranks. Thus, despite its great merits, the bureaucracy could not escape from the shortcomings of the people it was to guide.

IV

Russian society, too, differed profoundly from that of Western Europe. It reflected—and explained—the overbearing character of autocracy. In 1900 the bulk of the population consisted of peasants, the muzhiks, poor material indeed for citizenship. Serfs until 1861, they were still confined to a tightly knit collective mode of life within the patriarchal family and the village commune. Private property and personal initiative, or the Western awareness of individuality, were generally unknown among them. To be sure, a small and disliked minority, the kulaks (meaning "fists"), were rising by their ruthless energy above the level of the rural lethargy. But in 1900 the government had not yet decided how to treat them. It kept all peasants—and the industrial workers who remained tied to the village—legally and socially segregated from the other social groups. The distinction reflected a basic—and final—fissure in the Russian body politic. On one side stood the peasant masses, the "dark people"; on the other what we might call "privilege Russia," nobles, bureaucrats, the run of educated Russians, and even the merchants, who often had risen from the peasants. "Privilege Russia" looked on the village with profound contempt, and understandably so. Chekhov has aptly described the peasants in a story by that name, published in 1897:

> . . . these people lived worse than cattle, and it was terrible to be with them; they were coarse, dishonest, dirty, and drunken; they did not live at peace with one another but quarreled continually, because they feared, suspected, and despised each other. Who keeps the tavern and encourages drunkenness? The peasant. Who embezzles and drinks up the funds that belong to the community, the schools, the church? The peasant. Who steals from his neighbors, sets fire to their property, bears false witness at court for a bottle of vodka? At meetings of the Zemstvo and other local bodies, who is the first to raise his voice

against the peasants? The peasant. Yes, to live with them was terrible; but yet, they were human beings, they suffered and wept like human beings, and there was nothing in their lives for which one could not find justification. Crushing labor that made the whole body ache at night, cruel winters, scanty crops, overcrowding; and no help and nowhere to look for help. Those who were stronger and better-off could give no assistance, as they were themselves coarse, dishonest, drunken, and swore just as foully. The most insignificant little clerk or official treated the peasants as though they were tramps, and addressed even the village elders and church wardens as inferiors, and as though he had a right to do so.

These people furnished the soldiers of revolution in 1917 and the bulk of Soviet citizenry thereafter.

While the upper layers of Russian society had become Westernized, the peasants had remained in their traditional rut, unenlightened and sometimes given to weird and frightening superstitions. In the bottom of their hearts they carried an instinctive suspicion, if not hatred, of their Europeanized betters, for, in the last analysis, the Westernization of Russia since Peter the Great had been carried out at their expense. What did they care under which government they lived or what role it played in the world?

The Russian peasants, while stubbornly conservative in their ways, were at the same time far more revolutionary than their counterparts in Western Europe. Traditionally rebellious, they found their resentment increased at the end of the nineteenth century by rural overpopulation, the inroads of Western capitalism, and the expectation of a better life filtered down through city and town from Western Europe. The instinctive peasant response was to seize, by what was known as Black Partition, all lands not especially set aside for peasant use, that is, those of the state, church, and above all the landed nobility; more land meant a better life. The peasants lived by the ancient truth that he who does not work, and work by the sweat of his brow—no other type of labor counted in his eyes—neither shall he eat. They had long claimed a moral right to the land which, as sharecroppers or wage laborers, they cultivated for its owners. Of the discipline of citizenship under modern government—or of the complex superstructure of modern civilization—they naturally possessed only the vaguest notion; what they knew of it, they often hated. When their discontent exploded, as it occasionally did, they were apt to drive the landlord and officials out and run their affairs by their peasant wits until the troops restored order. By 1900, elementary education was beginning to penetrate the village, but it hardly bridged the fatal gulf between the peasant masses and "privilege Russia."

"Privilege Russia," however, did not enjoy the Western European boons of free and equal citizenship either. It was divided into a number of state-supervised and mutually suspicious collective organizations *(sosloviia):* the nobility, the bureaucracy, the priesthood, the merchant community (subdivided into two guilds), and what might very inadequately be translated as the "lower middle class" *(meshchanstvo).* The only group exempted from such corporate control was the growing number of individuals in the free professions. Higher education conferred the status of an "honorary citizen," whose position came closest to that of a Western citizen (which, incidentally, showed the government's solicitude for education).

Despite the ascendancy of the "honorary citizens" and the rise of a wealthy business community, the most privileged position in Russian society still belonged to the landed nobility. This group shared a common outlook with the tsar and set the tone in the bureaucracy and the armed services. It was, furthermore, the only recognized ally of autocracy in Russian society, and much pampered for that reason. Yet by 1900 it had long passed its day of glory. Increasingly impoverished and unbusinesslike, it even opposed essential measures of economic development. Moreover, some of its best members were disloyally hankering after a constitution. The decline of the nobility reflected the growing disintegration of the entire system of corporate organization. By 1900, "privilege Russia" inched toward the open society of the West.

V

Ever since the Great Reforms of the 1860s, the government itself had indeed contributed toward greater social freedom and mobility. The Russian defeat in the Crimean War (1854–1856) had taught a lesson: The energies of the individual Russian must be enlisted, after the pattern of Western progress, in raising the strength and welfare of the country. Thus serfdom had been abolished and new agencies of "self-administration" created: (1) the zemstvos, elected from various rural groups but nearly always dominated by the landed nobility, to take charge of rural development; and (2) the town dumas, dominated by the well-to-do urban taxpayers, to promote urban improvement. At the same time, Russian and foreign capitalists had been given a free hand for the development of a railway system and of up-to-date industries in general.

Yet the Western pattern was only imperfectly transplanted. Instead of genuine cooperation, a state of uneasy coexistence between autocracy and private initiative emerged. Autocracy continued its customary leadership, suspicious as ever of the spontaneity of its subjects. While it recognized the need for autonomous private initiative, particularly in the new economic and cultural pursuits essential to keeping up with Western Europe, it never granted its subjects a free hand. Zemstvos, dumas, and even business remained closely hemmed in by a thousand restrictions. What guarantees did the government have that the new opportunities would not be abused for political agitation or private gain at the expense of the commonweal? The public meanwhile complained bitterly about the unceasing bureaucratic meddlesomeness. How under such conditions could the individual acquire the experience and self-confidence necessary for constructive citizenship? Each side, no doubt, was right in its protestations, yet the result was frustration for both.

The clash between popular spontaneity and government leadership pervaded all facets of Russian life. It even reached down to the very source of human motivation, causing profound harm to Russian religion. Autocracy needed the support of the church, both as a unifying force throughout the empire and, in the traditional ideology of absolutism, as a conscience-saving restraint on its own unlimited secular powers. And the church—or more broadly, Orthodox Christianity—possessed deep roots in the population, which, however, was not without danger. In order to control the troubled religious stirrings among the people, the state, ever since Peter the Great, administered the church as a department of government. As a result, the church rendered more service to Caesar than was fitting for the vicar of Christ. Genuine godliness, to be sure, was not entirely sacrificed; Orthodox doctrine and ritual safeguarded spiritual vitality sufficient for survival. But the live core of religion was shut off from all outlets in social and political action. Thus crippled, it could develop no modern message. Here lay one of the deepest and most tragic flaws in the Russian tradition: Social and political action remained severed from the wellsprings of charity. The live religious urge atrophied in the hands of the government: It was driven underground into persecuted sects or revolutionary atheism (where it was speedily corrupted by political expediency), or it survived as a sterile solace for personal comfort unrelated to the great issues of the day and hence useless as a lubricant for social and political change. In the West, by contrast, religion remained a far more vital force, as the rise of evangelism or of "social Christianity" at the end of the nineteenth century proved.

It was a sad fact that after the emancipation of the serfs the tsarist government signally failed to win the loyalty of its subjects. In religion, economic development, and public administration the people found their goodwill rebuffed, their initiative blunted, and their spontaneity distrusted. As a result, they responded to government authority with a mood of sullen apathy, rejoicing at times over official blunders and in extreme cases, one suspects, even provoking them.

By 1900, the silent and tragic warfare between the government and "society" (the Russian term for the educated public that took an interest in the affairs of the country) had already reached an extreme form. A strict and often stupid censorship prevented free discussion of almost any political issue. Yet had there been free speech, it is safe to say, the government would have been drowned in a flood of protest, some of it utterly irresponsible. In order to protect itself from uninformed criticism, the government had long evolved an armory of repressive weapons, which in turn had driven all determined opposition underground. The revolutionaries were hunted down by the secret police and punished, when apprehended, by imprisonment, exile, forced labor in Siberia, and, in rare cases, even death, imposed mostly by administrative decision rather than court verdict. The continuous petty war aroused fierce passions on both sides and gradually ate away what was left of the good nature of Russian society carried over from a simpler age. That most despicable practice on the government's part was the fomenting (or condoning) of anti-Semitic riots, called pogroms, as a means of relieving popular discontent. Where else in Europe had domestic politics reached such a cruel impasse?

Where else in the civilized world was the body politic so deeply rent by internal discord? The country's ethnic and religious diversity was aggravated by the government's policy of forced assimilation. In addition there were the other two deep gulfs: between the government and "society," and between "privilege Russia" and the peasant masses. What was going to happen then in an age of political equality and democracy in which the people were bound to assert their spontaneity? It was clear by 1900 that in Russia (as elsewhere in Europe) the advance of mass politics could not be stemmed. The population down to the lowliest peasant was slowly becoming politically conscious and eager for a voice in the affairs of the country. Furthermore, their willing cooperation in all pursuits of modern civilization was vitally necessary if the country was to prosper. The stalemate between government and public only retarded progress. How then could the people of Russia be welded into a true community, transcending all their differences, and be reconciled to their government? Creating a cohesive, cooperative, mutually responsive polity was thus the first of the overriding necessities facing twentieth-century Russia.

VI

Yet even a greater challenge than mass politics confronted the tsar: Russian backwardness. Western Europe generally and most conspicuously Germany (not to mention the United States) collectively called "the West" by Russian intellectuals, set the model for Russian ambition and self-respect. Western science and technology spectacularly enhanced the well-being of the population and the power of the state. Russia, by contrast, stood far behind in the statistics of cultural and technical progress, whether measured by per capita mileage of roads and railways, number of telephones, letters carried by mail or messages sent by telegraph, infant mortality, or distribution of the national income. Critical observers would add to these indicators certain others: dirt, slovenliness, and corruption; widespread inexactness and unpunctuality; illiteracy; flagrant abuses of authority by police, or *chinovniki;* the enmity between the people and the government; and a thousand other detriments to modern efficiency. In the light of this evidence one can understand the depression or fierce indignation that overcame many patriotic Russians when they looked at the condition of their country.

Most Russians, covertly or overtly, had long assumed the existence of a cultural barrier between Russia and "Europe." They considered themselves, in fact although not potentially, inferior and backward. Maxim Gorky once ran into a police officer who, disgusted with his roaming through Russia, snarled at him, "This is not Russia, this is a pigsty." Some extremists went so far as to speak of the "Asiatic" character of contemporary Russia. Even the moderates were dissatisfied. As a well-known publicist and former defender of the Russian tradition, V. Vorontsov, wrote in 1906:

> Russia belongs to the family of civilized nations, and moreover has entered the 20th century of our era. This means that its needs and the forms of their satisfaction must be commensurate not with the cultural level on which it finds itself, but with those forms which have been devised and applied by western Europe. . . . We want to eat, dress, entertain ourselves and construct our homes, streets, and urban buildings on the model of what is being done in these areas by modern Europe, not by the Europe of the middle ages.

The burden of such wishful thinking was that Russia should catch up to Western Europe. Other and bolder minds even dreamed of Russia's becoming a paragon of political power and cultural leadership in its own right.

In this respect Russia's position before 1914 indeed resembled that of the non-European countries mentioned earlier which had fallen under the Western sway. Russian intellectuals, like some of the Indian intellectuals mentioned earlier, urged that their country be remade after "the model of what is being done . . . by modern Europe." The Russian way of life as one encountered it throughout the country was insufficient by comparison and thus bad. In short, the same outpouring of Western norms that undermined the various non-European civilizations also subverted the traditions and customs of Imperial Russia. The silent revolution from without hollowed out the traditional authority of Tsarist Russia long before it physically collapsed.

This "defeat by comparison" transferred Imperial Russia (at the same time that it was Westernizing its own colonial dependents within the empire) from the European context into the category of the underdeveloped countries. The universal norm was derived from those peoples who cultivated their own traditions, at their own speed, and exported them, seemingly without effort, as universal models. This was the enviable condition of the pacesetters among the European powers. All others were inferior, subject to a ceaseless "revolution from without" that subverted their indigenous creativity; they lacked true sovereignty. Here lay the deepest difference between Russia and the leading countries of the West.

VII

Considering the magnitude of the subversive inundation by Western norms, the Russian reaction was surprisingly complacent. Most educated Russians accepted the Western standards unthinkingly and turned them against their government. What specific anti-Western resentment existed was mostly focused on the foreign penetration of Russia's economy. After the emancipation of the serfs, Western business and business methods had indeed acquired a preponderant influence in Russia. For decades the government had borrowed extensively from abroad. It was no exaggeration to say that Russia was a Great Power on credit only. Nor could it be denied that this dependence did limit the tsar's freedom of action; he could not, for instance, freely vent his anti-Semitism. Foreign capital and enterprise also played a leading part in the development of Russian industry. The instruments of rapid economic growth came largely from abroad. No wonder then that the foreigners and their "capitalist greed" were blamed for all the pains of precipitous cultural change. The fiercest denunciations of foreign exploitation were voiced on the extreme right rather than on the left. Yet all these protests went unheeded. Neither the government nor Russian business nor Russian society could do without external aid, if any progress was to be made.

One of the glaring weaknesses of the Russian condition at the beginning of the twentieth century thus was the disparity between Russian ambition and Russian resources, between pretension and realities. In the eyes of its politically conscious subjects, including the emperor, Russia belonged to the family of civilized nations and was a Great Power destined to be a leader in the affairs of mankind. If they looked at Russian literature or music or all that Russia had already accomplished despite superhuman difficulties, they were convinced that it had much to offer. But how could their country play that forward role while it was still poor, uncivilized, and ruled by a government repudiated by most of its subjects?

Out of this discrepancy, which was as yet barely understood even by the more perceptive contemporaries (let alone most Western observers), emerged the overriding necessity facing the Russian people in the first half of the twentieth century: The fatal gap between ambition and resources had to be closed somehow, at whatever price. The great question which was to determine Russia's destinies for the next generation (and longer) was how the ever-rising costs of true sovereignty could be met out of the human and material resources of Russian-dominated Eurasia.

The riddle remained: How could that native endowment be made to bear riches equal to those of the West when it had produced only backwardness in the past? All modern Russian development was overshadowed by that riddle. And the statesmen who could find no answer perished like the victims of the Sphinx.

T H R E E

The First Crisis,
1900–1905

I

The age of the unforeseen and therefore revolutionary change in the Russian empire began not in the year 1905 but in the years preceding it. Western power and culture pressed vigorously against the country's backwardness, undermining the traditional order in state and society and provoking alarm over the country's future. The gap between Western prosperity and Russian poverty was daily becoming more obvious. The standard of living had to be raised for cultural advance and political stability. Survival depended on keeping up with Western Europe and the United States. Industrialism formed the economic base of Western power; industrialization furnished the key to Russia's survival in the competition of power politics. The first Russian statesman to recognize that critical necessity was Sergei Witte, the minister of finance (1892–1903).

Witte was the last of the great statesmen of the Imperial period, a complex man of great energy and quick mind, inspired by a sense of modern efficiency derived from railroad management; strong-willed, even headstrong, calculating and devious, blunt or charming depending on circumstances; worshiped by his subordinates, feared and hated by his enemies. Impatient to make Russia strong, he was a forerunner of Stalin rather than a contemporary of Nicholas II. His work revealed the basic problems that have haunted Russia ever since.

As minister of finance he was fully aware of the weakness of his country. Its economy was of the colonial type, exporting unprocessed raw materials, grain, oil, minerals; importing manufactured goods; and depending on a constant influx of foreign capital to keep the government

27

solvent. When Witte assumed his post, Russia's economic condition was particularly strained as a result of the Great Famine of 1891. In many parts of the country the peasants were starving; in the capital the treasury was empty, the government on the verge of bankruptcy. Yet despite such poverty, the routine obligations of a government that claimed to be a major power had to be met. Russia's armed strength had to match that of Germany and Austria-Hungary. The huge country had to be tied together by a modern network of communications. More and better schools were needed in order to lower the appalling illiteracy rate. The only way out of these miseries, it seemed, was to follow the Western example and increase the country's native wealth through industrialization. Under Witte, Russia thus became the pioneer of all modern experiments in deliberate economic development.

In 1900, Witte, the one statesman in Russia who was wide awake to the discrepancy between Russian pretension and Russian power, wrote an impassioned memorandum to Nicholas II, underscoring the necessity of industrialization and unwittingly formulating the leitmotif of twentieth-century Russian history:

> Russia more than any other country needs a proper economic foundation for her national policy and culture. . . . International competition does not wait. If we do not take energetic and decisive measures so that in the course of the next decades our industry will be able to satisfy the needs of Russia and of the Asiatic countries which are—or should be—under our influence, then the rapidly growing foreign industries will break through our tariff barriers and establish themselves in our fatherland and the Asiatic countries mentioned above. . . . Our economic backwardness may lead to political and cultural backwardness as well.

Economic organization, Witte further argued, was as important as spiritual valor for "the strength of the Great Powers which are called to fulfill great historical tasks in the world"—Russia, of course, being one of these key powers.

On first sight, Witte's prescription for industrialization seemed relatively simple; by itself it was hardly a revolution. He was to raise the productivity of Russia's economy by an extensive program of railroad construction (including the much-postponed Trans-Siberian line). This would result, he argued, in an expansion of Russia's heavy industries supplying the necessary equipment. The growth of these industries would in turn stimulate the supporting light industries. Through the increased demand and improved transportation, even agriculture would benefit. In the end, the new prosperity would yield more revenue to the government. There still remained the problem of funds for the initial capital investment, but Witte hoped that with the introduction of the gold standard (accomplished in 1897) foreign loans would become cheaper and more plentiful and that, eventually, the boom would feed on its own progress.

No one can deny the impressive results achieved by the "Witte system," as Witte's measures came to be called. Railroad construction and the heavy industries indeed boomed. The great Siberian railroad to the Far East was constructed on schedule, over 5000 miles long; and more mileage than that was added to the rail network of European Russia. With the help of French and Belgian capital, modern metallurgical industries arose in the Ukraine, making south Russia the chief industrial base of the empire. Other industries also began to flourish: machine building, textiles, chemicals. In the 1890s, Russian life was quickened for the first time by a rapid industrial upsurge.

Yet the economic advance was by no means an unmixed blessing. It ushered in a period of profound strain that aggravated all the ills of Russian society. In the first place, Witte's solicitude for industry did not appreciably raise the level of popular welfare; rural Russia was not lifted from its stagnation.

Crop failures and famines persisted, if in somewhat less catastrophic form; taxes bore heavily on the peasants, whose arrears piled up alarmingly in some areas; in many sections land became ever scarcer and more expensive. In 1902 the peasantry gave warning of its distress; in two provinces it rose against the landlords and the police. This was a danger signal indicating that perhaps not Russian industry but Russian agriculture should be the chief care of the government.

The industrial workers, too, were aroused. For the most part they were peasants who had gone to the factories in order to eke out a living that the village could not supply. Thus the sullen anger of the village spilled over into the factories and mills where it was heated further, sometimes to the explosion point. But the pent-up fury was not directed alone against the "capitalists" who ran the factory. Since strikes or public demonstrations of any kind were generally illegal, any outburst against the factory became also an outrage against autocracy. The workers thus were inevitably pushed on the road toward revolution. In the summer of 1903, all of southern and southeastern Russia from Baku to Kiev witnessed a strike wave that nearly grew into a general strike. It sounded an even louder tocsin than the peasant uprisings of the previous year.

Even the business community, pampered by government favors and more tradition-bound in its outlook than the landed nobility, grew restive under the accelerated change of these years. It felt the influence of Western business methods and began to appreciate the freedom that Western entrepreneurs enjoyed. Particularly after the onset of depression in 1899, Russian businessmen began to find fault with their government.

Indeed, all of Russian society shared a deep-seated resentment of the all-too-sudden jump into an uncongenial way of life. The hostility of the intelligentsia toward the Witte system was typical; very few writers and publicists accepted Witte's vision of Russia as a leading industrial nation. During the height of Witte's power as minister of finance, the revolutionary movement recruited its most fanatical leaders from the ranks of the intelligentsia. By 1900 they had established close contact with the workers of key industrial centers.

Even more disturbing, perhaps, was the opposition of the landed nobility to rapid industrialization. Russian noblemen derived their livelihood, constantly diminishing ever since the early nineteenth century, from agriculture. The current misery of rural Russia, unalleviated or even hastened by Witte's policies, further undermined their social and political significance; the smoldering peasant discontent, moreover, threatened their very life. Why under these conditions should the government lavish its energies on industry, an artificial creation in Russia and a patent luxury? Among certain landed proprietors, the hatred of Witte knew no bounds. They ranted not only against Witte but against foreign capital and its pernicious effects on Russian life as well. It undermined, they said, the deepest foundations of Russian state and society. The discontent among the landed aristocracy determined the outlook also of the zemstvos. Rural Russia, in short, had no use for the Witte system.

Through the intimate ties between the nobility and the court, the opposition of the nobility soon spread from the countryside into the capital, where Witte from the start had made many enemies, also because of his economic policies. Fellow ministers accused him of being an inveterate administrative empire builder, whose ambition knew no bounds.

II

His aggressiveness, to be sure, was not entirely his fault. The very logic of industrialization spurred him forward to domination. It demanded that all obstacles to economic progress be cleared away and the entire government cooperate in the great effort. For that reason Witte did not shrink from interfering in matters of foreign policy. Concentrating on economic development left no funds or energy for risky ventures in diplomacy; it called for a strict policy of peace. By the same token, Witte began to meddle in all aspects of domestic politics. If, for instance, illiteracy stood in the way of industrial growth, something had to be done about it, despite the widespread fear in government circles lest education intensify the subversion of popular loyalty (already so noticeable among the educated public). As Witte once addressed the emperor:

> Maybe education would lead the people to corruption. All the same, education must move forward vigorously. . . . Our people are coarse and unenlightened in their medieval frame of mind. But an unenlightened people cannot be made more accomplished. Not going forward it therefore falls behind as compared with people that do move forward.

Thus Witte pressed for better public instruction and took all advanced technical education under his jurisdiction.

But his ambition would not stop with small ventures. If the structure of Russian society obstructed economic progress, it too had to be changed. Witte advocated no less than recasting the upper layers of Russian society, putting the business community, tiny and unpopular though it was, ahead of the landed nobility. From the viewpoint of modern trade and industry, nothing was to be expected from the noble landlords (as Chekhov's *Cherry Orchard* well illustrates). Still more important to Witte was the revamping of rural society. Industrialization by private enterprise—such, despite his emphasis on government direction, was his ideal—required the dissolution of the peasant commune. Private initiative had to be introduced among the peasant masses as well. Thus he called for a huge transformation in the very depths of Russian life.

Yet he sensed that something even more basic stood in his way: the unseen motives and values that made men and women perform their daily routines. He had to replace the slow-minded, moody conservatism of an agrarian and almost medieval mode of life by the quick rationality of urbanism and the innate drive for hard work which has been called, since Max Weber, the Protestant ethic. The carelessness and nonchalance of many top officials in the government (not to mention the members of the imperial family) were the despair of Witte, who himself lived by an inherited Teutonic self-discipline. But a similar casualness and listlessness pervaded all other ranks of society as well. How could these deepest layers of human motivation be quickened?

Rapid Westernization, Witte gradually came to realize, was a comprehensive revolutionary process shaking Russian society to its depths and mobilizing all vested interests against him. Hence a final question arose for Witte: Could autocracy assume leadership over this vast and unpopular metamorphosis?

To his sorrow, Witte soon realized that Nicholas II was not meant to carry this burden. The tsar was temperamentally unfit to be autocrat in time of crisis. His weakness of will was obvious from the start, even to himself. As he observed to one of his uncles in the year of the coronation, "I always give in and in the end am made the fool, without will, without character." His uncertainty made him—and his wife Alexandra—all the more determined to uphold the dignity and power of his office. Yet how could he do this when he was never master of the situation? He winced in Witte's presence and always agreed with the person whom he had seen last.

It was not that Nicholas was devoid of goodwill or determination. Every day he dutifully applied himself, with a wistful glance at the weather outside, to reading and annotating the official reports. He meant to be a good father to his people, stern, even ruthless when necessary, but always sympathetic to their woes. The tragedy was that he could not master the harsh game of politics. Living in the splendid isolation of the imperial palaces, he was only dimly aware of the rapid changes in the Russian polity. Perhaps just because he felt that he could not master them, he was instinctively opposed to them; he remained a partisan of rural Russia. Commerce, banking, and industry were alien influences, replete with foreigners and Jews—like so many of his subjects he particularly loathed Jews. Significantly the figure among his ancestors whom he disliked most was Peter the Great. By contrast he inclined toward medieval Muscovy. And in time of adversity he sought solace not in a rational analysis of his mistakes, but in prayer. There could have been no more fatal opiate for an autocrat!

Yet even if Nicholas II had been endowed with a keener political instinct, his job, as defined by tradition, would have been too big for one man. The autocrat was the solitary and fragile keystone of government—head of state, policymaker, and chief administrator all in one—at a time when the functions of government rapidly multiplied and when, furthermore, they could be performed only with the help of a disciplined bureaucracy and a loyal populace. Not possessing inexhaustible vitality, the tsar was incapable of overseeing his vast establishment. What mockery of single-mindedness and unity of purpose was hidden behind the monolithic facade of autocracy! As the tsar did not lead, his ministers quarreled among themselves; cliques and camarillas interfered with the conduct of government. When no agreement between rival factions could be reached, the same imperial decree might announce two diametrically opposed policies. As for the people at large, Nicholas never deigned to take notice of public opinion, let alone invite his subjects into his confidence. His government, he was convinced, could handle its tasks as it had done in the past.

With this conclusion, Witte was inclined to agree. A single overriding will was necessary for carrying out the modernization of Russia. The people, while only too eager to consume the benefits of modernization, gave no indication of their ability—or willingness—to undertake the necessary changes on their own. Modernization and industrialization by public consent were therefore impossible. Were they then to be carried out against public opinion? This alternative Witte also denied. He hoped that under an inspiring leader the population could be aroused to the necessary pitch of enthusiasm. Solving the great national task of modernization, Witte hoped, would also impart to the body politic the tight, spontaneous cohesion required of a modern society.

It was a dynamic vision anticipating Soviet policies for which Witte, tragically, found no support among his contemporaries. He stood ahead of his time, attempting far more than a mere minister of finance could ever hope to accomplish, and far more than he himself knew. As one looks over the long list of changes that he started or at least suggested, one realizes that the essence of rapid industrialization was not establishing railroads, factories, or mills on Russian soil. The real task, of which Western Europe for once offered no model, was to provide the social, economic, political, and psychological framework in which Western technology could take root and flourish. What Witte had conceived as a relatively simple and innocuous economic policy tailored to the power of the minister of finance turned out to be an all-comprehensive scheme of industrialization. From a simple starting point it had grown into an ever more unmanageable and complex revolutionary leviathan that respected neither authority nor privilege, neither class interest nor even human dignity.

By 1902, the Witte system had become a political liability for autocracy. The peasants had shown their temper by revolting, the workers by staging ever more strikes, the students by joining the workers' demonstrations. The nobility was grumbling; even the business community was dissatisfied. There was ground then to believe that the foundations of the Russian state and society were giving way. In addition, Witte suffered a resounding defeat in foreign policy. He had been a protagonist of economic expansion (and of cautious political expansion as well) in the Far East, partly as a means of bringing business to his costliest project, the

Trans-Siberian railroad, partly as proof of Russian participation in the great historical tasks of the imperialist age. By 1902 this expansion had assumed, much to his chagrin, a predominantly political and military character. As such it had run into strong opposition not only from China but also Japan, which even concluded an alliance with Great Britain, likewise an opponent of Russian expansion. In the face of such danger, Witte inevitably favored retreat, which would have amounted to a patent defeat of Russian foreign policy. But the tsar was unwilling to aggravate the mounting domestic crisis by a humiliation in foreign affairs as well, and in August 1903, after much soul-searching, he graciously dismissed Witte from the ministry of finance.

III

Whether a failure or not—there is much to be said in its favor on purely economic grounds—the Witte system was the first tentative rehearsal of the major problems of industrialization in Russia. One crucial problem was the tempo of economic growth. At the turn of the century, two alternatives faced the Russian government. Russia's economic growth could either develop at a natural speed, organically, utilizing purely Russian resources, or it could be hastened by recourse to foreign aid. Which was the better course? The question was answered by one of Witte's supporters, the economist Migulin:

> Of course, limiting ourselves to our own resources and working with the help of savings accumulated by our own labor we could proceed more cheaply and gain more lasting results. But time does not wait. Life goes full steam ahead. Even so we are behind all the western countries. And by walking slowly one does not go far, our proverb to the contrary notwithstanding. We have to live at a more rapid clip and, whether we want to or not, must resort to the services of foreigners.

The first course meant slow but sound economic growth from the rural base upward. Large-scale industries would be built only when the rural market was ready to support them. The second course called for starting at the top, with exclusive emphasis on industry, particularly heavy industry, and drawing as much as possible on foreign capital and know-how. What ruled out the first alternative, admittedly the more desirable one, was the fact that it did not help Russia catch up to Western progress. The only hope lay in the other alternative, and what a dim hope it was! (The second alternative, incidentally, suffered from a flaw not previously mentioned. Just when Russia needed foreign aid most, it might not be available because of foreign hostility, the state of world economy, or a number of other reasons.)

The main problem was, of course, the high cost of the Witte system to the Russian people. The bulk of the investment capital for industrialization, so Witte himself admitted, must come out of the living substance of the people. How could the government justify the searing austerity under a program ostensibly aimed at increasing popular prosperity? And more broadly: How could the government sustain the morale of the population (and its own) during the almost interminable hardships, while the gap between Russian poverty and Western prosperity remained so conspicuous or possibly even widened as a result of the government's effort to catch up? Setting a trend for the future, Witte tried a variety of tricks to cope with that question, promising quick results, creating an atmosphere of optimism by a stream of statistics proving the success of his measures, and building up a sense of Russia's world mission. But how could a poverty-stricken country become a global model? If only he could have prevented the constant comparison with Western prosperity and success that made the enforced austerity in Russia so odious to its Westernized public!

But there were other insoluble problems. Witte knew that the spontaneous creativity of the peoples of Western Europe could only be matched (let alone surpassed) by the fullest release of the same energies in Russian society. For that reason he always deplored the red tape hampering Russian business. On the other hand, he manifested no faith whatever in the business community. Left to their own devices, obviously, Russia's entrepreneurs would never build up Russia's economic strength by the quickest means. If they had done so, there would have been no need for his efforts; Russia would be rich already. Thus Witte imposed his own regulations and pressures, guiding Russia's businessmen along an alien path dictated not by the profit motive but by a *raison d'état* they did not comprehend. His whole experiment (like its Soviet successors) suffered from an ingrained paradox. It tried to combine authoritarianism with the spontaneity of Western society. Witte was not aware of the dichotomy; yet even had he been, what could he have done?

Finally we must touch, as any consideration of industrialization in recent Russia history inevitably does, on the problem of political morality. Let us phrase the crucial issue in general terms: To what extent does state necessity, as pleaded by Witte, justify thwarting the will of the majority and violating the integrity of the individual by extreme demands on life, property, and human dignity?

IV

At this point we must ask a question crucial throughout this essay: Who has the moral right to set the standards of political morality? In the United States, and elsewhere in the West, we are apt to judge the affairs of nations from our own experience in countries that have managed, under exceptionally favorable circumstances, to combine freedom for the individual with security and global power for the state. Under these circumstances we have been able to concentrate our sensibilities and values to an unprecedented degree on the rights of the individual. Less favored countries, on the other hand, have had to recognize the priority of the state (or the group) over the individual. In their political history, external security had to be assured before the individual could be given a free hand. The survival of the group took precedence over the survival of the individual (as is the case in our own military codes).

Each set of political conditions over the long run has created its own moral absolutes. The holiest of American (and Western) political convictions center around the dignity of the individual. The equivalent among the less secure countries, one might say, is a searing all-or-nothing determination to make the community prevail regardless of the life or dignity of its members. Nothing, the spokespersons of this philosophy will argue, could be more degrading than invasion or foreign rule, not even callousness, exploitation, or injustice on the part of their own government; necessity makes hardness into virtue (an attitude by no means unknown even in the Western democracies, particularly in times of crisis). But lest we judge unfairly and assert our superiority too brazenly, let us remember that in the history of European power politics the responsibility for this adverse climate of politics in Central and Eastern Europe has rested rather with those Western powers that did manage to combine strength with a measure of freedom for their citizens. Their success threatened their weaker neighbors. In trying to make Russia strong, Witte certainly did not force a new heat of rivalry on the European state system. He merely tried to undergird Russia's position in a patently, ever-more-competitive struggle dominated by the Western powers. If for that reason he imposed considerable hardship on an uncomprehending population, was he morally in the wrong? Needless to say, the opposition, guided by the imported Western standards, shouted that he was.

V

Industrialization aggravated a deeper and more familiar problem with revolutionary implications: how to establish closer ties between the ruler and the ruled and between the privileged classes and the peasant masses. In order to be successful, industrialization called for a common pull uniting all, government and subjects, high and low. Yet the Witte system achieved the very opposite. By 1903, the relations between the government and the public were headed for crisis. Russian society found itself in a relentless rebellion against autocracy. The economic transformation of the country together with the influence of Western democratic ideals had speeded the political activation of the populace. Discontent was rife, and thanks to the new mobility the opportunities for discussing and inciting it were greater than ever. Political programs were being evolved, organizations planned, founded, and even tested in action. All the groups destined to play a significant part in the forthcoming age of revolution had their origin in these years.

While the policy of industrialization had done its share to arouse Russian society and to accentuate its divisions, autocracy remained the chief target of the opposition. The total exclusion of the public from politics, the brutality and arbitrariness of the officials, the lack of freedom of speech or of heterodox religious worship, the constant pressure of Russification on Poles, Finns, Ukrainians, Georgians, and nationalities in central Asia—*there* was the real enemy. A broad revolutionary front clamoring for a constitution was in the making. It ran the social gamut from peasants and peasant workers, religious and national minorities, a variety of professional groups—lawyers, physicians, agronomists, professors, and specialists of all kinds—and industrialists, to landowners active in the zemstvos and the clubs of the nobility. It even included "liberal" sympathizers in the ranks of the bureaucracy. From the start, however, an invisible flaw divided that impressive front: the traditional barrier between the educated on one side and the peasants and peasant workers on the other. It was reflected in the emerging variety of political organization, in the split between the liberals and the socialists, and, within the latter group, between the moderates and the extremists.

After the turn of the century, the revolutionary forces redoubled their effort in a crescendo of meetings, demonstrations, and strikes, syncopated at times by the assassination of particularly hateful officials. The government replied with more drastic repression and an occasional conciliatory gesture. The combination both embittered and emboldened the opposition. What finally accelerated the disaffection into revolution was the Russo-Japanese war, into which the government had drifted in order to avoid the diplomatic retreat favored by Witte. The minister of the interior at the time, V. K. Plehve, at first rejoiced over the diversion: What could be better than "a small victorious war"? He was quickly disillusioned (he was assassinated in July 1904). One defeat followed another, culminating in May 1905 in the annihilation of Russian sea power in the Straits of Tsushima. The dreaded discrepancy between Russia's power ambition and its resources was now made manifest to all. It was fortunate that Russia, thanks partly to Witte's skillful negotiations at the Portsmouth peace conference, had to pay a relatively small price affecting only a distant part of the country. Yet the damage to Russian prestige was profound.

The beginning of the Revolution is commonly dated from Bloody Sunday, January 22, 1905, a revolutionary event only because of what followed, not of what actually happened on that day. A group of workers and their families set out, with the blessing of some officials, to present a petition to the tsar. As they approached the Winter Palace, they were cold-bloodedly shot down by rifle fire. Such unwarranted breach of faith shattered the halo of awe still surrounding the tsar in the minds of peasants and workers. As the indignation spread throughout the country, the revolutionary surge became irresistible; the government gradually lost control over the course of events.

The gravest threat to the government emerged from the countryside where the peasants rose in an elemental, anarchic rebellion. But the striking workers in key industries and centers like St. Petersburg and Moscow were hardly less menacing. It was they who prepared the climax of the Revolution in October, when a railroad strike turned into a general strike and brought the government, the economy, and all public services to a complete standstill. At the height of this strike, the workers of St. Petersburg formed a workers' council (or soviet) acting as a central strike committee and also evincing a lively appetite for taking over governmental functions. The most significant aspect of this soviet was that it represented not the broad revolutionary front but only the underprivileged element in Russian society, the peasants and peasant workers. It was led, however, by revolutionary intellectuals including Trotsky.

Thus, in October 1905, in the aftermath of a resounding defeat in foreign policy, the relations between the tsar and his subjects had come to a complete breakdown.

FOUR

The Collapse of Autocracy, 1905–1917

I

The Russian crisis of 1905 hardly merits the term revolution; no new ruler ascended the throne, no power was transferred from one class to another. What occurred was more like a passing squall of bad weather— this was the tsar's view and not too far from the truth. A tide of popular rebellion brought the regime to the verge of collapse. But at that very point the government regained the initiative by a timely concession and gradually reestablished its authority; within a decade it had retrieved most of its losses. Nicholas II bent under the storm. When the emergency had passed and calm returned, he straightened out again, inwardly unchanged. The insurrections of 1905–1906 never came to a head. They were merely a preparation for the true revolution yet to come. The weaknesses of autocracy had to be revealed still more brutally.

The events that stemmed the revolutionary tide were the appointment of Witte as chairman of the newly constituted Soviet (Council) of Ministers, an institution resembling a Western cabinet, and—more important—the promulgation at the same time of the October Manifesto, his last great accomplishment. It granted basic civil liberties to all, regardless of religion or nationality; it even legalized political parties. This concession was capped by the creation of an elected legislative body, the Imperial Duma, sitting in the Tauride Palace built by Potemkin, the favorite of Catherine II. The October Manifesto also split the revolutionary front, reconciling the most cautious elements among the moderates, who had no heart for violence, with a government that promised to end the abuses of autocracy. For a time thereafter, the regime enjoyed a patent measure of support among the propertied classes in town and country, who formed the party called Octobrist.

Meanwhile Witte proceeded hesitantly and without his earlier mastery. Instinctively loyal to autocracy yet recognizing the need for public endorsement, he followed a wavering course. In mid-December he suppressed the St. Petersburg Soviet, yet soon afterward, at the height of a bloody revolt in Moscow, granted the vote to the industrial workers. Gradually, however, he began to employ the army to quell the continuing uprisings. It was the army that, in the last analysis, saved autocracy. Despite innumerable cases of mutiny, the discipline and loyalty of the peasant soldiers on the whole still held firm. When the powers of the Duma had been defined in a manner favoring autocracy and a large loan granted by France made the government financially independent of the new Duma, Nicholas dismissed his first prime minister. Thereafter the government's attitude hardened still further. Under the leadership of the strong minister of the interior, Peter A. Stolypin, summary measures were taken to put down the embittered violence that still flared up here and there and to punish the earlier misdeeds. As order was restored, the concessions granted at the moment of weakness were severely limited. Civil liberties were again curtailed, and after two elections had produced unmanageable majorities, the suffrage of the Imperial Duma was sharply restricted.

The Duma was not a Western parliament; neither was it an obedient sounding board for the government. It forced the ministers to collaborate with a small but important segment of public opinion and at the same time apprenticed the loyal opposition in the intricacies of running the country. The cooperation proved mildly beneficial to both partners. The government was spurred into greater efficiency, particularly in the armed forces, and the public was protected from the worst abuses of arbitrary power. One could almost speak of an aura of good feeling emerging from this partnership. After the revolutionary agitation was fought to a standstill, the Duma, under the leadership of the Octobrists, held the center of the political stage.

The statesman who impressed his personality on this brief period of stability was Peter Stolypin, minister of the interior and soon chairman of the Soviet of Ministers (1907–1911). He was a man of patent good sense, honest, endowed with amazing physical courage and tremendous capacity for work. He did not, however, possess Witte's insight into the depth of the Russian crisis, nor his vision. He merely thought of his country's needs in terms of agrarian reform and the consolidation of internal cohesion through further Russification.

Stolypin's most signal step toward that goal was peasant reform. The revision of the peasant order that Witte had vainly tried at the turn of the century was at last made possible by the Revolution. In 1905, the much-vaunted communal order had failed disastrously. Instead of buttressing autocracy it had fomented sedition. Stolypin adopted a moderate scheme based largely on Witte's earlier suggestions. Its essence was the encouragement of a prosperous and conservative element in the countryside composed of "the strong and the sober" (the kulaks). Through them, capitalist agriculture was to take root and act as an economic and cultural leaven. For this purpose Stolypin encouraged the changeover from the traditinal (and still popular) system of periodic communal redistribution of the land to hereditary landownership. He furthermore facilitated the peasants' withdrawal from the commune, strengthening at the same time the principle of individual ownership by vesting the title to the land in the head of the peasant household (thus wiping out, at the stroke of the pen, the claims of all other members). Finally, Stolypin promoted the formation of consolidated farm plots. Only in this manner was individual farm management with all its advantages made possible. These measures were accompanied by some improvements in the civic status of the peasantry which, however, did not abolish the barriers separating it from "privilege Russia."

The encouragement of individual farming affected the countryside only in small driblets of change. Even the withdrawal of households from the commune was a protracted, complex business; the creation of consolidated plots of land took decades and more to complete. Under these circumstances it was not surprising that by 1915 only slightly more than one-half of all peasant households (in European Russia) held their lands in hereditary tenure, and only one-tenth had succeeded in forming a consolidated plot of their own. Obviously the bulk of the peasantry was responding but slowly to Stolypin's experiment. Those peasants who managed to set up their own farms were not favored by their less energetic or less fortunate brethren, nor by democratically minded liberals.

On the whole, the years between 1907 and 1914 (and even a for a little while longer) were not bad ones for the peasants, nor for the other groups in Russian society. Even under the political restrictions reimposed by Stolypin and his successors, life was somewhat freer than before 1905, the legal security greater. More spontaneity of association was permitted, the area of self-help expanded; more groups gained experience of public affairs. The renewed economic upsurge after 1906, moreover, conferred a visible prosperity on the privileged members of Russian society and some improvement on the masses as well. Industrialization proceeded apace, its tempo being among the fastest in the world. Nor was the economic advance as dependent on the state as it had been in Witte's day, nor as intimately tied to foreign capital and enterprise. Illiteracy was being rapidly eliminated. If plans proceeded on schedule, the authorities predicted there would be enough elementary schools for every youngster by 1922. At the same time the contacts with Western Europe were close. Russia contributed freely to the contemporary European fashions in the arts, in literature, and in philosophy. These were golden years deserving the nostalgia of those who fled abroad during the subsequent revolutions or of many of those who stayed behind. Seen in this superficial glow, the tsarist regime as reconstituted after 1905 did not deserve its subsequent fate.

II

Yet, as for remedying the government's weakness in the mounting competition for power in the world, next to nothing was accomplished. The political compromise that imparted the air of good feeling had but a feeble foundation. It was never accepted by Nicholas II. At heart he always remained the autocrat, reducing the authority of the chairman of the Soviet of Ministers, sabotaging the work of a loyal servant like Stolypin lest he himself be eclipsed, and forever urging that the scant prerogatives of the Duma be further whittled away.

Moreover, the quality of imperial leadership, on which the future still depended, continued to deteriorate. These were the years when Rasputin established himself at court. What could have been more preposterous in the annals of modern government than the ascendancy of this incredible man? A dirty peasant with a stabbing, unforgettable glance, he was propelled into notoriety by his frightening magnetism, both spiritual and physical. Nothing in Western experience can make plausible this combination, so paradoxical yet so well authenticated, of saintliness and lechery. He was, indeed, a "holy devil." His debauches were of the grossest nature. They increased as his reputation for saintliness grew at court. The imperial couple at times worshiped him as a Christ, a Christ in the guise of a muzhik. Yet what proved to them his divinity was not only the spiritual solace he inspired but also his healing power. He was able, according to all witnesses (and there were many), to stop the bleeding of the hemophiliac heir to the throne, the Tsarevitch Alexis, for whom medical science had no cure. Because of this extraordinary gift, Rasputin ingratiated himself with the empress, who in her Victorian prudery could never see the rot in her idol. Through her, he became a political force. Of the complexity of government and modern society in general he had, of course, no idea. Yet at moments he manifested, as is also authenticated, a simple but penetrating understanding of events bordering on prophecy.

The tale of Rasputin's depravity spread as his influence at court became known. Soon it was the talk of the Duma and the ministers. Yet by 1914 no official dared to press the matter on the emperor's attention without risking disgrace and dismissal. Every time an honest man spoke out, the empress prevailed on her husband to go to the limit of his prerogative in order to protect "the holy one." Needless to say, the suppressed scandal festered and helped to alienate even the well-wishers of autocracy. And as the emperor also invoked the authority of the Orthodox church in Rasputin's behalf, it too was dragged into the mire.

There were other practices supported by the tsar and the church that boded ill for the future—for instance, the agitation of the Union of the Russian People, or Black Hundreds. It was an organization of reactionaries stirring up, in a manner later made notorious by the Nazis, anti-Semitism and other murky instincts in order to protect an unreconstructed autocracy. Immediately after the promulgation of the October Manifesto, the Black Hundreds set off a wave of pogroms and other riots; subsequently they tried their best to discredit Stolypin. Their political value to autocracy may be doubted. They fired rather than mitigated the hatred for the tsar among the revolutionaries. And they infused a new ugliness into Russian politics that later was to cost the country dearly.

Among the revolutionary opposition, of course, the political compromise of the Stolypin era also lacked support. The mass of the population continued in its sullen hostility, even though the revolutionary ardor had cooled for the moment. The peasants had no voice in the Duma; their outlook remained anarchic; it would be decades before Stolypin's reforms would work a change. Besides, the nobility's control of the countryside continued as before. The workers likewise persisted in their enmity. Labor organizations, briefly legalized after 1905, were soon again suppressed. In certain skilled crafts, to be sure, a moderate trade union outlook emerged. But for the majority the link with the village remained intimate and kept the traditional radicalism alive. Besides, the government did not significantly expand its labor legislation. Under these conditions, the militant revolutionaries easily retained their following. As for the moderate opposition, most liberals found themselves excluded from politics and exposed to persecution as well; many of them called for a republic. If one adds to these irreconcilables among the Russian-speaking population the various non-Russian nationalities—

Poles, Finns, Ukrainians, and others whom Stolypin resubjected to the odious chicanery of Russification—one can see how dubious were the prospects of the new order. No progress was made in identifying the peoples of Russia with their government.

Even during the quiet years after 1907, violence and strife were never far from the surface. Stolypin himself was assassinated by a revolutionary in the fall of 1911 (with the connivance, it seems, of the reactionaries within the government). The following year a massacre of peaceful strikers at the Lena gold fields revived the latent revolutionary energies. Before the end of July 1914, the revolutionary agitation reached a new peak, surpassing, in the number of strikes, the turmoil of the entire year 1905. Such events did not bode well for a peaceful evolution of the constitutional experiment, even under normal circumstances.

III

Nor was any progress made in building up Russia's external strength in the competition of the powers, as Witte had urged when he was minister of finance. This competition now loomed ever larger, as Europe headed toward war.

Russia was a Great Power set, as part of its harsh destiny, into the crosscurrents of European and global power politics. No Russian government, regardless of its ideology or class basis, could have abdicated from that role. Given the political ambitions of Germany and Austria-Hungary, or even of Poles, Ukrainians, and other border nationalities within the empire, the price of passivity in foreign relations was, as events were soon to prove, dissolution, foreign domination, and possible annihilation. Moreover, a power vacuum in Eastern Europe and northern Eurasia was not only murderous for Russia but also highly dangerous for the political stability of the entire world. Under any circumstances, war was an inescapable contingency for the peoples of the empire and their government.

There remained no alternative but to play the exhausting game like the other powers, offensively and defensively, as opportunity and Russian resources permitted. No one can accuse the tsarist government of conducting an extravagant foreign policy. The only area in which Nicholas II took a mildly active interest after 1905 was the Balkans, where Russia posed as the protector of the small Slavic states against Austria-Hungary and Germany. Still farther west the superior strength of Germany did not encourage any ambition threatening the status quo.

To be sure, like other governments the tsar and his advisers had their maximum as well as minimum goals in foreign policy. Russia's ruling circles, too, had caught the imperialist fever. Prince Radolin, the German ambassador, reported from St. Petersburg in 1895, "In every-thing which I hear they proclaim with one voice that it is Russia's mission to gain in due time the mastery of the world." Global ambition was not a Bolshevik innovation.

At their boldest, the hotheads talked of penetration into the Far East, into Ethiopia or South Africa, or even of unhinging the entire British Empire (a dream popular during the Boer War). Occasionally even an ideological note crept into these far-roaming ambitions. Autocracy was hailed as the spiritual rallying point for all the Asian peoples currently under Western domination. In the case of Ethiopia, the Russian inter-ests contained a religious appeal; in the Balkans they stressed the ethnic bonds. Such unlimited schemes, however, were not the sole property of the Russian ruling class. In those years, German statesmen and publi-cists were toying with equally overreaching plans of world power. They, too, thought of using the anticolonial and anti-Western agitation in Asia as a weapon against the British Empire and of building up an African domain of their own. They aimed at nothing less than replacing the *Pax Britannica* with German global hegemony. The British, of course—to limit the discussion to these three powers—needed no such fantastic goals. They *were* the dominant global power, the model for the political appetites of all the others. But one need only think of Cecil Rhodes, who is said to have wanted to annex the planets, to see the imperialist mega-lomania at work even among them.

The comparatively modest objectives of Russian foreign policy (as separate from the dreams) were voiced mostly in the inner circles of the government and shared by only a small segment of the public. The opposition generally denounced the government's foreign policy. Yet whether they admitted it or not, all politically conscious elements among the public paid close attention to the role that their country played in world affairs.

At the center of Russian foreign policy stood, of course, Russia's rela-tionship with Europe. What a tangle of contradictory interests and necessities it was! In the realm of economics and finance, the govern-ment had to consider the fact that central Europe—above all, Germany—was its chief market as well as its chief supplier of manufac-tured goods and commercial and industrial know-how. The Russo-German trade agreement was for that reason a most crucial factor in Russia's economic growth. France and Belgium, on the other hand, furnished the bulk of Russia's foreign capital needed for the same purpose. Russia's economic dependence on both these partners, needless to say, carried over into diplomacy as well. Here, too, painful contradictions prevailed. Dynastic interest tied Russia to Germany and Austria-Hungary. The monarchs of Eastern and Central Europe were dimly aware that they had to stand together if they did not want to fall separately. The dictates of the European balance of power, on the other hand, tied Russia ever more firmly to the Western democracies, a fact that cheered the revolutionaries but dismayed the conservatives.

In this maze of incompatible necessities the calculations of the balance of power finally prevailed. Russia could not advantageously have stayed out of the coming conflict over the emergence of German hegemony. Any advance of German power meant a threat not only to Russia's Balkan position, but, considering Germany's economic and territorial appetite, to its territorial integrity as well. Russia, therefore, had to take sides, regardless of its economic and dynastic interests.

Yet what frightful apprehensions the coming of war evoked! In February 1914, P. N. Durnovo, a high-ranking official of unimpeachably conservative views, wrote an alarming memorandum outlining the consequences of armed conflict with Germany. He called attention to the "embryonic condition" of Russian industry, to the country's "far too great dependence on foreign industry" (mostly German), to its "technical backwardness," and its "insufficient network of strategic railroads." War, Durnovo prophesied, would bring defeat as in 1905, and defeat in turn would bring revolution by the infuriated masses that would sweep all before them.

> The legislative institutions and the intellectual opposition parties, lacking real authority in the eyes of the people, will be powerless to stem the popular tide aroused by themselves, and Russia will be flung into hopeless anarchy, the issue of which cannot be foreseen.

Witte also spoke out, warning that Russia was less prepared for war than in 1904. These realists knew that however impressive the industrial advance of the previous years had been, it had not in the least remedied the basic discrepancy between Russia's resources and its power status.

IV

The course of the war that broke out on August 1, 1914, bore out the forebodings of the realists. No belligerent, to be sure, was ready for the much-prepared clash of arms. The need for adjusting state and society to the exorbitant demands of the front was a grueling test for the body politic of all participants, but particularly so for a deeply divided Russia. Russia also faced an additional handicap, being cut off by the German blockade from its allies and from "Europe" in general. Thus began, at a time of supreme danger, a period of deepening isolation (and isolationism) which has lasted, in essence, until Gorbachev's reforms. The pressure of European power politics remained in its acutest form, but the uncontrolled Western cultural influx, so prominent before 1914, now ceased. Henceforth Russia became more Eurasian than it had been for centuries. The war forced the indigenous peoples to solve their crises out of their own fund of ingenuity and temperament. For better or worse, the outbreak of the war ushered in a new phase of history in Russian-dominated Eurasia.

It was Russia's misfortune to join battle with the most powerful country of Europe. The German onslaught took a double form, a military and a political one. At the outset armed force stood in the foreground, as the German armies rolled back their adversaries in an almost constant advance. Within a year Russia lost Poland, in another year the Baltic coast up to Riga. By the end of 1917, the German armies were held in check only by the fact that Germany had to wage war on other fronts as well (which proved, incidentally, the benefit of Russia's alliances). The early retreats of the Russian armies also caused a disastrous breakdown of civil administration behind the front, aggravating the mounting internal difficulties.

The second onslaught, which became more effective as the war continued, was aimed at the unity of the Russian Empire and at the home front. From the start the German government (following common practice among the belligerents) tried to fan the varied internal discontent among its enemies in order to weaken them from within. In the case of Russia, the disloyalty of Poles, Finns, Ukrainians, Georgians, Jews, Moslems, and of the extreme socialist revolutionaries furnished particularly tempting opportunities. The German war aims, as they unfolded with the victorious advance, capitalized on all centrifugal forces in the Russian Empire. The national minorities of the entire western perimeter from the Baltic to the Caucasus were to be torn from Russia and placed under German protection. What was left of Russia was to be pushed far to the east. If in the meanwhile the Russian revolutionaries could be persuaded to undermine their country's ability to fight, all the better.

The Russian defeats, incidentally, were not caused by cowardice or lack of patriotism. At the outset one found magnificent courage and contempt for death among the Russian soldiers. What was lacking were equipment, supplies, transport, medical care—in short, the industrial and scientific sinews of modern war whose insufficiency Witte had long deplored. Equally wanting was a sense of modern efficiency and organization in the army command. So appalling was the mismanagement in the early months of the war that the minister of war, V. A. Sukhomlinov, was removed and eventually tried for high treason.

The military disasters of the first year of the war soon produced two major political calamities on the home front. The news of the retreat gave a spurt to public initiative. Zemstvos, town dumas, and other bodies tried to spur the war effort through the mobilization of industry and the reorganization of the medical service. True to tradition, the government frowned on such spontaneity, although it could not entirely stifle it. The public agitation also revived the opposition in the Duma, in which liberals of all shades now combined to form a coalition called the Progressive Bloc. It demanded that, at this moment of danger, the tsar confide in his subjects and appoint a government enjoying their confidence. Some of the most capable ministers indeed welcomed such cooperation with the Duma. Yet the imperial couple, the empress even more than her husband, turned a deaf ear to their pleas. Thus the fragile compromise of 1907, already weakened before the outbreak of the war, was terminated—which proved, alas, that nothing had really changed.

There was no hope even that Nicholas II would exercise his autocratic prerogatives constructively. The plight of his armies persuaded him, on moral grounds, that his place was at the front. In 1915, he therefore moved to army headquarters, leaving his wife in command at the capital (renamed Petrograd). This was the second political calamity to befall Russia, for the empress possessed not a shred of political sense. "Do not laugh at your stupid old wifey," so she reported to him from Petrograd, "but she has on invisible trousers. . . ." She proved that she wore the pants in the imperial family by fighting the moderates in the government who advised conciliation with the Duma. "I assure you," she wrote her husband, "I am yearning to show these cowards my own immortal trousers." In the end it was Rasputin who, behind the scenes, made and unmade the top officials of the empire, and a corrupt or inept lot they were, just when the country was asked to strain its efforts to the utmost. It was a telling paradox that the government which claimed the most extensive powers in all of Europe should prove least capable of mobilizing its country for total war. Official visitors from England and France were shocked by the contrast between the fierce exertions of their own countries and the slackness of the Russian war effort.

By 1916, the English and French had cause to worry about their Russian ally. The hopelessness of the fighting had begun to undermine the morale of the Russian soldiers; revolutionary slogans were circulating again. The dissatisfaction was greatest in the garrison towns, particularly the capital, where it was augmented by grievances of the civilian population. The war had never been popular with the peasants. The senseless slaughter for which they furnished the cannon fodder turned them increasingly against it. Nor was it a fighting cause for strikers drafted into service as punishment. On the home front, too, the backwardness of Russia was taking its toll. Food and fuel were growing scarce, money was losing its value, wages did not keep pace with the rising cost of living. Transportation and domestic trade were breaking down, and public order as well. Petrograd, Moscow, and the great industrial centers were among the places that suffered most. The hardships and the staggering inequalities of sacrifice before long eroded the patriotism manifest in the first months of the war. By 1916, the signs clearly pointed to another storm. In the fall, the police prefect of Petrograd reported that "the hostile feelings have attained a power among the masses which is without precedent, even in 1905–1906."

Yet, contrary to common expectation, the collapse did not come as a result of a mounting revolutionary upsurge. It began, almost imperceptibly, at the center of power. By the end of 1916, the imperial couple had become so estranged from the court and from the ruling circle, which for the most part had stayed clear of Rasputin, that a palace coup was freely advocated, even by members of the imperial family, as the only salvation for the monarchy. "If it is a choice between the tsar and Russia, I'll take Russia"—this was the opinion also of the generals in the field. The plans for the forcible deposition of the imperial couple failed; it took more courage than the titled conspirators could muster. Their only victim was Rasputin, who was murdered in late December. Yet the very idea showed beyond all doubt that Nicholas had wasted every last shred of goodwill that autocracy had ever enjoyed in Russian society. Any casual gust of wind could now smash its hollow pomp.

The portents of these alarms, however, were lost on the emperor. On January 12, 1917, the British ambassador, Sir George Buchanan, deeply perturbed over the turn of events, tried most tactfully to point out to Nicholas the need for public support: "Your Majesty, if I may be permitted to say so, has but one safe course open to you, namely to break down the barrier that separates you from your people and to regain their confidence."

Whereupon Nicholas drew himself up and, looking hard at the embarrassed diplomat, replied, "Do you mean that *I* am to regain the confidence of my people or that they are to regain *my* confidence?" And this in the age of an aroused and politically awake populace!

Within two months, history pronounced its verdict. On March 7, 1917, the grumblings of women waiting in line before the food stores of Petrograd suddenly flared into a major demonstration. When after two days of ever more rebellious rioting the authorities called on the garrison to defend the regime, the soldiers simply melted away. Late on March 12, the tsar's orders had ceased to command in Petrograd and within a few days the same was true throughout the empire. On March 15, sitting in his train at Pskov, the headquarters of the northern armies, he meekly signed his abdication to the emissaries of the Duma group which now claimed power.

Autocratic government as conducted by Nicholas II in the tradition of the Romanovs had been found wanting. It had not given the Russian people the leadership that they needed in either peace or war. But more than autocracy stood condemned: the entire hybrid system, in effect since the 1860s, of autocratic leadership combined with a limited and forever suspect volume of private and nongovernmental public initiative. Neither singly nor supported by a halfhearted measure of public spontaneity had autocracy been able to provide the country with the strength and cohesion required at the moment of supreme peril. The future would decide what other system would work, whether spontaneity unhampered as in the Western democracies, or a revitalized and ever more totalitarian autocracy.

FIVE

The Training of
the Heirs

I

In order to emphasize the fact that the tsarist regime collapsed under the strain of war—and collapsed, furthermore, spontaneously rather than under deliberate revolutionary assault—this essay has said little so far of the opposition groups that in March 1917 conjointly inherited the responsibilities of government. Yet ready they were, with programs, ambitions, and leaders, the product of a long and often raw apprenticeship dating back several generations.

The revolutionary opposition grew out of the intelligentsia, a typical by-product of the outpouring of Western European civilization into Russia, a group without parallel in the West but common enough among the underdeveloped countries. It bore the brunt of the encounter between Russia and Western Europe. Its mission was to transmit cultural stimuli from the West and to relate them as best it could to native conditions. In its ranks one could potentially find all educated Russians regardless of their social origin, for education in itself meant Westernization, and Westernization demanded that Russians see themselves in relation to the West. More specifically, the term intelligentsia stood for the elite that devoted itself fervently to finding answers for the manifold questions raised by the confrontation. Its members were ingrained ideologists, thinkers without self-evident native truths searching for sound foundations in comprehensive theories of historical development (all borrowed from the West). These theories were a matter of life or death to those who held them, to be defended fiercely and intolerantly against friend or foe.

As Toynbee remarked, "Intelligentsias are born to be unhappy." Forever suspended between the "ideal," derived from the philosophies of Western Europe (usually the more extravagant ones), and the "real," which denoted the sordidness of Russia, the Russian intelligentsia (like its counterparts elsewhere) was a profoundly tragic group. It belonged neither to the West nor to Russia. In its isolation it sought solace in extreme visions of human happiness. Nothing less, it seemed, would satisfy its longings than utopia realized. In its misery it also felt a strong kinship with other outcasts: peasants, workers, and all suffering and alienated humanity. This theme, introduced by Belinsky in the 1840s, became one of the leitmotifs of Russian literature. None knew human misery so deeply as the Russian writers.

The intelligentsia's halfway position between Russia and Europe accounted for several congenital incongruities in its outlook. For instance, it displayed a double reaction to Western influences. On the one hand, instinct prompted imitation of the superior norms of the West and the patterning of Russia's future after the Western model (viewed most often in idealized form). Considering the continuous and all-comprehensive superiority of Western Europe, this was the dominant reaction. In Russian literature one meets a tragicomic witness of this penchant, the ardent disciple of every latest fad in European thought who never arrived at any independent views. On the other hand, an almost equally strong instinct, also mobilized by the Western example, bade Russian intellectuals safeguard their native inheritance and the sovereignty of spontaneous and original creativity. They wanted a *Weltanschauung* all their own. This second tendency, called Slavophile, extolled, often in blithe disregard of fact, the Slavic genius over an inferior Western one. Or, in a more reasonable mood, it favored the organic reconstruction of Russian life out of Russian tradition over a continual rash borrowing from abroad. Russia, the Slavophiles said, had to go its own way. The split between the Westernizers, who thought of Russia's future in terms of Western development, and the Slavophiles was all pervasive. It ran crosswise through all political points of view. Yet it was never final. The same person might hold one or the other view at different times of life or even both at the same time in regard to separate aspects of Russian tradition. One could hardly be Slavophile, after all, in matters of military technique, literacy, or sanitation.

The ambivalence appeared in still another form, as a love-hate relationship with the West. It was love, for the West gave the Russian intellectuals their distinction in Russia society, their skills and their sense of direction. Yet there was also bitter hatred, for the West constantly humiliated them. They were borrowers, not contributors of equal standing. Whichever emotion seemed to be on their minds' surface at the moment, its twin was never far below.

Whether viewed with love or hate, the West shook the intelligentsia's self-esteem to the depths. As compared with the French or the English—although perhaps not with an almost equally touchy American of the mid-nineteenth century—Russian intellectuals wore their egos on their sleeves. Yet their sensitivity also sharpened their perceptions. Better than those Europeans, they could see the built-in necessary arrogance of Western society. As Dostoevsky, who knew well the agonies of the Russian intelligentsia, enviously observed:

> Every great people believes and must believe if it intends to live long that in it alone resides the salvation of the world, that it lives in order to stand at the head of the nations, to affiliate and unite all of them, to lead them in a concordant choir toward the final goal preordained for them.

No Russian intellectual could rise to such magnificent self-confidence. Yet Dostoevsky did not think of conquest as the balm for injured pride. Drawing on the deep religious undercurrent in Russian thought, he wanted Russia "to become cosmopolitan." As he wrote in 1880:

> The Russian destiny is incontestably all-European and universal. To become a genuine and all-round Russian means, perhaps, . . . to become brother of all men, a universal man, if you please. . . . Our destiny is universality acquired not by the sword, but by the force of brotherhood and our brotherly longing for fellowship of men. . . . To become a genuine Russian means to seek finally to reconcile all European controversies, to show the solution of European anguish in our all-humanitarian and all-unifying Russian soul, to embrace in it with brotherly love all our brethren and finally, perhaps, to utter the ultimate word of great, universal harmony, of the brotherly accord of all nations abiding by the law of Christ's Gospel.

In this vision Dostoevsky, however, was by no means original. In the face of the French Revolution, German thinkers long ago had claimed a superior spiritual role for their nation. Under English domination, Vivekananda, as cited earlier, similarly tried to rally the Indian intelligentsia. It was a natural reaction of humiliated idealists to glorify the spiritual gift of their people as the instrument of universal salvation.

Most Russian intellectuals, while always keenly sensitive to Russian prestige abroad, were not concerned with Russian might. Power politics was part of the hatred reality from which they hoped to escape. They dreamed of transforming their country into a paragon of social justice and human happiness, where swords were wrought into plowshares. Yet as patriots they were still trapped in the relentless power contests of international relations.

II

The revolutionary impulse in Russia had a long history. It was born, one might say, late in the eighteenth century when educated Russians began to observe the divergence of Russian conditions from the ideal norm derived from the West. When the differences deepened, as they did in the course of the nineteenth century, and when the tsars permitted no public discussion of them, the revolutionary movement waxed stronger. In any comparison the Russian realities stood condemned, foremost the tsar and his bureaucracy, but also all official Russia, including the church. But how to change the regime?

It could never be done, so the great majority of those who wanted a better Russia agreed, by the liberal prescription of persuasion, debate, and majority vote. Even if liberalism had fitted the emotional needs of an alienated intelligentsia (or, in a larger sense, the conditions of Russia), autocracy ruled it out with an iron fist. "All constitutional change," so Count D. A. Tolstoy, the minister of the interior, said in 1884, "must be reconciled with the basic foundation of state order—the absolute Imperial power." To the end, the very word "constitution" remained *non grata*. What liberal tendencies survived under persecution (until easier conditions came to prevail after 1905) did so in the wide and dim border between legality and illegality, a well-meaning but ineffectual force devoted more to cultural enlightenment (for which there was always great need) than to political conquest. Thus the good-natured rationalism and procedure-mindedness with which liberalism might have smoothed the course of social and political change just when the tempo of change was fastest possessed no roots in Russian life.

Russia could be transformed, so the futility of liberalism showed, only by illegal and revolutionary methods. This was the creed of the revolutionary intelligentsia that emerged after the Crimean War. Its revolution, however, was no longer concerned with limited political objectives. The new revolutionaries were socialists aiming at a profound social and moral regeneration in the body politic. Their extravagant visions were matched by their gigantic capacity for moral indignation expressed in terms borrowed from church Slavonic rather than Western idiom. Inspired by the loftiest ideals, they constantly knocked their heads against the inhumanity of Russian life without finding legitimate remedies for their hurts.

The clash between the "ideal" and the "real" nearly always involved the powers that be. Rebellion might start in the family, particularly where discipline was harsh. It always found ample opportunity at school, often amounting to a veritable war between pupils and teachers. It came to climax at the universities or technical institutes, where youthful exuberance ran strongest and the restrictions were most galling. The worst hotbeds of revolution were probably the theological seminaries, where authority was buttressed by religion. But the rebellion did not stop there. Behind a provoked father, teacher, priest, professor, or dean always loomed the policeman or the Cossack acting for the tsar. The chain of authority all too easily transformed juvenile defiance into treason. The Russian rebels were joined by others from the suppressed religious or national minorities for whom the contrast between ideality and reality was still more revolting. Considering the senseless brutality in which the authorities occasionally indulged, the boundless moral indignation of all these idealists might well soar to an immoral and nihilist intensity.

Experience showed that political action was possible only through illegal organization; the revolutionaries had to go underground. Those who chose this calling—both men and women, often of the best families—led a dismal but exciting life. Their careers followed a common pattern. They were hunted by the police. When captured they were imprisoned for long terms often without trials, interrogated until they betrayed their secrets, and sentenced to exile in Siberia where loneliness and isolation undermined body and mind. Some were executed. In order to endure in his calling, the revolutionary had to become hard, as a revolutionary organization told its members in 1878:

> Promise to dedicate all your spiritual strength to the revolution, give up for its sake all family ties and personal sympathies, all loves, all friendships. If necessary give up your life without regard for anything and without sparing anything or anybody. Do not keep any private property, anything that is not at the same time the prosperity of the organization of which you are a member. Give all yourself to the secret society, give up your individual will. . . .

Besides steeling and depersonalizing themselves, the idealist conspirators had to master all the dirty tricks of the craft: forgery, theft, deceit, betrayal, even murder. As Chernyshevsky, a revolutionary who left a deep impression on Lenin, wrote in 1862, "A man with an ardent love of goodness cannot be but a sombre monster." Thus the highest spiritual ends were wedded to the basest means.

The Russian revolutionaries have often been reproached for this unholy combination. Yet it was hardly of their free choice. It was the regime that drove any determined and idealist opposition underground, the policeman who apprenticed the amateur rebel in the arts of conspiracy. The secret police agent found his counterpart in the professional revolutionary. Indeed, between the two an oddly intimate relationship sprang up that made their roles almost interchangeable, as some notorious cases of men serving both causes were to prove. Of the two, the revolutionary was the more heroic, a martyr who served mankind under the most treacherous conditions; no wonder he sometimes flinched and surrendered. He had many admirers in Russian society, particularly among the youth. And he never lacked disciples.

To most Americans, of course, the fusion of idealism and criminality, of the highest ends with the most sordid means, is as repugnant as the mixture of the saint and the sinner in Rasputin. Ends and means, to be sure, rarely interlock even in the best political system. In the Russian revolutionary tradition, however, they were eternities apart—just as in the Russian government which so often had tried to civilize the country by the knout. The professional revolutionary, the overbearing *chinovnik*, the war between ends and means—all these were but symptoms of the same Russian disease of backwardness and of the struggle against it. They marked both autocracy and revolution.

One should not assume, however, that in the revolutionary movement (or in autocracy, for that matter) the extreme was the rule. The majority of Russian youths in the institutes of higher learning, while opposition-minded and sometimes toying with sedition, did not join the outcasts. Even among those who did, many eventually lived abroad, thinking revolution rather than carrying it into action. Or, if they remained in Russia, they preferred tilting with the censor to battling with the police. Much of Russian literature carried revolutionary overtones. And the revolutionary intelligentsia was forever haunted by the "accursed question": What is to be done? Revolution, so incessant failure taught the underground movement, required not only activists; it needed theorists as well. It could succeed only if it had a sound program and a proper underpinning of revolutionary strategy and tactics in the Russian setting. How could a small band of revolutionaries, no matter how dedicated, overthrow the autocratic leviathan and create from Russian realities a haven of justice, prosperity, and peace?

Since no industrial labor force worth mentioning existed until the 1890s, it was natural that the revolutionaries should think in terms of the peasantry. For centuries, the peasants had been an endemic revolutionary force. In their commune furthermore, so Alexander Herzen taught a whole generation of intellectuals in the 1860s and 1870s who called themselves *narodniks*, lay the seed of the future socialist society. The *narodnik* movement was the most influential revolutionary force before the advent of the Marxists in the 1890s. The commune kept private property, capitalism, and all the evils of industrialization out of the village. Hence Russia could be spared the spiritual and material corruption that, according to socialist theory, they caused. Once autocracy was overthrown, the peasants would build, from the grass roots up, a new type of society embodying their deep spiritual wisdom (which most intellectuals worshiped from a distance).

The task of the professional revolutionaries, according to a school of thought led by Bakunin, was to heat the peasant discontent to the explosion point and then to let matters take their course until autocracy, the church, and all the other trammels of established authority had been destroyed. The best society, they proclaimed, was that in which no government existed at all and the people settled their affairs by their own local arrangements. Anarchism (in this or milder form) understandably had a powerful appeal to those who suffered from a highly centralized state. It was deeply ingrained in the revolutionary movement as well as in the peasant mind.

Unfortunately almost all who carried the revolutionary agitation into the village soon discovered that it was impossible to establish a working relationship with the peasants; the gulf between peasant Russia and "privilege Russia" stood also in the way of the revolutionaries. How could it be bridged? The more patient revolutionaries began to devote themselves to humble cultural work among the peasants in order to mend the fatal rift. The impatient ones experimented with terror as a means of shocking the people into rebellion in order to unhinge autocracy. For over two years (1879–1881) a wave of assassination, directed against the most hated officials, swept the country. It culminated in the murder of Alexander II in 1881. Yet when the bomb exploded under the autocrat, autocracy as an institution did not even tremble.

This failure, which chastened the revolutionary movement for years, lent support to those few theorists who had never put their faith in the people. A small elite of professional revolutionaries, they argued, should seize power in the name of the masses and hold it in trust until society had been prepared for the benefits of socialism. They did not believe, in other words, that the spontaneous actions of the peasants held any promise for the future. What counted was organization and the ardor of the revolutionary elite.

Whatever the numerous experiments of revolution during the second half of the nineteenth century, none had any result except slowly to refine the infamy of political warfare between the police and the radical opposition. The great advance in the revolutionary movement came only after the turn of the century. The era of mass politics began, even in Russia, to offer new opportunities for revolution (without, however, resolving the old problems of theory or practice). At the end of the Witte system the bulk of the population had become politically activated as never before. This fact, for the first time, provided the revolutionary circles with a potential mass following. The relaxation of autocratic power after 1905 permitted a much larger volume of publicity and agitation.

III

The expansion of the political stage mobilized at last the moderate element in Russian society. The Imperial Duma offered a public forum for a legal opposition encouraged by the vigorous models of liberal democracy in France, England, and the United States. Russian liberalism, considered to be the natural heir to autocracy, drew its strength from two small but influential groups, the advanced elements of the landowning nobility that had long called, through the zemstvos, for some form of central parliament, and the growing element of a new and more substantial intelligentsia—a middle-class intelligentsia—composed of lawyers, doctors, teachers, professors, and the like who played a crucial part in the modernization of Russia. In the course of the Revolution of 1905 these two groups merged in the party of the Constitutional Democrats (Cadets). Their most forceful leader was Paul Miliukov, who had made a reputation as a historian before he ventured into politics. The Cadets believed in the sanctity of private property and in individual enterprise, but they also favored a measure of social regulation, provided it was imposed by parliamentary procedure and hedged in by due process of law. Open-minded toward the wishes of other groups, they insisted above all on legality in public action and, by implication at least, on the leadership of the educated few. They were ready to cooperate with the revolutionary underground, realizing that the overthrow of the autocracy called for a broad political front; yet they themselves eschewed violence. Many of them indeed feared the anarchism of the Russian masses. Their ends and means were to be cut from the same cloth. Their most congenial stage was therefore the Duma (despite its restricted suffrage), not the street.

Although opposed to autocracy, the Cadets were still nationalists in moderation. They thought of Russia as a Great Power carrying out its historic mission as protector of the Slavic peoples and playing a proud role in Europe and the world. A liberal regime, they expected, could do this much better than the benighted autocracy. In politics admittedly they were content to let their country be a follower of Western development rather than a leader in its own right. But in science, art, and above all in literature, they were proud of what Russia had already accomplished.

These complacent perspectives made optimists of the Cadets. The natural course of political evolution, as demonstrated by Western Europe, would inevitably prepare their ascent to power, an assumption that called for neither extensive inquiry into the suitability of democratic government for Russian conditions nor elaborate organizational preparation.

Looking back in March 1917, the Cadets might indeed conclude that history was going their way. Despite setbacks, the liberal current had run strong since 1905. Russia was allied with a democratic England and France against Germany militarism and reaction. In the Progressive Bloc of 1915, Miliukov and his party had assumed the leadership over the entire opposition in the Duma, including the bulk of the Octobrists. Miliukov's Duma speeches of 1916 had helped more than anything else to undermine what public confidence the government still enjoyed. Now the autocracy was dead, who but the liberals had the necessary experience in public affairs to take over the government? Would they also have the necessary mass support? When they began to think about ways and means, they became sadly frustrated and divided. This was most obvious during the war. Could autocracy mobilize Russia for victory? No. Were the liberals then to do away with autocracy? No, for revolution in time of war would bring out the worst instincts of the rabble. When it came to the prospect of government by the Russian people, Miliukov essentially thought like Durnovo or Witte. He was condemned to stand by passively.

As the Duma liberals and their allies in the Progressive Bloc gathered on March 12 when the rebellion in Petrograd was at its height, their offices in the right wing of the Tauride Palace remained ominously silent and empty. The din of insurrection centered in the left wing of the building, where soldiers and workers under the leadership of the Social Revolutionaries and the Social Democrats were forming the Soviet of

Workers' and Soldiers' Deputies. Frightened by their isolation, the liberals hurriedly proclaimed a Provisional Government to hold power until the meeting of a democratically elected Constituent Assembly, lest power slip into less competent hands. Thus, at the moment of its triumph, liberalism was challenged by the older and more radical revolutionary groups, each considering itself a more appropriate mouthpiece for the will of the people, which now had become tsar.

IV

The Social Revolutionaries were the heirs of the *narodnik* movement and of the revolutionary organizations of the previous century. Constituted as a political party shortly after 1900, they possessed a core of professional revolutionaries—for a time it even boasted a "maximalist" terrorist faction—yet it suffered from constant persecution and lost its best leaders. The relative freedom of agitation after 1905 diversified the membership. It was not easy for Victor Chernov, the surviving leader of stature (who by nature was no leader), to hold together the moderates, who differed little from the liberals, and the impatient radicals who pressed for peasant seizure of the nobility's lands.

By its principles, the party was pledged to obey the will of the toiling people, that is, the peasants. No one could deny that the Social Revolutionaries knew their rural Russia. After 1905, peasants and intelligentsia were no longer so far apart as in the previous century. The Social Revolutionary program voiced their common aims. Once autocracy was overthrown, it stated, the reconstruction of Russian society was to proceed spontaneously, rising from the village to higher organs of government and culminating in a federal center. The same preference for decentralization, incidentally, also applied to their party organization, which, as a result, always remained loosely knit and ineffectual.

The democratic principle was carried over into economic life. If the peasants wanted the land, so the Social Revolutionary program said, all land was to be theirs, without compensation to former nonpeasant owners. Yet the title to the land was to be held "socially" (whatever that meant in terms of law—the concept of private property was to be kept out of Russia). Each peasant household was to cultivate with its own resources as much land as it could, aided by whatever cooperative ventures it might wish to join. Nothing, however, was to violate the basic rule of equality in peasant society.

The Social Revolutionary party, it has been said, represented a state of mind rather than a program. It suffered from the vagueness typical of all efforts to rebuild Russia from the peasant base upward. How, for instance, could the regional differences of income caused by different climate and soils be equalized without the intervention of a strong central authority? What, furthermore, of the peasant commune condemned by Stolypin—should it be resurrected or allowed to disappear? And what of industry? Most Social Revolutionaries were willing to let private enterprise in that branch of the economy continue for an indefinite period. They subordinated industry to agriculture, presuming that it would develop only as the countryside prospered.

Nor could the Social Revolutionaries explain how peasant Russia might preserve its sovereignty in the power competition of an imperialist age. One writer in the *narodnik* tradition, S. N. Iuzhakov, had suggested that by nature Russia was predestined to lead the worldwide revolt of the preindustrialized societies against their capitalist exploiters. But nothing had come of this thought. Preoccupied with peasant Russia, the Social Revolutionaries did not think in terms of power politics. They complacently followed the common socialist belief in the international solidarity of the toilers which, after the revolution, would permanently end all power conflicts. During the war they remained on the sidelines, neither wholeheartedly supporting the war nor condemning it.

When their opportunity came in March 1917, the Social Revolutionaries reaped the benefits of their long agitation among the peasants. The Petrograd Soviet, composed largely of soldiers who were but peasants in uniform, gave them a clear majority. If numbers were to decide the succession to autocracy, the party of the peasants would certainly be the chief heir.

V

In everything but numbers, however, the Social Democrats had a clear advantage over the Social Revolutionaries, chiefly because they drew on the infinitely greater intellectual vigor of Marxism. Marxism had much to offer to Russian revolutionaries. Perhaps its greatest attraction was the imposing scope, the magnificent presumption of a philosophical system based on a knowledge of the "scientific" laws of history. Here at last the Russian intelligentsia found the comprehensive ideology for which it had been yearning, and one, moreover, that lifted it, as on the wings of religion, from despondency to the gates of omnipotence and fulfillment.

What spoke especially to their conditions as revolutionaries was the fact that Marxism made the industrial proletariat the preordained vehicle of social and human regeneration. Throughout the nineteenth century, the Russian peasantry had failed to heed the revolutionaries' call. Marx taught his Russian followers to take the workers as their comrades in arms. The Marxist appeal to the Russian intelligentsia was greatest of all in the 1890s, when the growing volume of strikes first called attention to the workers' political potential.

The revolutionary comradeship with the proletariat suited, moreover, the intellectuals' spiritual need for identification with suffering humanity. They were carried away by the expectation of a socialist (or communist) society in which, for the first time in all history, individuals would be truly masters of their destinies. At the same time Marx's emphasis on the strife and ruthlessness of the class struggle responded to the fighting mood of men and women harassed by daily persecution. It cheered them, too, for through Marxism they saw themselves glorified in a great historical tradition running from the French Revolution to the deliverance of mankind from evil.

When it first became a force among the Russian intelligentsia, Marxism expressed the temper of the times. Industrialization was making rapid strides in Russia; it was the wave of the future. Unlike the *narodniks* and their Social Revolutionary successors, the Marxists were modernists, at least in part. They welcomed the cultural advance that came with the rise of large-scale industry. Yet at the same time they continued the *narodniks'* moral aversion to the evils of industrialism, saying that those flaws were merely the result of "capitalism."* They would disappear after the socialist revolution, when large-scale production and the perfection of society would combine to produce an earthly paradise. Under communism competition, division of labor and professional specialization would disappear; people would be their natural selves— which amounted to an idealization of preindustrial life or, put more crassly, of backwardness, a subliminal attraction to Russian romantic intellectuals.

As the Russian intellectuals steeped themselves in Marxism, however, it became clear that their creed, so largely based on Western European precedent, did not readily fit Russian realities. The exact location of their Russia in the Marxist chart of history was a tough

* In this essay the terms "capitalist" and "capitalism" are set in quotation marks when used in their Marxist sense.

theoretical problem. Autocracy, Marxists would agree, was a feudal
rather than a bourgeois institution. Russian capitalism was still weak.
Marxism thus might seem to require that its followers first strive for a
capitalist Russia—a preposterous suggestion; to a Russian Marxist the
rise of "capitalism" in Russia always signified the rise of the proletariat
as a revolutionary force and a step toward socialism. They were always
one step ahead of history.

And was the proletariat to be tool or master of the revolutionary intelligentsia? Seasoned Marxists answered that naturally the proletariat fashioned its own mentality (or "consciousness," according to their lingo)
and thus shaped its destiny. The revolutionary intelligentsia merely
acted as a vanguard, which took its orders and its very outlook from the
main force. Yet would the revolutionary hotspurs be willing to mark time
if the "consciousness" of the proletariat were not ready for either revolution or socialism? And was its "consciousness" ever to be trusted?

In the bitter disputes that arose over these issues, two distinct points
of view emerged, the "soft" and the "hard." Both were advanced by revolutionaries familiar with the vicissitudes of their calling. For years the
difference was one of emphasis and inclination, not of fundamentals.
Only gradually did the rift ripen into schism. By 1912 the breach was
complete; by 1917 it was irrevocable.

The "softs" inclined toward the liberal-humanitarian strains in
Marxism. They were willing to listen to the views of the industrial workers (but never of the peasants!) and to adjust themselves to their spontaneous activities. They cheered when the workers formed the St.
Petersburg Soviet in 1905. For the same reason they preferred a party
structure allowing a maximum of mass participation, after the model of
the German Social Democratic party. They looked forward to the day
when all their work could be legal. Necessity drove them underground,
but they never felt comfortable with the conflict of ends and means that
ensued; they shrunk from fanaticism. Since in their estimate Russia was
not ready for socialism—it would come to Russia only after it had been
achieved in the West—they leaned toward patience and tolerance. Their
goal was the overthrow of autocracy and the establishment of a liberal-
democratic regime with a strong labor party and a powerful trade union
movement.

The "soft" position was generally adopted by the faction called
Menshevik (the minority), so named after an entirely unrepresentative
ballot at a party congress in 1903, when it had lost out to the "hards."
With a quick eye for the propaganda advantage, the latter forever thereafter hailed themselves as Bolsheviks (the majority), although in fact the

Mensheviks always had a larger following right down to March 1917, when they formed the second largest faction in the Petrograd Soviet.

VI

The "hard" position was the creation of Vladimir Ilich Ulianov (1870–1924), better known as Lenin, one of the great political figures of the twentieth century. From Western and native sources he fashioned the first great Western anti-Western movement, with a style suited to the temper of the outer reaches of the urban-industrial West.

The tensions of the times pushed the two eldest sons of the Ulianov family into the revolutionary movement. As a supervisor of schools in the chief towns of the lower Volga region, Lenin's father had risen high in the ranks of the imperial bureaucracy, advancing even into the hereditary nobility. If his sons turned rebels after his death it was, presumably, because of the discrepancy between their humanitarian ideals, innocuously—and perhaps too ardently—cultivated in their home, and the harsh reality of the autocratic regime. For his protest, Lenin's older brother soon paid with his life. While a student at the University of St. Petersburg he took part in a plot against the tsar's life and was executed in 1887. His fate committed the younger boy to the same cause.

In constant trouble with the authorities from the start of his university studies, Lenin was trained as a lawyer. In 1893 he moved to the capital and at once immersed himself in the revolutionary agitation among the factory workers, who welcomed the solicitude of the intelligentsia (although not necessarily their revolutionary extremism). In a short time he assumed a position of respect in the Marxist circles. Inevitably the police began to take notice, and in December 1895, he found himself arrested. Sentenced after some delay, he was exiled to a village in the depths of Siberia. Neither jail nor exile diminished his prodigious capacity for work. Barred from all revolutionary action, he wrote an impressive scholarly tome, *The Development of Capitalism in Russia*, and translated Sidney and Beatrice Webb's volume on trade unionism, not to mention many pamphlets, articles, and letters. In Siberia he married a fellow revolutionary from St. Petersburg, likewise under sentence of exile, named Krupskaia—she continued to be called by her maiden name—who served him as a devoted and selfless companion to the end of his days. She bore him no offspring—how could they have fitted children into a revolutionary career?

After his release in 1900, Lenin went to western Europe, soon to be followed by his wife. There they stayed until 1917, with the exception of a brief Russian interlude during the Revolution of 1905, rootless aliens, unwanted and unassimilated. When Trotsky after his first escape from Siberia visited Lenin in London, Lenin showed him the sights. "This is *their* famous Westminster," he said, pointing at the Houses of Parliament. Alas, to Lenin the good things of Europe were all *theirs*, the capitalists' and exploiters'. Ill at ease amidst their comforts, Lenin never acquired an inside view of Western democracy or of "capitalism." He remained close to his Russian heritage, a secret Slavophile in the Marxist ranks. With the single-mindedness of genius he pined for Russia, for revolution, and for getting the better of the "capitalists'" easy superiority, the cause of which he, like Marx, never understood.

By 1902, the revolution seemed as distant as ever. Two generations of revolutionaries had passed and accomplished nothing. Their accumulated failures now taught a still more impatient third generation, of which Lenin made himself the spokesman, to become yet hardier and craftier professional revolutionaries. More intensively than even Chernyshevsky's "monster," Lenin armed himself to the depths of his personality for this task. Softness in any form was the supreme sin. As he once observed to Maxim Gorky:

> I can't listen to music too often. It affects your nerves, makes you want to say stupid nice things and stroke the heads of people who could create such beauty while living in this vile hell. And now you must not stroke anyone's head—you might get your hands bitten off.

The previous generations of revolutionaries had had their hands bitten off by being too emotional, too kind, too careless with their impulses. By contrast Lenin permitted himself only the most rational and cold-blooded calculations of revolutionary opportunity. In case of failure he allowed no despair, but counseled self-criticism, analysis of the mistakes, and a new and still more earnest beginning. In case of success he shunned exultation—that too was a form of weakness and courted disaster.

What counted "in this vile hell" was discipline, method, accuracy, precision, and infinite patience with detail in all the black arts of revolution. A revolutionary had to be *toujours en védette*, ready to advance when possible and to retreat when necessary, to endure above all, and to preserve intact the vital revolutionary resolve. Throughout his life, Lenin retained an almost masochistic fierceness toward the gentle voices that might weaken this hard-won determination, whether generosity, sentimentality, or any form of what he called "petty-bourgeois" morality. The only moral guide that a revolutionary recognized, he preached, was success in his calling. Considering the emotional and undisciplined ways of the Russian intelligentsia in which it had its origin, Lenin's code was a remarkable monument to the human will. Yet it still remained a product of human flesh and blood. It could be upheld—and the doubts suppressed—only by the utmost exertions of fanaticism. Thus rationality of purpose was carried to the point of a rigid irrational compulsion. And human nature demanded a price for such outrage. All too often Lenin, who in his heart remained tuned to the music of kindliness, complained that his nerves played him tricks that kept him from working. Revolutionaries with coarser temperaments, of course, would have better nerves. And the fourth generation—the commissars—would laugh at such weakness; the trend favored the primitives like Stalin.

The code of thought and feeling that Lenin prescribed for himself and other revolutionaries was accompanied by a set of rules for the organization through which they must work. These rules again can best be understood as a response to past failures. The revolutionaries had had their hands bitten off, Lenin charged, because they had been amateur organizers. Their desire to imitate the mass organizations of the German Social Democratic party had allowed the police to penetrate their ranks. What had been created with heroic effort was thus wiped out in short order; the best revolutionaries were sacrificed for nothing. His plea therefore was for a revolutionary organization capable of outsmarting the police (which at this time, under the direction of an ex-revolutionary, Colonel Zubatov, was beginning to apply the methods of modern crime detection to the revolutionary movement).

Survival—not to mention success—under these conditions was impossible, Lenin argued, so long as the Russian Marxists believed that the revolution must proceed from the workers themselves. He angrily proclaimed the contrary view. "The history of all countries shows that the working class, exclusively by its own efforts, is able to develop only trade union consciousness."

Revolutionary consciousness, Lenin proceeded, could be carried to the workers only from without, by the revolutionary intelligentsia, an altogether different category. Whether this was universally true may be questioned. But who could deny that the Russian workers were singularly unsuited to cope effectively with the complex tasks of bringing socialism to Russia? As Lenin pointed out in 1902 in regard to forming a Russian workers' party similar to the German Social Democratic party, "What is to a great extent automatic in a politically free country must in

Russia be done deliberately and systematically by our organizations."
What counted in the Russian setting was organizational leadership. The
brittle relationship between the intellectual vanguard and the proletarian
masses remained a crucial ingredient in Lenin's political theory. It
betrayed his ineradicable suspicion of all spontaneous, unorganized
humanity, even of genuinely proletarian organizations like the St.
Petersburg Soviet of 1905. This secret contempt of spontaneity sheltered
him from the influences of the Western democratic model, yet it also
perpetuated the old cleavage between the educated classes and the Russian masses. (Could there have been a more disdainful approach to the
man in the street than this heartless collective term, "the masses"?)
Physically and spiritually, Lenin (like Marx) always kept aloof from the
workers. Did he ever set foot inside a factory?

Revolution, then, was the concern of the Marxist revolutionary leaders, the heirs of both the Russian and European revolutionary tradition
and the masters of the scientific laws of historical development. They
alone possessed the proper "consciousness." They devised the appropriate policy for every new set of circumstances and formulated what eventually became known as "the party line." It had to be defined precisely
so as to avoid misunderstanding and to enable the members of the party
to carry it out to the letter. The elite, Lenin further insisted, must be
organized like a miniature army, a human machine expressly designed
for revolution, disciplined and loyal to the commander. He therefore
demanded that the party's Central Committee have plenary power over
the entire organization, like a commanding general over all officers and
troops in the field. And like a general in time of war—war and revolution were much akin—the revolutionary leader could not afford to be
choosy in his methods. In 1907 Lenin wrote:

> Revolution is a difficult matter. It cannot be made with gloves and
> manicured fingernails. . . . A party is no girls dormitory. Party mem-
> bers should not be measured by the narrow standard of petty-bourgeois
> morality. Sometimes a scoundrel is useful to our party precisely
> because he is a scoundrel.

During the low years after the failure of the Revolution of 1905, Lenin
even approved of bank robbery, euphemistically called "expropriation,"
as a means of financing the Russian Social Democratic party. The most
spectacular of these "ex's" was carried out in Tiflis under the supervision of Stalin. Later, during the war, he had no scruples about taking
German money for his faction. All means were fair so long as they
promoted the revolution. Needless to say, Lenin's conception of what a

Russian Social Democratic party should be, so contrary to the liberal-humanitarian tradition of Marxism, did not go unchallenged. As early as 1903, Trotsky predicted what would happen if Lenin's views prevailed:

> The organization of the party takes the place of the party itself; the central committee takes the place of the organization, and finally the dictator takes the place of the central committee.

This, precisely, was the way in which the Bolshevik party evolved (and after the summer of 1917 even with Trotsky's active support).

Lenin, however, would never see the danger. He believed that in the comradeship of the common struggle no conflict could arise within the party. The flow of commands from above would be modulated by the flow of information and suggestion from below; no constitutional safeguards were needed. At all events, his chief reply to his critics was unanswerable. Under autocracy—and he never believed that the October Manifesto made any difference—only a secret and highly trained organization of militant revolutionaries could prevail. It was either that or catastrophe again. Under Russian conditions, he further contended, the masses could be properly won to the party and made conscious of their role only if the party attained the quality of a tight-knit revolutionary elite. Striking workers, he wrote, would hardly risk their lives for an unwieldy, spy-ridden mass organization. They needed efficiency and the leadership of reliable underground agents to guide their work in street and factory. Successful mass action indeed depended on the expert core.

VII

Combining the highly centralized leadership of the revolutionary elite—of Lenin himself—with large-scale action in the age of mass politics, was a many-sided and highly problematical challenge. The secret of success in this squaring of the circle lay in constant agitation by the elite among the masses. By propaganda and a thousand other forms of directing revolutionary discontent, including irrational means of mass manipulation, the revolutionaries were to shape the "consciousness" of the masses. Lenin early recognized the benefit of slogans and other simplified appeals geared more to the emotions than to the understanding of the man in the street. Thus the Bolsheviks learned the techniques of modern mass politics under the frontier conditions of revolutionary warfare. Never, so Lenin preached, could they afford to lose touch with the masses. In this lay their strength.

Yet, in the last analysis, the identification was never quite complete. With all their skills of manipulation, the Bolsheviks could never lure the masses into the proper consciousness. The gap between spontaneity and revolutionary consciousness remained unbridged—the circle, after all, could not be squared. The Bolsheviks thus shared the predicament of the tsars. Unlike the other opposition parties, which bowed, in theory as well as practice, to the will of the people, they could not admit the population into the political decision-making process, which is the essence of democracy. By his own theory Lenin was cast into the role of a counter-tsar, and the Bolshevik faction into that of a counterautocracy. Thus did the tsarist regime perpetuate itself, illegitimately, yet with improved skill; for despite the innate flaw, Bolshevik political practice was vastly superior to that of the tsars, who had never learned to work with an aroused populace.

One positive strand tied Lenin, however obliquely, to the tsars—his nationalism. As one reads his famous pamphlet of 1902, *What Is to Be Done?* which sets forth the basic concepts of Leninism, one is struck by his allusions to the superiority of the Russian revolutionary movement. Fighting the most reactionary government in Europe, it was the vanguard of the international revolutionary proletariat.

> The role of the vanguard fighter can be fulfilled only by a party that is guided by the most advanced theory. To have a concrete understanding of what this means, let the reader recall such predecessors of Russian Social Democracy as Herzen, Belinsky, Chernyshevsky, and the brilliant galaxy of revolutionaries in the 1870s, let him ponder over the world significance which Russian literature is now acquiring; let him . . . but be that enough.

The incomplete "let him" speaks volumes for the soaring national pride in Lenin, who yearned for world recognition, not on behalf of the empire—that was moribund—but for revolutionary Russia. His thought leaped far ahead into the future. Lenin undoubtedly was guilty of what Trotsky once called "that national revolutionary messianic mood which prompts one to see one's own nation state as destined to lead mankind to socialism." And he forcefully expressed the burning hope for an escape from backwardness voiced earlier among Russian intellectuals. In Lenin, Russian nationalism and the Marxist foreknowledge of history combined in the most powerful stimulant to the Russian ego yet evolved. Let "capitalist" Europe beware!

The obvious objection to such utopian ambition, according to Marxist theory (as well as to common sense), lay of course in the fact of Russian backwardness. Russian "capitalism" would not complete its appointed course for a long time. But for a third-generation revolutionary like Lenin such perspectives were intolerable and, fortunately for him, not entirely supported by the evidence. As the events of 1905 showed, Russia possessed a revolutionary thrust that might well carry it quickly beyond a purely bourgeois phase to global preeminence.

Marx already had advised the revolutionary vanguard to take any available revolutionary force as its ally. Lenin expected no help from the Russian *bourgeoisie*, a class far weaker than its Western counterpart. At least one stratum of that class had been bought off by the October Manifesto; the others had not acted vigorously enough (and never could, by their very nature). It was rather the peasantry that had accounted for the revolutionary ground swell. And to the peasants Lenin turned in 1905, despite the fact that Marxist theory rated them as hopeless, Marx himself having spoken of the "idiocy of the countryside." Whatever the economic convictions of the peasants—Lenin always remained suspicious of their "petty-bourgeois" bent of mind—the explosive impact of Black Partition was invaluable revolutionary capital, too important to be spurned. Thus he began to speak, over the protest of the "softs," of a revolutionary democratic dictatorship of the proletariat and the peasants (the poorer peasants particularly), which was to emerge from the overthrow of autocracy.

The new perspectives also implied an adjustment of the normal Marxist pattern of social progress to Russian conditions. The peculiarities of Russia prevented a clear-cut succession from feudalism to capitalism and from capitalism to socialism. In Russia, as in other backward countries, a combined development was apt to be the rule. Feudal elements mingled with capitalist and socialist ones; a weak bourgeoisie and a powerful underclass of peasants and workers existed side by side even under autocracy. Thus, Lenin foresaw that after the overthrow of autocracy the toiling masses would already have the upper hand, giving the new government the character of a powerful revolutionary democratic dictatorship rather than of a bourgeois democracy in the Western style. Such a regime, he thought, might also have a startling effect outside Russia. It might act as a spark, setting off the proletarian revolution in the advanced "capitalist" West, riper for socialism than Russia. Having created a socialist society of its own, the West would then rush, with socialist zeal, to introduce socialism into Russia, well in advance of the natural course of its development. Trotsky, who was gradually drifting closer to the Bolshevik position, formulated an even more articulate theory—the theory of "the permanent revolution"—for those who wanted to march forward to socialism regardless of whether Russia was ready or not. Such implacable revolutionary determination in theory and practice, incidentally, ranged the Bolsheviks on the side of the irrationalists in European politics, despite their guise of Marxist rationalism; backwardness was not easily overcome.

VIII

When war broke out in 1914, Lenin watched with choking rage the collapse of international socialist solidarity. Workers now fought workers for the defense of their national interest, for their bourgeoisie. During these bitter months, after settling down in cheap lodgings in Zurich, he set the basic concepts of Bolshevism into the largest possible context of global politics. Russian revolutionary theory had traditionally suffered from its ignorance of the realities of power politics. Lenin, in his famous pamphlet *Imperialism the Last Stage of Capitalism* (1916), now remedied this deficiency. In the last stage, he argued, giant capitalist monopolies competed all over the world for new markets. In their rivalry they set nation against nation, people against people. Thus they had caused World War I. Yet the very violence of the imperialist competition advanced the revolution in a double movement. The war, Lenin predicted, would make the European proletariat rise against its masters. Ever since the outbreak of hostilities, he himself had urged the European socialists to convert the international war into a civil war. Yet—and this was a new feature—it would also drive the colonial peoples, who in the period of imperialism had been enslaved by "capitalist" rule, to rise against their exploiters (among whom Lenin included Imperial Russia). This grand conception of imperialism provided a ridiculously distorted account of both "capitalism" and the origins of the war. Yet it contained a prophetic insight. In it Lenin fused the traditional socialist revolutionary movement in Europe with the incipient Anti-Western global revolt, which he had keenly eyed for several years. The "internal" and the "external" proletariat, the industrial workers of Europe and the backward peoples, were joining forces against the Western ruling classes then locked in mortal combat. Posing the question of what he would do if the party of the proletariat came to power during the current war, Lenin confidently replied (1915):

> We should have to prepare and undertake revolutionary war, that is, not only should we fully carry through in the most decisive ways our entire minimum program but we should systematically begin to draw into revolt all peoples now oppressed by the Great Russians, [and in

addition] all colonies and dependent countries of Asia (India, China, Persia, and so on), and also—and primarily—the socialist proletariat of Europe.

It was a sweeping vision of a counterpower to the great outpouring of Western civilization, a counterpower centered around the revolutionary potential of the European proletariat. Thus Leninism helped to carry the seed of the French Revolution into the non-European world. Liberty, equality, and fraternity—the revolutionary quintessence of European civilization—now were set to work against the Western domination of the global community.

Before March 1917, however, all of Lenin's plans for effective revolutionary action in the imperialist age remained a matter of theory. They merely reflected his effort to keep Marxist analysis—the correct version—abreast of the rapidly unfolding events. However crucial for the political education of the "hards," they did not advance the cause. Representing the extreme left of the Russian Social Democratic party and counting few adherents, the Bolsheviks were even more unsuccessful and divided than the other opposition groups. Despite Lenin's talk of the superior efficiency of his revolutionary elite, the secret police had succeeded in planting an agent, Roman Malinovsky, in its inner circles; he enjoyed Lenin's confidence. Paradoxically, the Bolsheviks became an effective political force only after the collapse of autocracy.

At the time of the March Revolution, the Bolsheviks were still a negligible group. Their leaders were scattered: Lenin in Switzerland, Stalin in Siberia, Trotsky (whom we may henceforth include among the "hards") in New York. They possessed but a handful of delegates in the Petrograd Soviet. Yet when Lenin heard of the fall of autocracy, his mind was made up. A socialist revolution in Russia—and perhaps world revolution too—was within reach. The Provisional Government of Russia, he wrote,

> is in no condition to escape collapse, for it is impossible to tear ourselves out of the claws of that terrible monster begotten by world capitalism—the imperialist war and the famine—without leaving the soil of bourgeois relations, without going over to revolutionary methods, without appealing to the greatest historical heroism of the proletariat of Russia and the whole world.

He arrived in Petrograd toward the end of April 1917, after having crossed Germany with the assistance of the German government. At once he set the course of his small band of followers toward the seizure of power in the name of the proletariat, staking all on the monstrous effects of the war.

1917: March to November

I

The year 1917 was one of agony and mounting crises for all European belligerents. The strain of war, now stretching from the third into the fourth year, became well-nigh unbearable. England, governed since December 1916 by Lloyd George's strong war cabinet, was brought to the verge of starvation by German submarine warfare. France, after the failure of the Nivelle offensive in May, saw its troops mutiny on critical sectors of the front and its government falter until, in November, Clemenceau (the Tiger) took over the reins as head of the government. In Germany, where more than elsewhere the exertions of the war had caused drastic government control of the economy and, under the "Hindenburg program" of December 1916, of manpower as well, the ravages of the "turnip winter" reopened and deepened the prewar political schism. As a result, the government became a virtual dictatorship under the High Command. For Italy, the year, which had witnessed much demoralization and unrest, ended with the disastrous defeat of Caporetto. As for Austria-Hungary, which of all major powers resembled Russia the most, the situation was summed up by the advice that Count Czernin, under the impact of the news from Russia, gave to the new Emperor Charles: "If the monarchs of the Central Powers cannot make peace in the coming months, it will be made for them by their peoples." The Emperor's Czech, Croat, and Italian soldiers were indeed hastening the peace by deserting to the enemy.

While stalemate on the western front persisted despite the use of ever more savage weapons, there was still hope of victory: for the allies in their association, after April, with the United States; for the Central

Powers in the imminent collapse of Russia. This hope, combined with a patriotism often bordering on hysteria, produced in England, France, Germany, and—after Caporetto—in Italy, the grim determination to endure to the end. Elsewhere defeatism rapidly gained ground. Among the countries that stood up under the strain, government became more authoritarian or dictatorial. At the same time war propaganda became more messianic. At the start of the war, men had thought of its aims in concrete terms of territories or boundaries. As it dragged on, they began to think of it ideologically, as a war for human freedom and justice, and even a war to end all wars, involving the very future of civilization or of mankind. After the entry of the United States into the war, Woodrow Wilson became the leader of the ideological crusade. Yet while they talked of humanity, governments and people became self-centered as never before, sacrificing the last shred of cosmopolitanism to the furies of combat. Russia could thus expect little sympathy from even its allies for its trials in this decisive year.

II

The collapse of the autocratic regime left the Russian empire without effective government and its people open to intense political agitation—with unforeseen consequences. Never did the Russian people enjoy greater political freedom than after March 1917. Apart from the pressure of the German and Austro-Hungarian armies (which remained passive for most of the year), they were masters of their fate. In their new freedom would they be able to manage bringing state and society into alignment and constructing a more effective government? Would they be able to raise the strength and prestige of Russia in the world? Out of the efforts of the heirs to cope with these key questions arose the next and more drastic revolution.

The new regime did not get off to an auspicious start; the government that took over in March was deeply divided. Until the meeting of the Constituent Assembly, the Provisional Government considered itself the legitimate successor. It staffed the ministerial posts, made plans (many of them eminently sensible and necessary), formulated policies, and tried to carry them out as best it could without civil service or police. It was the government in everything except the essence: executive power. This attribute was rather in the hands of the other government, the Petrograd Soviet, which derived its mandate from the garrison and workers of the capital who had made the March Revolution. Its leaders, moderate socialists all, repudiated any thought of the Soviet taking over the reins of government. They conceived of the Soviet merely as the guardian of the toiling masses under a regime that was bourgeois in nature. Yet, under pressure from their constituents, they were all too often forced to assume the functions of government in crucial issues of domestic and foreign policy.

The solitary link between the uneasy partners was Alexander Kerensky. As an important member of both bodies, he became the central figure in the new era (although not prime minister until July). A young man of inexhaustible energy, an idealist of moderate Social Revolutionary views, gifted with superb powers of speech, and driven by an exalted sense of mission, he alone was capable of whipping up the consensus of moderate opinion necessary for a democratic regime. He was the first of the great orators of revolutionary mass politics in the modern age. The exalted quality of his appeal, so lofty and yet so devoid of political realism, fitted the mood of expectancy that reigned in the early weeks. He reminisced in exile about the dawn of the new era:

> New fires of hope and aspiration were kindled and the masses were drawn together by mysterious bonds. We have lived through many beautiful and terrible events since then, but I can still feel the great soul of the people as I did in those days. I can feel their terriffic force which may be led to perform great deeds or incited to horrible crimes. As a flower turns to the sun, so the newly awakened soul of the people longed for light and truth. The people followed us when we tried to raise them above material things to the light of high ideals.

Yet persuasive as Kerensky's oratory was in those days, it could not close the gap of ideology and outlook that separated the Provisional Government from the Petrograd Soviet. From the outset, conflict between them was continuous, erupting in a series of crises. The first of these arose in early May over foreign policy. Miliukov, who had taken control of foreign affairs, favored continuing the policy of the tsarist government, its alliances and secret treaties (one of which promised to Russia the Straits of Constantinople). He—and all moderates—assumed that Russia would fight on to victory. The Soviet, however, fearful of unnecessarily prolonging the war and for the wrong ends, entertained a different conception. Already in late March, it proclaimed:

> Conscious of its revolutionary power, the Russian democracy announces that it will, by every means, resist the policy of conquest of its ruling classes, and it calls upon the peoples of Europe for concerted, decisive action in favor of peace.

This was the first of the revolutionary appeals for peace that "Russian democracy" (a title the Soviet arrogated to itself despite the fact that it represented only soldiers and workers) addressed to the toilers of all countries. When Miliukov persisted in his course, the Soviet became restive. On May 6, the enraged soldiers and workers poured into the street and demanded not only the ouster of Miliukov but peace at once, without annexations and indemnities. The crisis ended with Miliukov's resignation and the reorganization of the Provisional Government, which now included six members from the Soviet executive committee. The moderate socialists thus entered into an uneasy coalition—the First Coalition—with the "capitalists," a move that constituted a drastic departure from socialist etiquette (at least as practiced in Russia).

Even the new arrangement did not overcome the dualism that frustrated the conduct of government just when a strong central authority was urgently needed. The cause of the split lay deep in the nature of the two institutions. The Provisional Government tried to represent the will of all Russia until the Constituent Assembly would relieve it of its task. As an interim government it felt itself debarred from settling the basic issues, such as the form of government, the land question, the position of the non-Russian nationalities, or war and peace. It should, of course, have conducted elections for the Constituent Assembly at the earliest moment. But considering the state of the country, were the people quite ready yet for deciding their future calmly and fairly? Sound liberal instinct led to one delay after another, until it was too late.

The Petrograd Soviet, on the other hand, particularly after it was reinforced in June by a delegation from the first All-Russian Congress of Soviets, could never give its full support to a representative government. By origin and composition it was a class institution, bound to maintain its separate identity as spokesman of all the revolutionary soviets that mushroomed throughout the country in the wake of the March Revolution. And how they multiplied: 400 in May, 600 in August, 900 in October!

The rift in the government proved unbridgeable because, in the last analysis, it had its cause in the age-old division of Russian society itself. On the side of the Provisional Government we may group the public institutions of educated Russia, foremost the town dumas and the zemstvos, now reconstituted on a democratic basis, and with them all educated and Europeanized Russia; in short, "privilege Russia." On the other side we find "soviet Russia"; that is, the peasant masses consisting of the peasants themselves, the peasants in uniform (the soldiers), and the peasants in the factory (misnamed, for the most part, proletarians).

"Soviet Russia," to be sure, formed by no means a uniform pressure group. The peasants set up their own soviets, hesistantly and under the prompting of citified elements. They did not really need soviets for what they wanted from the revolution. Under Social Revolutionary leadership, however, they rallied in periodic all-Russian peasant congresses in order to safeguard their political interests. The soldiers at the front banded together in their own soldiers' soviets. Garrison troops, however, most commonly sat together with the workers, the soldiers outnumbering the workers, particularly at the outset, and the workers by an even larger margin outnumbering the peasants, when eventually the latter were included. What mattered, however, was not proportionality of representation but authenticity of opinion. Deputies who ceased to reflect the temper of their constituents were apt to be recalled at once. Thus the moderate spokesmen commonly drawn from the educated classes after March were by summer and fall replaced with extremist intellectuals.

As may be imagined, the soviets were huge and unwieldy bodies; for a time the Petrograd Soviet numbered about 3000 members. The proceedings, too, were apt to be chaotic, which at an early point caused the withdrawal of the decision makers into the executive committee or even smaller caucuses. Each soviet, and particularly the Petrograd Soviet, which in June absorbed the executive committee of the first All-Russian Congress of Soviets, created its own administrative apparatus. This, unfortunately, tended to remove the leaders from close contact with the masses. The real strength of a soviet always lay in its identification with the local community. There were weak and strong soviets, the latter arrogating to themselves ever more functions of local government, some becoming veritable tyrants. And the soviets always displayed more zeal and energy than the town dumas and zemstvos in the same area, and more contempt too for legality and public order. At worst they became an instrument of class war at its most ruthless. Yet all soviets acted on the assumption that in them, and in them alone, resided "Russian democracy"; the other groups, which had shared with autocracy the burden of modernizing Russia, were exploiters, "capitalists," parasites. The distinction implied a clear repudiation of the Europeanized upper strata and of much they stood for.

It was for these reasons—their class character and their turbulence— that the soviet leadership (and Kerensky too) did not predict a long life for the soviets as an institution. They were unfit for government and would disappear when the Constituent Assembly had done its work.

The split between "privilege Russia" and "soviet Russia" was the most dangerous rift in the body politic but, unfortunately, not the only one. All existing fissures were opened up and widened. In her new freedom, Russia suddenly experienced all the frightening consequences of modern mass politics. Never before had there been such political fermentation. For the citizens, particularly the semiliterate simple people, life became an unending series of meetings, assemblies, and debates. They were bombarded with political appeals by pamphlet, poster, newspaper, and speech, all flattering them with a new importance. The Western democratic values in the programs of the parties now holding sway were broadcast as a thousand tiny explosives shattering old habits of submission or apathy. Every view, every feeling hitherto unnoted became articulate and called for action. After March, Russia thus witnessed a gigantic awakening of heady political fantasies. Old hopes and resentments were mobilized and reinforced by present hardships of hunger, cold, uncertainty, and a thousand frustrations. Out of this awakening, a new age of rampant political spontaneity was born.

Everybody now spoke their minds, bluntly and imperiously as had been the custom of the authorities in the past. The resulting cacophony revealed how weak under the autocratic monolith had remained the bonds of community and how small the fund of political rationality. The conservatives, to be sure, lay low for a while; their Russia was discredited. All the others pressed their rival claims on each other *fortissimo:* manufacturers and workers, landlords and peasants, liberals and socialists, moderates and extremists, Russians and non-Russians (sometimes the non-Russians among themselves), Christians and Jews, fathers and sons. The arguments soon ceased to be reasonable. Everywhere one could detect a penchant for maximalism, an irresistible urge to go to the limit. Why else should a prominent employer have threatened his striking workers with "the bony hand of hunger" to bring them back on his terms, or a powerful landlord have preferred Black Partition to a timely accommodation with his aroused peasants?

From late spring onward this maximalism spread from the capital and the urban-industrial centers into the length and breadth of Russia, stirring its 1.5 million inhabitants to their very depths. Its effects were strongest where the accumulated grievances were greatest and current suffering most acute. The pain brought to a boil all the ugliness of temper that centuries of humiliation and degradation had engendered. Russian politics from May 1917 to the spring of 1921, when the riot of spontaneity died out in utter exhaustion, cannot be understood by the concepts of Western democratic practice. They must be viewed primitively, in terms of Hobbesian social mechanics, in terms of crude violence among masses uprooted by war and revolution.

In the late spring and early summer, the peasants grew restive. They craved to be masters of the countryside at last; they wanted the land right away. Hesitantly at first and then more boldly they began to seize it by themselves, deporting their landlords or hanging them by their necks. By fall, all restraints were thrust aside. No force on earth could have stopped the vast agrarian revolution (which, in the end, netted the peasant only a minute increase in his holdings). The soldiers, meanwhile, had become active too. They deserted in large numbers, "voting for peace with their legs," as Lenin called it. By October their numbers had swelled to about 2 million. They— and most of the population—were sick of the war, regardless of the consequences for Russia (and who cared about the Allies?). No restoration of the death penalty could restore army discipline. Other groups likewise took the law into their own hands, workers throwing out their employers, or national minorities preparing for independence.

The temper of the times may be illustrated by a cruel tale about a group of soldiers who sometime during these months shot their officers, mutilating some of them beforehand by cutting off their noses. When asked about the noses, they explained that during rifle inspection in the old days these officers had put their fingers first into the muzzles of the rifles and then on the soldier's nose. If there was soot on the officers finger, it showed up on the soldier's nose. "You must have felt deeply offended," the Countess Kleinmichel (who told this story) said to a soldier, trying to fathom his motives. "Oh no," said he, "in those days nobody felt offended. We did not think about it. But later"—and here he drew himself up—"later we understood that it was an offense to our dignity." Indeed, by the new values much in the Russian past had been an offense to human dignity. Some months later, after the Bolshevik coup, the sailors of Sevastopol seized anyone with clean fingernails who crossed their path, stood him against a wall as a *burzhui*, a "capitalist," and shot him dead. The worm was surely turning.

That was the tide with which the soviets of soldiers, workers, and peasants were swimming. Here lay their strength. Conversely, the weakness of the Provisional Government and increasingly also of the moderate leaders in the Soviet bureaucracy lay in their aloofness from it. After the May crises, the crucial issue in Russian politics was whether that tide would destroy Russia or whether, perhaps, it could be checked before it had run its fatal course.

III

The hope that it might be checked emerged as a result of the next great crisis, the "July days," in which, for the first time, the masses of the capital were pitted against both the Provisional Government and their own moderate leadership in the Petrograd Soviet. They had reason to be angry. Since May, no progress had been made in any of the issues crucial to the workers, peasants, or soldiers. Their impatience grew as economic conditions deteriorated and the war continued. Furthermore, on July 1, Kerensky, who in May had taken over the War Ministry, launched a powerful offensive against the Austrian army. In its political aspects it was intended to consolidate the Provisional Government and to reassure the Allies (now including the United States), whose economic aid was badly needed. Yet at the height of the offensive, the government coalition patched together in May collapsed. The "capitalist" ministers suddenly resigned over an issue of agrarian policy, and on the following two days, July 16 and 17, the soldiers, sailors, and workers again poured into the streets. About half a million strong they made their way, shooting and looting, to the Tauride Palace, demanding that the Soviet take power from the Provisional Government. When they discovered that the Soviet leaders opposed such a step, they nearly lynched Chernov, who tried to calm them. Yet their fury spent itself vainly, for not even the Bolsheviks, who reluctantly had furnished some leadership for the uprising, felt that the time for action had come.

The reckless outburst had its effect on "privilege Russia." As the revolutionary masses withdrew, the propertied elements likewise took to the streets and vented their wrath on the Bolsheviks, who as a result were driven underground. Thus the drift to the extreme left was halted for a while. Yet the period of reaction that ensued hardly bettered the position of the government. The Kerensky offensive collapsed, as it was bound to, and Kerensky, soon raised to the prime ministership, met with great obstinacy in shaping a new cabinet. It took him nearly three weeks— three weeks while Russia hovered on the brink of anarchy—to bring the liberals and moderate socialists into alliance again. The delay demonstrated how deeply the forces of liberal democracy were divided among themselves. Nor did they command mass support, as the July days had conclusively shown. They were powerless in the face of the tidal wave of revolutionary spontaneity. In these fateful weeks, the competition for the succession to the tsar was decided against the Cadets, the

Mensheviks, and the run of Social Revolutionaries—against all the truly democratic parties.

Liberal democracy in Russia—using the term broadly—had proved unequal to the task. Since March it had given the country every opportunity to speak its will, and the result had been division, violence, and a breakdown of government. Spontaneity, leaving the population to its own devices, had produced anarchy. The invisible resources of unity and social discipline, which in the Western democracies restrained liberty from degenerating into license and made possible not only effective government in peace but also unprecedented voluntary sacrifices in war, were found wanting in Russia. A few years later they were equally found wanting in Italy, Spain, Poland, and Germany (to mention but a few parallel cases). None of these countries had had a chance in the past of knitting the tight habit of subconscious unity before they copied Western democracy. Russia was merely the first case in a long series of similar breakdowns, the one that occurred in the largest country in the world under the most exceptional circumstances.

Viewing the events of the summer of 1917 in this perspective, we must conclude that the failure of democracy in Russia was inevitable, if not in 1917 then surely in the years following (assuming that a Russian state still survived). Only decades, if not centuries, of relative immunity to the pressures of power politics and an active internal melting pot might have helped the discordant elements to grow together. Now there was no time. In the extreme moments of the twentieth century, a country either possessed that cohesion or had to create it artificially, if it did not want to fall apart.

After the July days, the sole question of Russian domestic politics was whether the heir to autocracy would be a dictator of the right or of the left. The wave of reaction favored the former. It brought to the fore General Kornilov, a distinguished officer whom merit had raised from the peasantry to his high rank and who was by no means a reactionary. He was convinced that only a military dictatorship could save Russia from Germany and from disintegration, an opinion that by now many members of "privilege Russia" (including some socialists) shared. With such backing he began, toward the end of August, to move supposedly reliable army units toward Petrograd, ostensibly in order to strengthen Kerensky but secretly prepared to go further if opportunity opened. Yet as his men approached the capital, they were met by agitators sent by the Soviet, under whose persuasion even the most loyal soldiers lost heart. Against the Petrograd Soviet, Kornilov's troops melted away as had the armies at the front, and his coup collapsed. No dictatorship of the right could stem the tide of revolutionary spontaneity as embodied in the soviets. On the contrary, Kornilov revived its impetus, somewhat checked after July, and prepared the way for the dictatorship of the left.

IV

The dictatorship of the proletariat had, of course, been the goal of the Bolsheviks ever since Lenin returned to Russia. At every opportunity, he pressed home the argument that the war was an imperialist war and that it could be stopped, with all its savage hardships, only if the "capitalist" governments in Russia and elsewhere were overthrown. In his eyes, all those Russians who sought to continue the war—and this included Kerensky, the Mensheviks, and most Social Revolutionaries— were "capitalist" warmongers. He gambled on the inability of the Provisional Government to carry out its staggering tasks and on the growing revulsion against the war.

Thus of all political parties, only the Bolsheviks cast their lot with the revolutionary torrent. Their slogan was "All power to the soviets" until July, when the Soviet leadership turned against the masses. Then they allied themselves with the more radical elements represented in the Petrograd district soviets and the factory committees. In the fall, when they gained control of the city soviets in many parts of Russia, they proclaimed as their goal the dictatorship of the proletariat. They alone dared to profess what the unruly masses wanted and were already trying to achieve by themselves: immediate peace for the soldiers, land to the peasants by Black Partition, self-determination for the minority groups, bread for the hungry, and social justice on their own terms for all those who felt oppressed and exploited. They alone were willing to descend to the language of the *Lumpenproletariat* and, when necessary, to incite its passions to fever pitch. "The Bolsheviks," Trotsky wrote in retrospect, "not afraid of those backward strata now for the first time lifting themselves from the dregs, took people as history had created them." Mercilessly they exploited the ignorance of the masses.

Yet while they placed themselves midstream in the revolutionary tide, they would not be carried away by it. As a revolutionary elite, they had a will of their own. They thought of themselves as the engineers of revolution, harnessing the revolutionary steam power created by the historic conditions of the moment to its true purpose, which only revolutionary Marxists could perceive. Whatever the Bolsheviks would do, for their own benefit and that of Russia, they would do through the masses, never against them. But they would also remain inwardly apart, as manipulators, not agents, of the popular will. In this manner, they solved the first of the underlying necessities of modern Russian development, identifying the people with their government and in turn identifying themselves with the people.

Falling in line with the drift toward the extreme, the Bolsheviks (who were taking German money) were able to grow from a small minority to the dominant party in the soviets. In May they already controlled the majority of the soviet at Kronstadt, the naval base near Petrograd. Their big windfall, however, came in the wake of Kornilov's march on the capital. The Bolsheviks led in the defense of the city and, as a reward, soon controlled the soviet. The trend was reflected in the changing membership of practically all soviets throughout Russia. On the eve of the second All-Russian Congress of Soviets, meeting in early November, Lenin's party could claim majorities in the soviets of Petrograd, Moscow, and the great industrial centers, of the Ural towns, and of the garrisons of the north and northwest. In Siberia they shared control with the Social Revolutionaries, whose left wing throughout the country inclined toward the Bolsheviks. The latter lagged behind the Social Revolutionaries, their closest rivals, only in the central black soil provinces, the Ukraine, and the western and southwestern fronts. The Mensheviks had completely dropped out of the running, except for their stronghold in Georgia. The trade unions, apart from the railway, post, and telegraph workers, went over to the Bolsheviks. Even in the city dumas of Petrograd and Moscow they made impressive gains, proving the strength of their appeal in the metropoles. There was no reason to doubt that the majorities would increase and the trend extend into all the regions of Russia. By the indices of practical politics, the time was ripe for the Bolshevik seizure of power.

Yet by the traditional indices of Marxist orthodoxy, Russia was still a backward country unfit for a socialist revolution. The Russian "proletariat and the poorest peasantry," to use Lenin's term for the forces at his disposal, were too weak a basis for building the most advanced social system. And even if the Bolsheviks succeeded in taking power now, they could not hold it for long, except by non-Marxist methods of terror. What was the benefit, so the "softs" asked, of such irresponsible adventurism?

Arguments like these, however, did not detain the impatient Lenin. He saw the straws of evidence from the West all pointing toward a general conflagration. Everywhere in Europe the people wanted peace; they would achieve it by revolution. A Bolshevik revolution might indeed provide the spark, as he had argued earlier. Much of the confidence that buoyed the Bolsheviks in these months—and years—stemmed from their anticipation of a European revolution. But Lenin also pursued another line of thought. The war itself, he argued while still in Switzerland, was preparing socialism by imposing ever more drastic controls. This was happening in Germany under the "Hindenburg program" and would happen in Russia, too.

> These steps are quite inevitably prescribed by those conditions which the war has created and which the postwar aftermath will make even more acute in many respects; and in their totality as well as in their further development, these steps would be a transition to socialism, which cannot be realized in Russia immediately, with one stroke, without transitional measures, but which is perfectly feasible and scientifically necessary as a result of such transitional measures.

Lenin, then and later, was never very precise about the prospects of socialism in Russia, but he did offer concrete ideas as to what he would do if the Bolsheviks came to power. He expected to have the bulk of the population behind him. The dictatorship of the proletariat would therefore be an even more democratic regime than capitalist democracy, which benefited only the rich. He also would find at his disposal the vast creativity of the Russian people, liberated for once from all exploitation, and the newly created administrative machinery of the soviets for putting it to work. "Capitalist" techniques, he announced, had so simplified modern administration that even proletarian housewives would take their turn in the central offices. Lenin, moreover, intended to nationalize the banks and syndicates, utilizing their organizations and skills for running the economy. Experts in all fields would flock to Soviet power, because of the greater opportunities for constructive work that it offered. In addition, he would make use of the "best models from the experience of the progressive countries." It seems incredible that so tough-minded a thinker as Lenin could indulge, with patent sincerity, in such utopian fantasies.

But his Bolshevik hardness had not left him. For those who would not cooperate, Lenin hinted, the shackles of social control were ready: food rationing and compulsory labor service. Still more ominous was his statement that under the new regime "all citizens are transformed into hired employees of the state which is made up of the armed workers. All citizens become employees and workers of one national state syndicate." The emphasis, one notes, rested on the overriding power of the state under a dictatorship that would wither away only when the superior social discipline that it required had become the self-discipline of the individual citizen—a vain hope.

The combination of utopianism with the harsh practicalities of power indicates the central paradox in the Bolshevik program. On the one hand, the dictatorship of the proletariat, so it promised, would launch the Liberation of Man. On the other, it called for discipline and restraint, for closely intermeshed cooperation in the huge workshop of socialist society. It held out freedom as the goal but took away its essence, the spontaneity of the natural man. Thus Lenin prepared his party for coping with the second of the overriding necessities of Russian development, the necessity for rapid updating of state and society. And no mean future he envisaged for his country. As he wrote in September, looking back to the fall of the monarchy:

> Owing to her revolution Russia in a few months has caught up to the advanced countries in her political organization [a fine bit of megalomania]. But this is not enough. War is inexorable and puts the question with unsparing sharpness: either perish or catch up and overtake the advanced countries economically as well.

In short, a Bolshevik Russia, unwilling to perish, was to surpass the glories of the "capitalist" countries which had been the global models for so long. It was Soviet Russia that would spearhead the human advance to freedom and justice. Thus, Lenin competed with Woodrow Wilson, who had brought the United States into the war in order to make the world safe for democracy American-style. Americans never forgave Lenin (or his heirs) for striking at the jugular of their own global mission.

V

With his high-flying assurances Lenin spurred his party to take the fatal plunge. On October 23, with some hesitation and after the defection of several doubters—even now the party lacked the unity for which Lenin had pleaded since 1902—the Bolshevik Central Committee voted for the seizure of power. The preparation and execution of the coup, however, were not to be Lenin's work—he remained in hiding from the end of July until early November—but Trotsky's.

Leon Davidovich Bronstein, alias Trotsky, was a far more dashing and versatile revolutionary than Lenin. He had escaped from Siberia twice, had been president (for a time) of the St. Petersburg Soviet in 1905, had traveled farther and kept his eyes wider open to the fascinations of life than Lenin. He lacked Lenin's doggedness and practical common sense, being apt to carry points of doctrine to an extreme, but he outshone him as a writer and speaker. If Lenin may be called the Grand Strategist of the Revolution, Trotsky in these weeks was the Grand Stage Manager, an artist of genius in revolutionary action. As skilled a dialectitian as any Marxist, he excelled as a revolutionary journalist and pamphleteer; as a revolutionary orator, he had no equal. He could throw himself wide open to the varieties of human experience and fuse them into service to the Revolution; he could fall in with the mood of any audience, capture it, and bend it to his will. In his words, the abstractions of Marxism came alive with the body warmth of humanity. Yet despite his almost febrile sensitivity he was a brilliant organizer of action, as hardheaded and cruelly cold-blooded in the crucial moments of revolution as Lenin. The one great flaw in this plethora of gifts—apart from the repulsive fusion of idealism and expediency—was his pride. He could not depersonalize himself as a Bolshevik should and never inspired the selfless loyalty that bound men, including himself, to Lenin. Yet in these weeks Trotsky was at his best.

The "objective conditions," he agreed with Lenin, were right for revolution. The Provisional Government was discredited. Kerensky's rhetoric, now strained sometimes to the point of incoherence, had lost its spell over "the great soul of the people." The stalemate within the moderate center was more frustrating than ever. As a leading Menshevik observed in mid-September during the Democratic Conference, one of several ad hoc public bodies convoked to bolster the Kerensky regime, "The praesidium . . . has unanimously decided that there is within the organized democracy no unanimity of will that could be translated into action." Could there have been a more damning admission? Meanwhile, the German army was advancing on the Baltic coast, which heightened the sense of crisis in the capital.

If the Bolsheviks did not seize the propitious moment now, another and more successful Kornilov might arise. Under the pretext of defending the masses against the forces of reaction Trotsky set to work. Using the machinery of the Petrograd Soviet, regardless of the opposition of the moderates, he armed the Red Guards (the Bolsheviks' own fighting force), won over wavering units of the garrison, and incited public opinion to fever pitch by ruthlessly fanning the phobias and hopes of the masses. An eyewitness has left us an account of Trotsky's power over his audience in those days:

> Around me was a spirit close to ecstasy. It seemed that the crowd would, at once, without any urging or leadership, sing some sort of

religious hymn. . . . Trotsky formulated some sort of short general resolution, or proclaimed some sort of general formula like "we will stand
for the cause of the workers and peasants to our last drop of blood."

Who is in favor? The crowd of thousands, as one man, raised their
hands. I saw the raised hands and the burning eyes of men, women,
youngsters, workers, soldiers, muzhiks, and—of typically lower middle-class persons. Were they in a soulful passion? Did they see,
through the raised curtain, a corner or some sort of "holy land" toward
which they were striving? Or were they imbued with a consciousness of
the political moment, under the influence of the political agitation of
the socialists?

The coup was planned for the eve of the second All-Russian Congress
of Soviets, known in advance to have a Bolshevik majority. The
Bolsheviks did not wish to be given power by that congress, but rather to
take it by themselves and to present the delegates with the *fait accompli.*
They were determined to preserve their separate identity.

While the preparations were in progress, Kerensky remained inexpli-
cably passive. He did not seem to be worried by the ill-concealed talk of
insurrection. When at the last moment he took a few precautions, it was
too late. Through the Red Guards and a few radical elements in the garrison, the Bolsheviks, early on November 7, occupied the key points of
the city and after much hesitation late on the same day laid siege to the
Winter Palace, the seat of government. There followed some aimless
shooting; yet before long they gained entry peaceably and arrested the
ministers whom they found there drafting and redrafting an appeal to the
people of Petrograd (Kerensky had already left to seek help outside the
city). Little blood was shed, and the city was spared the terror that had
characterized the July days. Indeed, life in Petrograd remained strangely
normal, for the deed was done, on the whole, according to schedule—
with some competence, as befitted a revolutionary elite, although hardly
with the precision and command of the situation of which party history
was to boast subsequently. In Moscow, however, the Bolshevik seizure
of power took place only after a week of bitter fighting. The country was
far from won.

On November 7, even before the coup was completed, Trotsky
announced to the Petrograd Soviet that the Provisional Government was
overthrown, and Lenin, appearing again in public, gave a brief explanation of the meaning of these events:

What is the significance of this revolution? Its significance is . . . that
we shall have a social government, without the participation of the
bougeoisie of any kind. The oppressed masses will of themselves form

a government. The old state machinery will be smashed into bits and in its place will be created a new machinery of government by the soviet organizations. From now on there is a new page in the history of Russia, and the present . . . Russian revolution shall in the final result lead to the victory of socialism.

On the same day, the second All-Russian Congress of Soviets assembled in the Smolny Institute, a former school for aristocratic young ladies which also served as the Bolshevik headquarters (despite Lenin's quip that the party was no girls dormitory, there was a girls school in the revolution after all!). The congress was no longer a gathering of the cream of the revolutionary intelligentsia, as it had been in June, but of the unwashed, suspicious, and sullen "black people" from the depths of Russia who, as Trotsky put it, "grasp a phenomenon wholesale, not bothering about details and nuances." As the delegates, among whom the Bolsheviks comprised slightly more than half, voted a Bolshevik Central Executive Committee, the Mensheviks and moderate Social Revolutionaries (but not the left Social Revolutionaries) walked out in protest. "So much refuse thrown into the garbage pail of history!" Trotsky shouted after them. During the following night, November 8–9, Lenin, stepping into his role as head of the new government, announced two decrees, the first declaring the war at an end, the second handing the land to the peasants largely on their own terms. The third and last item of business, after which the delegates were sent home again, was the ratification of the Council of People's Commissars, the new executive organ that was to carry out all the other promises of the Bolsheviks.

VI

Let us ignore at this point the fact that the Bolsheviks were not firmly established for several years, but rather draw a few conclusions about their ascent to power. In the first place one can hardly deny that theirs was a democratic revolution. It established a government that could hope to speak—at least at this fleeting moment—for a majority of Russians. It was a government of "Soviet Russia," as this term has been used here, close to the political instincts of the bulk of the people.

Second, the overthrow of the Provisional Government—and of "Privilege Russia" in general—was not entirely of the Bolsheviks' own making. It was the result of the elemental torrent of liberation that had broken loose after March. The existing bonds of government and society were all snapping by themselves, in the countryside, the army, the factories, the national minorities, everywhere. No authority was strong enough to stem that tide. All that could possible be attempted—and that with great difficulty—was to direct it from within until it had run its course.

Third, the elemental revolt aiming at the smashing of the old state machinery was a phenomenon possible only in Russia (or underdeveloped countries like China). Only there did the run of the population still live in relative self-sufficiency, with hardly a stake in the government. "Soviet Russia" had little to lose from the overthrow of the government, neither protection of property or status, nor social security, nor extensive public education, nor any other boon of government. In urban-industrial Europe, on the other hand, the majority of the population had long since acquired such a stake. State, society, and the economy were interwoven a thousandfold; all citizens were patently interdependent for their very livelihood. Thus all the people had a vested interest in order and security, regardless of their political views. Threaten them, in time of crisis and internal disunity, with the overthrow of the government and they would rush headlong into the arms of a Mussolini or a Hitler. And if they longed for a change of regime, they would still insist that the transition be accomplished "legally," without disturbing the continuity of the public services. There would never be a chance, in other words, of a Bolshevik revolution in the West.

The Bolshevik seizure of power marked for Russia the end of a decade of revolution from below. The tide of liberation, which assumed hurricane proportions in the fall of 1917 and continued to rage for several years more, had been rising since the start of the century. Autocracy had sacrificed the "Witte system" to it but had itself been forced to give ground in 1905. While seemingly recovering most of its losses, it never succeeded in reestablishing its authority. The trend continued to run against it, even under the pressure of the war. The defeats deepened and strengthened the upsurge until it finally broke all bounds after the sudden fall of the monarchy.

The new freedom liberated the long-suppressed spontaneity of the peoples of Russia. It did not lead, unfortunately, to the self-discipline needed for an effective democratic policy or an industrial economy. Liberation meant throwing off the hated restraints of the old order and being able, for once, to act according to one's deepest feelings.

VII

The Russian Empire was the first country to experience the world-shaking effects of the war that had broken out in 1914. That war, the first *world* war, escalated the international rivalry to global dimensions, imposing unprecedented strains on the resources of state and society everywhere. In support of their war aims the Allied powers proclaimed freedom and democracy as worldwide ideals. Now the collapsing Russian empire faced a double challenge: how to absorb the elemental appeal of these ideas while adjusting its traditional ambition to the intensified worldwide power competition. The challenge brutally sharpened the perennial tension between collective security provided by a country's power in the world—the ultimate guarantee of individual survival—and the value of individual life. The battles of the war had devoured lives by the hundreds of thousands, setting appalling precedents for human sacrifice in the twentieth century: What did individuals count when the glory, or especially the survival, of their country was at stake? While the political and psychological security of the winners in the war—and certainly of the United States—was never really in danger, the peoples of the Russian Empire were the first helpless victims of the crucial paradox of the twentieth century: the disregard for human life in the global search for the wealth and power guaranteeing freedom and equality.

The Russian Empire was a backward country at the mercy of powerful neighbors. The essence of its backwardness rested in the fact that its people, left to their own devices, could manage neither effective government nor a productive modern economy. Was the Russian Empire then to be dissolved? For the Bolsheviks, at any rate, and many non-Bolsheviks as well, the answer was a passionate *no!* They craved power for their own survival, for the future of world socialism, and for the integrity of their territorial base in Imperial Russia which they dearly loved. Thus, as the survival of the Russian state grew ever more uncertain in 1917, the suppression of spontaneity began anew, slowly at first under Lenin, furiously at last under Stalin. The new harness of Communist rule proved to be far tighter than the tsarist one. The dangers to the country were greater, the ambitions of its rulers bolder, and the progress of the "advanced" countries undiminished; they would not mark time while Soviet Russia tried to catch up.

The essence of industrialism, which stands at the base of modern power, is interdependence and voluntary cooperation throughout the length and breadth of society. Lenin's sociology, although clumsy and extreme, took its cue from the "capitalist" order. Every advanced industrialized sociey constitutes a vast workshop. Its members voluntarily coordinate their activities under a common law and government—never perfectly, to be sure, yet sufficiently so as to produce a remarkable flow of goods and services. They do this with no more drastic compulsions than submitting to majority rule and earning a living, and sometimes with much nonpecuniary zeal. Submitting to the discipline of their jobs and their political order, they ordinarily do not even feel constricted in their freedom; they are spurred on by the opportunities.

As Gorbachev has learned, a country that craves the benefits of modern industrialization without possessing among its inhabitants the necessary motivation and self-discipline is headed for endless misery. Faced with the threat of their country's annihilation in World War I, ambitious Russian patriots had no choice but to substitute an artificial external discipline in place of the spontaneous self-discipline of the West. The scope of Communist totalitarianism, as it developed over the years, indicated to what extent, in the judgment of its leaders, the Soviet population lacked the spontaneous motivation needed for competitive power in world affairs.

The Soviet leaders' judgment deserves respectful consideration. Collective security from foreign political and cultural domination is the precondition for individual freedom—a factor commonly overlooked in countries long enjoying the civic freedoms derived from their global preeminence. Cultural backwardness entails individual unfreedom; it compels people to submit to an uncongenial foreign mode of citizenship for the sake of building the collective strength needed to overcome cultural dependence. Only equality in human skills and material resources can provide the political security guaranteeing the sense of freedom felt by most Western peoples. In a backward but politically ambitious country like the Russian Empire, political leaders following the trend of the times would naturally give top priority not to individual freedom, but to the prerequisite social cooperation assuring power and security.

Given the elemental appeal of the ideal of freedom, the Bolsheviks of course could never admit that they were sacrificing freedom for the sake of power. Their determination to become a superior universal model required that they make an additional effort to represent their Russia as the embodiment of a freedom greater than that found in the "capitalist" West. They had to overtake their model in *all* attributes of superiority, even as the price of perverting the vocabulary of freedom and spontaneity beyond all recognition.

The First Months of the Soviet Regime

I

The Bolsheviks, to return to the story of the Revolution, had seized power; the Communists, as the Bolsheviks under Lenin's urging now began to call themselves, had to hold and consolidate it throughout the empire and spread it beyond if they could. What they had learned in their struggle against autocracy and the Provisional Government they now had to apply even more recklessly and on the grandest scale. They aimed at nothing less than overthrowing the entire world order, both in the capillaries of socioeconomic relations and in the coarser tissues of global politics, and replacing it by a superior, more finely meshed society and a more advanced civilization suited to the highest potential of man. As they saw it, mankind was entering a crucial phase of development. The age was one of final solutions: Capitalism was giving way to socialism with all the bloody alarms of a great historical earthquake. Taking this heroic view, the Communists were emotionally steeled for the grimness that lay ahead.

Communism's greatest asset for the realization of its far-reaching ambitions was no doubt its ideology. Marxism-Leninism was a true myth, a potent capsule mixing vital political insights with profound psychic drives and releasing spectacular energies for revolutionary action.

Many ingredients recommended this myth to the condition of Russia. Marxism was an ingenious mixture of German romanticism with British industrialism, a fusion of the slow and moralizing mentality of an agrarian (or preindustrial) society with the fast rationalism of a superbly integrated and technically oriented community. Modern Russia found itself in a transition ever more rapid than that through which Germany had passed in the days of Marx; it wanted an appropriate ideological synthesis. Marxism also offered concrete advantages. It was most knowledgeable in fields in which the tsars had been notoriously deficient: economics, sociology, industrial relations, and mass politics. To their Marxist inheritance, the Bolsheviks added their own store of revolutionary experience and their insight into the psychology of frustrated idealists, displaced and uprooted factory workers, and the underdog in general.

Marxism-Leninism also supplied certain useful specifics. Its concept of the classless society justified the elimination of all the accumulated divisions and schisms in Russian society. It recognized only one class—the proletarian toilers regardless of race, religion, nationality, or level of culture. Its slogan of the dictatorship of the proletariat, moreover, allowed for a more vigorous assertion of governmental leadership than had been possible under the recent autocrats. At the same time, it stressed the identity of the rulers and the ruled. The new regime had grown out of an uprising of the masses. The Communists were determined never to lose touch with that base.

New opportunities were also contained in the more general concept of Marxist-Leninist philosophy. More temptingly than the church, it held out hope for a better life for all mankind. And in stressing the interdependence of all social phenomena, it opened up vast vistas for experiments in social engineering designed to give reality to that hope. The economic base and the superstructure of government, law, art, literature, religion, the family, education—of the entire culture and the innermost consciousness of the individual—were all of one piece. Change the first and you would have license to tamper with all the rest. By its very nature, socialist sociology encouraged totalitarian practices.

Marxism-Leninism, moreover, provided a principle of international organization. Its doctrine of imperialism gave militant expression to the yet vague longings for independence in non-Western countries overrun by "capitalist" civilization. It dignified their quest for prestige and power with a global significance, offered an outlet for action, and held out, in the vague distance, a promise of world government capable of guaranteeing peace and prosperity for all. The greatest reassurance in the Communist myth was reserved for the Russians themselves (if they could but convince themselves of its reality!). They now assumed leadership in the global anti-Western revolt, proud of having been the first to leap forward into the new era of human history, sure of possessing the foundations for the most advanced social order in the world. Both their myth and their nationalism compelled them to concentrate all their energies on catching up to and overtaking the "capitalist" countries, not only politically but in every other respect as well.

The appeal to Russian patriotism could be lifted out of the Marxist-Leninist context and be used separately, like a second language, for communication with those whom the myth could not reach. Yet the traditional pride of country could not supply the myth's universal sweep. Nor could it bestow the victorious uplift imparted by Marxist dialectics, which were the myth's most powerful ingredient. Marx, so the myth read, had discovered the laws of historical evolution, and his followers—his true followers like Lenin—could employ these laws with scientific accuracy in order to guide the world toward its socialist goal. This faith gave the Communists their arrogance and their imperviousness to failure. If history was with them, who could prevail against them?

The suitability of this myth for Russia's condition lay in the grand conceptions articulating government and society, Russia and the world, reality and ambition, in a manner inspiring self-confidence and a will to action. Yet there was one crucial proviso attached to it. While there might be slight adjustments in detail, the myth capsule had to remain intact. The irrational resolve to succeed must never be relaxed. Reasonableness and softness in any form quickly corroded the potency of the myth and were to be shunned like poison. If one ingredient gave way, the others lost their savor too. And if the myth collapsed, the revolutionary determination would wither, the dynamic drive stall, and all would be lost. The preservation of the myth was the central condition for Communist survival.

The rigid ideological dogmatism, however, would never have sufficed for survival had it not been mated with an amazing pragmatic flexibility in the development of suitable political techniques. This continued unscrupulous agility in the choice of means bordering on adventurism was the result of several factors: the acute danger to their power that forever harassed the Communists; the continued discrepancy between their ambition and their resources; and finally, and perhaps most important, the wholesale rejection of all liberal-democratic models, which left them with only their own wits to face Russian realities. Not even Marxist doctrine offered concrete guidance for the construction of a socialist society. The constant improvisation in Communist practice brought into Russian statecraft an element of originality peculiar to that brief era of rampant revolutionary spontaneity.

II

The Communists' capacity for social and political experiment was put to a severe test after November 1917, not only in Russia but in the world. Their very first act as a government, the decree on peace, placed their revolution in the global context. While bidding the governments of the belligerent countries to arrange an immediate armistice, it incited their subjects to revolution. All warring governments at the time were fomenting strife behind the enemy lines; the German gamble in funding the Bolsheviks had indeed paid off most brilliantly! Why should the Communists not play the same game? They were better apprenticed in the arts of subversion than any liberal or conservative regime. And years before, Lenin had already set the basic course: revolution in Europe and in Europe's colonies and dependencies throughout the world. Now the chance had come to put the revolutionary myth into effect and build up the counterpower to European imperialism in all its form.

In this foreign policy, Lenin played a double game. He dealt with the "capitalist" governments so long as they possessed effective power. But over their heads he also pushed for revolution by any means at his disposal. Immediately after taking power, he published the secret treaties of the Allied governments in order to expose their imperialist character. He sent out inflammatory radio appeals and put agitators to work on the soldiers of the Central Powers through both fraternization at the front and indoctrination in the prisoner-of-war camps. Where diplomatic channels were available, he used his ambassadors (or lesser emissaries with diplomatic immunity) as agents of the revolutionary contagion. In fomenting revolution everywhere, the Communists drastically broke with the social solidarity of the European state system that had become customary in the nineteenth century. They set themselves apart as the center of a new global order, thereby also settling old scores in the field of foreign relations. With what relish they repudiated the foreign debts of their predecessors (which most likely would have been cancelled anyway)! With what insolence they addressed the "capitalist" governments when they thought they could do so with impunity!

And how they railed against the "colonial exploiters"! Within less than a month, they issued the rousing "Appeal to the Working Moslems" (among whom in their zeal they included even the Hindus of India):

> The working people of Russia burn with the sole desire to get a just peace and to help the oppressed people of the world to conquer freedom for themselves. . . . Russia is not alone in this cause. The great watchword of liberation . . . is caught up by all the workers of the West

and the East. . . . The reign of capitalist pillage and violence is crumbling. The ground is burning beneath the feet of the bandits of imperialism. . . .

Thus began the deliberate mobilization of all dissatisfaction and bitterness throughout the world that could possibly be put to political use. The Communists drew on the widespread postwar pacifism; they probed into the deeper layers of disaffection with "capitalist" society expressed before the war; and they cultivated the frustrated ambitions of the native intelligentsia of Asia.

In times of stress, modern mass politics tends to become psychopolitics; it favors the absorption of the emotional needs of an aroused and often bewildered populace into political programs and political action. The Communists were pioneers in the arts of activating and manipulating the fears and hopes of the common people. They raised extravagant illusions and held out a promise, certified by the laws of history to become true, of a world order free from anxiety, hunger, exploitation, injustice, and, most important in these years, from war. They even appropriated the pacifist ideal of a peaceful world federation and incorporated it into their first constitution. Said one speaker in July 1918, while commending that document:

> Our constitution is of world-wide significance. As the workers and peasants from different countries take advantage of favorable circumstances and follow the example of Soviet Russia, the Russian Soviet republic sooner or later will be surrounded by daughter and sister republics, which united will lay the basis for a federation first of Europe and then of the entire world.

There would be no occasion for war in the commonwealth of peaceful toilers.

III

In terms of modern power politics, the emotions of the masses were novel political raw material. No one could accurately gauge their strength in the final stages of an unprecedented war and in the agonies of its aftermath. The war had created a new climate of politics. As the clash of arms ended, the clash of political creeds mounted and new political armies descended into street and parliament. The Communists set high hopes on the effectiveness of the new instruments of power, and apprehensive conservatives often flattered them by taking their estimates at face value. The manipulation of public opinion abroad was the most effective foreign policy instrument that Lenin had at his disposal when all conventional tools of Russian power had been dissolved by defeat and revolution. He was determined to employ these tempestuous weapons as much as the blockade of Soviet Russia and its limited resources would permit, particularly as the Communist experiment within Russia encountered many unexpected obstacles.

As it turned out, the Bolshevik seizure of power in Petrograd was a rather minor event, important only in retrospect. They still had to conquer power in every locality. This was fairly easy where they possessed solid support in the Great Russian heartland. But the course of events ran differently in the rural expanses along the mid-Volga, the Ukraine, the south and southeast, in Siberia, and in the fringe territories inhabited by non-Slavic peoples. And even where they held power, they did so tenuously, having to combat not only political enemies as desperate as themselves but also incredible disorganization, hunger, cold, exhaustion, explosive anarchy, and all the miseries of backwardness compounded by defeat and revolution. The tidal wave of popular spontaneity, which was to make the dictatorship of the proletariat a truly democratic regime for the vast majority of the inhabitants of the empire and release untold creative social energy, soon proved to be a tricky, many-channeled, chaotic flood whipped to white fury by the acts of the new regime. How under these conditions was a small minority like the Communist party to make itself master of Russia?

There was unexpected trouble from the start. The new regime was boycotted by the entrenched civil servants in the ministries and banks on which it still had to rely. Step by step, it was forced to turn on them, and on their allies among the public, the terror edge of the proletarian dictatorship. It suppressed the liberal press and instituted what it called revolutionary justice, summary proceedings against all class enemies. It even created a new political police, the dreaded Cheka, to fight the counterrevolution whose leaders were drifting to the Don Cossack territory to prepare for civil war. Among fellow socialists, too, Lenin met with rancorous hostility which was not so easily countered. Faced with opposition within the Soviet ranks, he bowed to political necessity and formed a political coalition of Bolsheviks and left-wing Social Revolutionaries in order to give a somewhat broader base to his regime. Yet the smallness of even that foundation was soon made painfully evident.

Having joined, for propaganda reasons, the clamor for elections to the Constituent Assembly before he came to power, Lenin could not afterward prevent their being held. Nor could he rig them to hide the fact that majorities in these soviets of soldiers and workers did not signify majorities among the population at large. The results, as he anticipated, were distinctly disappointing. "Privilege Russia," to be sure, was completely routed. Even the Mensheviks had come off very poorly. The Social Revolutionaries (of all shades) and Bolsheviks together counted for four-fifths of the vote, which again showed where the majority of Russians stood. But the bulk of that block belonged to the Social Revolutionaries, the Bolsheviks reaping slightly less than a quarter of the total. The left Social Revolutionaries had not run separately from the Social Revolutionary party; hence the numerical strength of Lenin's Bolshevik-left Social Revolutionary coalition could not be tabulated. But as the few ballots of the Constituent Assembly subsequently indicated, it clearly did not command a majority.

Nor could Lenin, who had no use for parliamentary institutions, prevent a meeting of the Constituent Assembly. After much sparring, it was allowed to gather on January 18, 1918, in the Tauride Palace, surrounded by Red Guards. It at once showed its anti-Bolshevik orientation, whereupon the Bolshevik delegates walked out. The remaining members did, however, endorse the Bolshevik decree on land and declare Russia a democratic federative republic. When the session dragged on into the early hours of the next day, the commandant of the Tauride Palace informed Victor Chernov, who happened to be speaking, that the guards were tired and wanted to go home. Thereupon the assembly adjourned. When the delegates returned the next day, they found the doors barred by order of the Central Executive Committee of the second All-Russian Congress of Soviets, which, meanwhile, had declared the Constituent Assembly dissolved. Thus ended the brief experiment of democratic parliamentarism, the posthumous child of the Provisional Government.

Was there any possibility that it might have succeeded where its parent had failed? It would hardly appear so. The Social Revolutionary party, to be sure, would doubtless have been able to form a government of its own, thus escaping the wrangles of coalition. But modern peasant parties have been notoriously weak and unsuccessful, and neither the Social Revolutionary party's program nor its organization held out a promise of superior efficiency (to put it mildly). Moreover, the weakness and disunity of the moderate elements in general and the absence of a common set of convictions, which had destroyed the Provisional Government, would still have troubled any parliamentary regime emerging from the Constituent Assembly. In short, even though the tide of spontaneity no longer favored the Bolsheviks as it had before their seizure of power, their dictatorship still represented the best balance of social and political forces possible under the circumstances. The suppression of the Constituent Assembly did not, therefore, alter the political scene, although it made the dispossessed opposition more militant and thereby contributed to the outbreak of civil war. Afraid of such repercussions, Lenin immediately afterward convoked the third All-Russian Congress of Soviets, which passed a "Declaration of the Rights of the Toiling and Exploited Peoples" designed to reassure the Soviet masses. And soon more urgent problems, requiring a strong and resourceful government, moved into the foreground.

IV

For now the negotiations for peace were in their final stage. Lenin's call for a general armistice had been accepted only by the Central Powers. If the Communists wanted to end the war, they had to break Russia's treaty obligation to its allies not to conclude a separate peace. The negotiations with the German government were held at Brest-Litovsk in eastern Poland. They continued for several weeks, under the full glare of publicity, for the Communists wanted to practice what they proclaimed to be the people's choice in international relations: open covenants openly arrived at. And with the help of Trotsky's quick tongue they often managed, in the drawn-out exchanges, to best the German generals and diplomats, laying bare their aggressive designs.

The German conditions were indeed stupendous. Russia was to lose its Baltic provinces, all of Poland, the Ukraine, and vital territories in the Caucasus, which were to be ceded to Turkey. Against these demands Lenin played for time in order to let the German Revolution, on which he had staked much, come to his aid. Despite the publicity of the negotiations, however, the German proletariat did not rise against its imperialist masters. In late February the German High Command, impatient with the Communists' procrastination, ordered the German armies to march deeper into the defenseless country. Thereupon the Communist leaders, who in fear of being captured had just moved the capital from Petrograd to Moscow, were forced to come to terms. The delay had already cost them dearly. It had given the Germans a chance to conclude a separate peace with the government of the Ukraine, which had seceded from Russia after the November coup and had not been brought to heel again by the Communists. Thus, for the time being, the Ukraine escaped from Soviet control seemingly by self-determination rather than by German power.

Signing the peace was a painful decision for the Bolsheviks. Their party was deeply divided over the issue. The most militant elements preferred what they called revolutionary war—fighting the Germans by any means that came to hand and kindling among the entire population the passions of a last-ditch stand. In this they had the support of the left Social Revolutionaries. Lenin, on the other hand, argued that a disastrous peace was still preferable to further chaos in Russia. He was not willing to risk the tenuous position of the Communist regime in an all-consuming holocaust which, in any case, might not stop the German juggernaut. On his plea the treaty of Brest-Litovsk was signed and ratified in early March 1918.

A greater humiliation could hardly be imagined. By its provisions Russia lost the gains of two centuries of expansion, its greatest and most modern industrial center (which included most of its coal and iron), its food basket, most of its oil, and almost one-third of its population. It was reduced, in terms of traditional power at least, to third-rate significance.

Thus did the peace treaty reveal the hollowness of Imperial Russia's great power pretension, as realists like Witte had prophesied long ago. The Germans roamed freely through the richest parts of the empire, for a brief while even occupying Baku. And at home German industrialists laid their plans for the economic penetration of Soviet Russia as well, through the control of its means of communications. In the East, indeed, the German dream of a powerful *Mitteleuropa* seemed to have come true. Soviet Russia could consider itself fortunate that it had not lost far more. Had the bulk of the German armies not been diverted to the western front by the combined onslaught of France, England, and the United States, Russia would have become a German colony.

The peace of Brest-Litovsk was an exceedingly grim event in Russian history. But Lenin, whose work had braced him for just such situations, knew how to draw strength from its very grimness:

> We must plumb to the very depths the abyss of defeat, dismemberment, bondage, and humiliation in which we have been plunged. The more clearly we understand this, the more firm, hardened, and steeled will be our determination to achieve liberation, our striving to rise once again from bondage to independence, and our indomitable resolve at all costs to make Russia cease to be wretched and feeble and become mighty and abundant in the fullest sense of the term.

Fortitude was indeed sorely needed. While the treaty of Brest-Litovsk represented the nadir of Russian state power in modern times, there was still worse to come for the Communist regime. It was an evil omen that as a result of the peace the left Social Revolutionaries drifted away from the

Communists, who henceforth carried the burden of power alone, thereby hastening again the outbreak of the civil war.

V

For a moment, however, the treaty of Brest-Litovsk allowed Lenin a brief breathing spell. By mid-March the Communists had concluded peace, given the land to the peasants (albeit with many mental reservations), and made some progress toward the recasting of Russian government and society according to their program. In the spring and early summer, despite a gradual deterioration of the regime's position, the outlines of the new order were beginning to show. The institutions of "privilege Russia," zemstvos, town dumas, press, universities, learned societies, clubs, and social centers—the whole web of its economic and social power—were demolished. The bourgeoisie was harrassed, terrorized, subjected to special capital levies, drafted for compulsory labor, treated like outcasts, and annihilated as a class. Thus began a long martyrdom for the Europeanized upper strata of Russian society. They suffered not only with their bodies but in their souls as well. The great majority of them had been patriotic Russians. Why should the impersonal sins of Russian history (which so few of them understood) be suddenly visited upon those who felt entirely innocent? Some of them turned against the Communists and fought back. Others—more than is commonly realized—succeeded in seeping into the Soviet establishment where their skills were wanted, a few even attaining important positions. None, however, could escape being dragged down into the gray, shapeless Soviet masses.

The egalitarianism of the communal tradition now began to set the official tone of the Soviet regime. No one was allowed to rise above his fellows. Even the People's Commissars, the ministers in the Soviet government, were paid only a skilled worker's wage (exceptions were made, however, for famous specialists or artists). No individual was allowed to enrich himself by the labor of others; only the state was permitted to hire and fire workers. The Soviet regime, however, never tampered with the right of individuals to own a minimum of private property such as household furnishings, books, a bicycle, and, later on, a savings account or even an automobile.

In the essentials of life too, the "black people" began to call the tune. The former instinctive receptiveness to Western influences was replaced by a deeper tradition of xenophobia and suspicion of all things European (the abstract internationalism of many leading Communists notwith-standing). Speech, rhetoric, fashion, and a thousand other details of life and thought changed flavor as the new regime adapted itself to the mentality of the Soviet masses. It was a shocking descent from previous standards, yet an inevitable corollary of modern mass politics. Soviet teachers, writers, scholars, and the party itself, were now faced with the endless uphill struggle to educate, refine, and civilize those who had hitherto distrusted all culture as the work of aliens or exploiters.

The new order was formally embodied in the Soviet constitution promulgated in July 1918 for the territories left to Soviet rule, now called the Russian Soviet Federated Socialist Republic. It created a hierarchy of soviets as the basis of government, continuing the heavy overrepresentation of the workers and the system of indirect representation, both of which had evolved in the previous year. Representation proceeded from the grass roots upward. Yet government authority descended strictly in the opposite direction. The Council of People's Commissars, the true executive in the Soviet system, acted with quick dispatch. Its decisions were binding on the executive committees of all lower soviets. They and their staffs constituted the new Soviet bureaucracy, in which one could recognize quite a few familiar faces held over from the old Russia, as well as its red tape and officiousness. In this manner the government of Russia became a strictly centralized Soviet government backed up, of course, on every level, by the Communist party.

At the same time, the Communists also brought Russia up to date in the relationship between church and state. They dissolved the monasteries and confiscated their properties (as once upon a time Henry VIII had done in England), made religion a private concern of the citizen, and left to the clergy and their flock only the church buildings (and often not even those). As militant atheists, the Communists were ruthless in pruning the power of the church. Moreover, they made their fight against the church into a war against all religion, avenging all the sins into which the Russian state—or Russian history—had led the Orthodox church. But knowing full well that the church is strengthened by the blood of the martyrs, they pressed their persecution with some caution.

Other innovations were legal equality for women; greatly liberalized laws on marriage, divorce and abortion; solemn safeguards against racial discrimination; and constitutional pledges of extensive social services, of free education, and of improved housing, all guaranteeing the toilers access to the best of contemporary civilization. Needless to say, most of these measures remained on paper because of the continued penury of the state. The Communists also introduced, at long last, the Gregorian calendar, bringing Russian chronology up to that of the "capitalist" West by skipping 13 days. Even the alphabet was simplified.

The Communists, finally, began to feel their way toward a socialist economy. The great banks were nationalized and industry (some of it in private hands until the summer of 1918) grouped by branches into syndicates under the authority of a new Supreme Economic Council. In economics, too, the Communists pursued ambitious goals. Marxist doctrine had long proclaimed the superiority of a centrally planned economy over the anarchy of the capitalist market. Its heirs were now preparing to draw up a general economic plan for a Soviet Russia. Ever since the Witte system many Russian economists, industrialists, and scientists had recognized the necessity of central planning as a means of developing Russia's lagging economy and argued about its details. Only in one respect did the Communists far exceed their prerevolutionary predecessors: They were ready to extend their economic plan to all other peoples who might adopt the Soviet socialist system. Lenin himself, however, fancied a somewhat plainer scheme (derived from a German source). He was to advance the socialist economy by providing cheap electricity to the whole country, arguing rather naïvely that Soviet rule plus electrification produced communism. All these schemes, however, remained only vague expectations. Effective planning required a more integrated and stable community than the Communists possessed in 1918 (or for years to come). The immediate problems were more elementary.

VI

The economic deterioration that had begun with the war still continued, and at a disastrous clip. In the spring of 1918, the Russian economy was approaching the point of complete collapse. Money lost all value; manufactured goods disappeared from the shops; the shops themselves closed down as the normal channels of trade ceased to function; speculation and corruption were rife. The greatest need in the urban-industrial centers, where the Communists enjoyed their most solid support, and in many other places as well, was for food. More bread was the one item in their prerevolutionary appeals that the Communists had not been able to provide.

Supplying food for the urban population was not only a matter of central control over distribution and consumption, which was begun by the Provisional Government and carried to an extreme by the Communists, but above all of stimulating grain production in the villages. But when "boughten" goods could not be obtained even by barter, why should the peasants raise food for the market? In their extreme need, the Communists soon took to extorting what grain there was in the villages, using "committees of the poor" to pry it from the more prosperous peasants or, even more drastically, sending armed workers into the countryside to take it as a prize of war. The effect of these measures on the peasantry can be imagined; yet they lasted until 1921.

The proper remedy, obviously, lay in stimulating industrial production. But here the Communists encountered another serious problem. How could the revolutionary workers, who had just seized the factories, be persuaded to work even harder than under capitalism and for a smaller return? In the last analysis, as Lenin was fully aware, socialism had to prove its superiority over capitalism by outproducing it at lower cost. Labor productivity was the crucial issue that loomed behind much of Soviet domestic policy from 1918 to the end.

In theory, there should have been no difficulty. The destruction of the capitalist system was presumably carried out by a proletariat which, having learned the best that capitalism could teach, stepped forward with a superior discipline. Russian realities, however, did not fit the doctrine. The Marxist term "proletariat" when applied to the Russian preindustrial masses, smacked of an ideological fraud. As Lenin himself admitted in April 1918, "The Russian worker is a bad worker compared with the workers of the advanced countries." The Soviet regime thus had to instruct its toilers how to work properly. And this meant using, in the name of the higher stage of development, all the tricks of the capitalist employer: piece wages, competition between work gangs, and time-and-motion studies according to Frederick W. Taylor. Lenin's advice to workers' delegations in these months might well have shocked less flexible Marxists. "Now we'll learn from the capitalists, because we don't know enough." And he treated his listeners to a dose of the Protestant ethic to boot: "Keep books punctually and conscientiously, manage economically, don't be lazy, don't steal, preserve strictest discipline in your work."

But he used still another and more ominous line of thought. As he put it, modern large-scale industry, by which the Communists set such store, required an "absolute and strict unity of will which directs the joint labor of hundreds, thousands, and tens of thousands of people":

> The revolution has only just broken the oldest, most durable, and heaviest fetters to which the masses were compelled to submit. That was yesterday, but today the same revolution demands, in the interests of socialism, that the masses unquestionably obey the single will of the leaders of the labor process.

Almost simultaneously, the seventh Communist Party Congress with its usual Bolshevik shrillness demanded "the most energetic, unsparingly decisive, draconian measures to raise the self-discipline and discipline of workers and peasants." These were alarming prospects for the Russian toilers. It was one thing to bring Russian state and society into alignment and do away with all class barriers. But it was quite another to train the Russian proletariat for industrialization.

Obviously, the so-called Russian proletariat was not yet ready to submerge its newly awakened wills into one single will, or, more generally, to assume its governmental duties. A deep disappointment over its response to the Communist dictatorship ran through Lenin's speeches in the spring and summer of 1918. As he observed in July:

> The workers and peasant masses possess greater constructive talent than might have been expected. . . . But at the same time we have to admit that the chief shortcoming of the masses is their timidity and reluctance to take affairs into their own hands.

Two weeks later he admonished party workers, "We must broaden our sphere of influence among the working class masses." The spontaneity of the latter, alas, left much to be desired. What Lenin really meant was, to paraphrase one of his classic statements, that the Russian proletariat, exclusively by its own efforts, was apt to develop only the petty-bourgeois habits of backwardness. The social energy released by the revolutionary masses, by those "backward strata now for the first time lifting themselves from the dregs," was not by itself going to build socialism. His Menshevik critics had been right after all: On such foundations no socialist order would last.

Yet the impatient Lenin was to be stopped neither by the Russian workers' spontaneous trade-union consciousness nor by their backwardness. The obstacles merely affirmed his determination. As he announced in what was probably the crassest statement of Leninism:

> The habits of the capitalist system are too strong, the tasks of reeducating a people educated in these habits for centuries is a difficult job which demands a lot of time. But we say: our fighting method is organization. We must organize everything, take everything into our hands. . . .

Ever more total organization and comprehensive social engineering were Lenin's ultimate answers to the staggering challenge of matching the spontaneous civic cooperation prevailing in Western society.

VII

Lenin, however, benefited from that visceral, anarchic excitement of revolution set off by the Bolshevik tocsin—as expressed by Alexander Blok:

> Life is only worth living when we make immense demands on it. All or nothing! A faith, not in what is not found upon earth, but in what ought to be there, although at present it does not exist and may not come forth for quite a while! . . . A true revolutionary cannot aim at anything less, though we cannot yet say whether this aim will be accomplished or not. Its cherished hope is to raise a universal cyclone which will carry to the lands buried in snow the warm winds and the fragrance of orange groves, and will water the sun-scorched plains of the south with the refreshing rain from the northern regions. Peace and brotherhood of nations is the banner under which the Russian revolution marches on its way. This is the time of the roaring flood. This is the music which he who has ears should hear.

In the early stages of the Revolution, such exultation was a source of Communist strength, particularly among the intellectuals.

For coarser and more easily guided natures, the Communists unhesitatingly beat the vile drums of greed, hatred, and sadism. Lenin wholeheartedly endorsed the slogan, coined by an anonymous revolutionary, "Let's loot the looters." He also recommended revolutionary justice carried out on the spur of the moment, without process of law. And he did not shrink from putting the revolutionary dynamite into the deepest bonds of social life.

In granting freedom and equality to all women, the Communists made the ambition of women and the discontent of wives into a powerful political force. A Bolshevik virago was sometimes more frightful than the fiercest member of the Red Guard. They also revamped the traditional relationship between the sexes. Bourgeois marriage was a fraud, the Communist Manifesto had declared. It was now to be replaced by "the free union of men and women who are lovers and comrades," in the words of Mme. Kollontai, the Communist authority on the "woman question" (who freely practiced what she preached). Marriage in times of revolution was bound to suffer. But the new gospel helped to undermine it even more.

As for the care of children born from these free unions, Mme. Kollontai supplied the following answer:

> The worker mother who is conscious of her social function will rise to a point where she no longer differentiates between yours and mine; she must remember that there are henceforth only *our* children, those of the communist state, the common possession of all workers.

Alas for the socialist mothers; they must remember that the maternal instinct was merely a bourgeois relic (even *their* spontaneity was not suited to the new age)! And alas for the waifs entrusted to the care of a society at war!

The new regime also tended to set the children against their parents, particularly if the latter did not belong among the toilers, and the pupils against their teachers. The teachers, by Lenin's own admission, felt rather lukewarm toward the Revolution, all the more reason to transform education into a tool of revolution. The curriculum as well as classroom discipline suffered, and the institutions of higher learning, now open only to the toilers, lost their former luster.

Thus the universal cyclone began to take its toil. But deliberately unleashing it against all customary order and stability was a dangerous game. It nearly brought down even the Communist regime.

The Universal Cyclone, 1918–1921

I

The breathing spell after Brest-Litovsk barely gave Lenin time to come to grips with basic issues of socialist reconstruction before he was confronted with all the unfinished business of revolution now grown to gigantic proportions. By their unilateral coup in November and their continuous instigation of revolutionary terror, the Communists had set the example of deliberate violence. Under such prompting, the anarchic spontaneity of the previous year, already tending toward bloodshed, turned into an open and universal civil war. Starting in a minor way before November had ended, it smoldered under the surface during the following winter and spring. In May 1918, the fury suddenly leaped into the open and raged for almost three terrible years in every community of the Russian Empire with unforgiving finality, pitting Reds against Whites (as the defenders of the old Russia were called), poor peasants against kulaks and Cossacks, city dwellers against villagers, uneducated against educated, socialists against capitalists, Bolsheviks against Mensheviks or Social Revolutionaries, non-Russians against Russians, Christians against Jews, men against men in the frenzy of raw spite. In this orgy of fratricide, certain clearly defined fronts stood out. In the border regions of the north, west, southwest, south, and southeast, non-Russians fought for independence or genuine autonomy. In Siberia and the same border regions, Reds fought Whites. In addition, peasant forces called the Greens fought both Whites and Reds in many parts of the country, but particularly in the Ukraine.

Oddly enough, the first and most dangerous threat to the Communist regime came not from the army officers who were gathering in the south or Siberia but from the Bolsheviks' former allies in the underground, the Social Revolutionaries. Excluded from power, they turned their conspiratorial methods against the Communist dictatorship. The left Social Revolutionary party, in opposition after March, was even bolder, plotting within the Cheka (to which it had been admitted as member of the coalition) for an uprising in the capital.

The Social Revolutionaries, as well as other opposition elements, received aid from an unexpected quarter. A rather large contingent of Czech soldiers, sifted from the Austro-Hungarian prisoners of war for volunteer service in France, was to be evacuated via the Siberian railroad and Vladivostok. As the Czechs gathered in the latter part of May along that far-flung line, the Communist leadership, suspicious of their motives, suddenly demanded that they disarm. In reply the Czechs seized control of the Siberian railroad and thereby encouraged various opposition groups in the vicinity to similar defiance. These events decided the fate of the imperial family. Transferred in August 1917 from Petrograd to Tobolsk in western Siberia, they were shifted in late April to Ekaterinburg, an industrial town under Soviet control. In the night of July 16, ten days before the Czechs occupied the town, they were murdered in the cellar of their house, together with their physician, two servants, and a spaniel.

Now events moved thick and fast. In western Siberia, two anti-Communist centers sprang up. Closer to Moscow, in Samara, several prominent Social Revolutionary deputies of the Constituent Assembly created an anti-Bolshevik government of their own and began to rally an army. On July 6, a group of the left Social Revolutionaries, after their party's final break with the Communists, assassinated the German ambassador at his Moscow residence and tried to seize the city. At the same time, some towns on the upper Volga ousted their Communist-led soviets. Elsewhere, factory workers revolted and railway workers threatened to strike. At the end of July, Lenin, thoroughly alarmed, declared "the socialist fatherland in danger."

To the internal uprisings, foreign intervention was added. In late June, the British government, eager to preserve the Russian front by any means at its disposal, reinforced the port of Murmansk, which British troops had occupied in March. In early August, with American help, it seized Archangel as well, thereby cutting off Soviet Russia from its remaining outlets to the sea. The British also dispatched a small force to central Asia, and, in order to speed the evacuation of the Czechs, the three Western Allies and Japan occupied Vladivostok and the stations along the Siberian railroad as far west as the Urals, giving aid and comfort to all anti-Bolshevik groups on their way.

The climax of the crisis came in August. The month began with the capture of Kazan on the mid-Volga by the Samara regime. It ended with the assassination of Uritsky, the Petrograd chief of the Cheka, and the severe wounding of Lenin by an assassin in Moscow. Never was the Communist regime closer to collapse.

Pressed against the wall, the Communists fought back with cold fury. The reverses strengthened the discipline of the Red Army which Trotsky had begun to train after Brest-Litovsk; now it began to show its fighting qualities. The Cheka, too, swung into action. Large-scale terror became the order of the day, as thousands and thousands of hostages picked from all strata of society and all opposition groups were shot. Others were sent to the Gulag, which originated under Lenin not Stalin. Thus began the horrors of the civil war, destined to last until the spring of 1921.

By September 1918, the Communists had successfully beaten off the uprisings of the Social Revolutionaries, only to encounter the more effective onslaught of the tsarist officers who now entered the field as champions of the dictatorship of the right; in Siberia, they established their first stronghold under the leadership of Admiral Kolchak. As "Supreme Ruler" of the empire he claimed command over all armed forces of Russia. In the winter and spring of 1919, his troops were slowly advancing northwestward in order to achieve a junction with the British at Archangel, thus creating a second crisis for the Communists. The German revolution in November 1918 brought Lenin a blissful moment of elation, but little relief. The armistice in the West, which preceded the German revolution, annulled the treaty of Brest-Litovsk and reopened the Baltic and the Ukraine to Soviet forces. But at the same time it intensified Western intervention, which now assumed a clearly anti-Communist orientation. While the retreating German troops guarded the Baltic littoral against the Red Army, British ships entered the Baltic Sea. British troops also appeared on the Caspian Sea, and French forces occupied key Black Sea ports.

The Communists succeeded in turning back Kolchak's offensive just in time to prevent diplomatic recognition of the "Supreme Ruler" by the Paris peace conference. But as his fortunes ebbed, the White "Army of the South," commanded by General Denikin, an abler man than Kolchak, began its advance into Soviet territory. In October 1919, it drove to within 250 miles of Moscow, producing yet another spell of tenseness in the Kremlin, particularly as a third White force under General Yudenich, operating from the Baltic, simultaneously penetrated the outskirts of Petrograd. Comforted by the virtual withdrawal of Allied intervention in September 1919, the Bolsheviks also survived these alarms. But as they drove Denikin's army to its doom (Yudenich never constituted a serious threat), the government of the newly established Poland declared war on Soviet Russia. After some amazing reversals of the fortunes of war, the Polish armies penetrated deep into Byelorussia before peace was made. The last battles of the civil war were fought during the fall of 1920 in the Crimean peninsula, from which General Wrangel, Denikin's successor and the most capable of all the White commanders, had conducted a futile campaign into the mainland before being evacuated with French help.

In the winter of 1920–1921, the war with the rebellious non-Russian minorities in the steppes and deserts of the southeast also came to an end. The Tatars and Bashkirs between the Volga and the Urals were granted a measure of autonomy under strict Soviet control, as were the Kirghiz people further to the southeast. Turkestan in central Asia was likewise subdued, although a few rebellious tribesmen still held out. It too received autonomy as a Soviet Socialist Republic. And in the Transcaucasian region the Red Army reconquered the three republics, Georgia, Armenia, and Azerbaijan, which had proclaimed their independence earlier in the civil war, and subjected them, as a Soviet Socialist federation, to Communist rule.

II

We cannot, however, view these murderous events in isolation, for from the start the principal fronts of the civil war had been extended far beyond Russia. The Russian civil war was the center of the universal cyclone that shook all of Europe—a Europe wanly emerging from the war—and jolted the world as well, as Lenin had predicted.

What a dismal spectacle the chief regions of Europe presented at the end of the war, and what an opportunity for revolutionary agitation! In Eastern Europe a great landslide was underway. German, Austro-Hungarian, and Russian empires which had given order and stability to the marches of Europe had collapsed (not to mention the Ottoman Empire, whose final dismemberment spread the cataclysm into the Near and Middle East). As a result, not only Russia (as we have seen) but also the broad stretch of liberated lands from the Baltic to the Black Sea and Mediterranean found itself in a profound state of flux, traversed by two revolutions.

The first was the revolution of national self-determination, which created a series of new sovereign states, Finland and the three Baltic republics, Poland, Czechoslovakia, and Hungary, and greatly augmented two older states, Rumania and Serbia (eventually renamed Yugoslavia). Constituting (or reconstituting) their governments, drawing their boundaries, and settling the fate of innumerable national minorities in regions that history had not predestined to form nation-states, were difficult if not superhuman tasks. In the process much blood was spilled.

The other revolution, compounding the first, was a social one. In the lands carved from the former empires, the monarchical order of life was overthrown and Western democracy introduced, yet not without some competition from the Soviet model. Particularly where large landed estates had been the rule, land reform was hastily pushed through lest it be accomplished, Soviet style, by the peasants themselves. In its wake peasant parties, akin to the Russian Social Revolutionaries, sprang up and gained numerous adherents. The Marxists, both "soft" and "hard," were also active, demanding a better lot for the workers in the scattered industrial centers, and clashing, like the peasants, with liberal and conservative parties. How the various social, regional, and national groups in the new parliaments could be yoked together under a democratic government capable of solving the problems of the postwar era was at best an open question, except in Czechoslovakia, where democracy really took hold. Unsatisfactory indeed was the subsequent history of the fragmented and weak *Zwischeneuropa* caught between Germany and the Soviet Union.

The vanquished peoples of central Europe were likewise shaken by social revolution. The defeat of their country and of their political ambitions in Europe and the world had come as a terrible shock to most Germans. It had set off not only a widespread revulsion against the Bismarckian system of government—this was the cause of the November Revolution which created a democratic republic—but also a clash of extremist groups on the right and left. The Bolsheviks had many allies among Spartacists, Shop Stewards, and Independent Socialists, but also fanatical opponents. At the outset the radical left took the offensive, staging many uprisings in the winter and spring of 1919. In April, a Soviet-type government ruled over Munich. Who in these months could have been sure that the German republic would not go the way of the Kerensky regime? And who, furthermore, could foretell whether the workers of Vienna would remain loyal to their moderate socialist leaders? In Hungary, indeed, democracy took the Soviet turn under the dictatorship of Béla Kun, one of the prisoners of war whom the Russian Communists had converted.

Not even the victorious Allies in Western Europe were immune to the revolutionary fever. For a week in January 1919, the red flag flew from the municipal flagpole in Glasgow, and at least one British radical ventured the hope that it would also be hoisted over Buckingham Palace. The British government, in addition, had its hands full with rebellions in Ireland, Egypt, and India, as Soviet propaganda gleefully noted. South of the Channel, Clemenceau was wounded by an assassin of anarchist leanings in February, while French workers were preparing, now that the war was over, to resume the class war. The federation of French trade unions declared a May Day holiday amounting to a general strike. It wanted "to impress the French public with the strength and the unity of the working classes." Red flags adorned many a local parade; in Paris bloody scuffles ensued. Plans were laid in the summer for a common general strike of English, French, and Italian workers (which, however, never took place). Italy, where the right and left clashed as in Germany, seemed even closer to revolution. Italian socialists staged sit-in strikes in the industrial centers of the north and talked of seizing power, profiting from the universal letdown of political morale.

Everywhere, demobilization produced a profound disillusionment. Wartime oratory had raised extravagant expectations of a better future, greater national glory, and a higher standard of living. But after the war all governments were hopelessly overburdened with debts, as the astronomical costs of the war were carried over into the peace through inflation, taxation, and widespread unemployment. Even victory was hollow; the promises could not be kept. The war, furthermore, had destroyed the interdependence of Europe on which everyone's prosperity depended. It would be years before the prewar levels of well-being could be reconstituted on a new basis. Meanwhile, men grew impatient. Their minds were agitated as never before by the problems of war and peace, prosperity and socioeconomic organization, government and politics. In their ignorance they now searched for quick, soothing explanations of the recent holocaust and their present frustrations; they craved culprits and scapegoats. The political irrationalism that had arisen before the war now found many new converts. The political passions thus aroused imposed a heavy strain on the democratic order inherited from prewar reforms or introduced, as a result of Western victory, into all the defeated and newly created countries of Central and Eastern Europe.

Even the United States, which had saved the Allies from defeat and now entered global politics in full force, felt the tremors of the cyclone. In 1919, 4 million workers went on strike (which, however, signified far less revolutionary zeal than similar events in prewar Russia). In the Pacific Northwest, the center of some of the most violent unionism in the country, the city of Seattle experienced a brief general strike in

February. In the same months the "Friends of the New Russia" staged a dinner party in Washington. In September not one but two Communist parties were founded in Chicago (both tiny). And the year ended with a prolonged steel strike, which brought William Z. Foster, the future leader of American communism, to national prominence. The anti-Communist rebound was even more vehement, as Attorney General A. Mitchell Palmer led the charge against "the red menace."

The unrest was felt even further afield. All around the world, perceptive observers sensed a break in the traditional global order. A new era was beginning in which Europe no longer stood at the center. The United States, Japan, the British dominions, and even the "colonial" peoples in Asia loomed larger now that Europe had demeaned itself by its great war. New hopes and ambitions were aroused. The Indian scene, as described by Nehru, was typical.

> The end of the world war found India in a state of suppressed excitement. . . . Political agitation, peaceful and wholly constitutional as it was, seemed to be working itself to a head, and people talked with assurance of self-determination and self-government. Some of this unrest was visible also among the masses, especially the peasantry. . . . The soldiers back from active service on distant fronts were no longer the subservient robots that they used to be. They had grown mentally, and there was much discontent among them.

In China, the universal unrest flared up with unexpected suddenness. When on May 4, 1919, the news arrived that the Paris peace conference had failed to protect China against the Japanese demands that had grown out of the war, the people of Beijing, led by the students, poured into the streets in violent protest. The agitation continued for months afterward and spread to other cities as well. The May Fourth Movement, as this first outburst of a new Chinese nationalism became known, eventually led to the formation of a Chinese Communist party. In short, the political ambitions of the Western model, having already swayed Japanese society for two generations, were now beginning to influence Chinese life as well.

How discouraging were the toils of statesmanship under these conditions! At Paris, where in the winter and spring of 1919 the statesmen of the victorious powers and their clients were assembled, a multitude of baffling problems presented themselves. Their subsequent compromise, which led to the "dictated" peace of Versailles, provided a basis for a fresh start after the war but hardly for a lasting settlement. Yet it was fortunate, perhaps, that the German representatives were not invited to that conference—and still more fortunate that the Communists were kept out. The participation of both, however conforming to precedent and general interest, would certainly have precluded any settlement whatsoever.

III

In the light of all these conditions it was no irresponsible fantasy to say, as did the program of the Communist International founded in March 1919, that "the imperialist system" was breaking down.

> Ferment in the colonies, ferment among the former dependent small nations, insurrection of the proletariat, victorious proletarian revolutions in some countries, dissolution of imperialist armies, complete incapacity of the ruling classes to continue to guide the destinies of the peoples—this is the state of affairs throughout the world.

Against this somber background, the Communists projected their own apocalyptic oversimplification: "Humanity, whose entire civilization lies in ruin, is threatened with complete annihilation. There is only one force that can save it, and that is the proletariat."

At the height of the civil war in Russia, Lenin created the Third, or Communist, International, also called Comintern (an organization of European left-wing socialist groups). It was to guide the manifold stirrings of revolution in the direction of the Communist myth and to use them for the benefit of Soviet Russia. Within the next two years, the new organization won over most of the extremist elements in the European socialist movement, while the moderates rebuilt the Second International scattered by the war. Thus European socialism (always divided) was forever split and thereby robbed of its future. Despite the formation of the Comintern in 1919, one could hardly speak, however, of an international Communist conspiracy. What linked the various revolutionary plots and rumors of plots in those chaotic months was their common revolt against a discredited order and a vague identity of slogans and symbols. All left-wing groups desperately needed support and sought it in a common solidarity, despite profound differences in philosophy and organization. The Comintern, paradoxically, became a reasonably reliable tool of Soviet foreign policy only long after the cyclone of revolution had subsided.

Yet it was clear from the start that Lenin viewed the revolutionary tinder elsewhere as a natural opportunity for extending Soviet control. He was ready to ignite it by any means within reach, making little distinction between conventional power based on arms and revolutionary power derived from a genuine local revolutionary situation such as had existed in Russia in November 1917. When Béla Kun's Hungarian regime was faltering, Trotsky dispatched two divisions of the Red Army to succor it. And in the summer of 1920, when the Red Army for a brief moment besieged Warsaw and the Communists hoped for assistance from the Polish workers, Lenin quipped of "breaking the crust of the Polish bourgeoisie" with the bayonet. Sometimes the bayonet alone seemed to be the decisive factor. In October 1918, hoping to liberate the territories still held by the Germans, Trotsky inspired the Red Army with bold talk of Communist expansion:

> Free Latvia, free Poland and Lithuania, free Finland, on the other side free Ukraine will not be a wedge but a uniting link between Soviet Russia and the future Soviet Germany and Austria-Hungary. This is the beginning of a European communist federation—a union of the proletarian republics of Europe.

Trotsky's ambition, incidentally, seemed almost like a Communist replica of Germany's *Mitteleuropa*.

The militant revolutionary outreach thus encouraged conferred another boon on the Russian Communists. It proved to them (who were acutely aware of their weakness) the accuracy of their myth and hardened their self-confidence. As early as the fall of 1918, Lenin wrote:

> Bolshevism . . . has shown by the example of Soviet power that the workers and peasants even of a backward country, even with the least experience, education and habits of organization, have been able for a whole year amidst gigantic difficulties and amidst a struggle against the exploiters (who were supported by the bourgeoisie of the whole world) to maintain the power of the toilers, to create a democracy that is immeasurably higher and broader than all previous democracies in the whole world and to start the creative work of tens of millions of workers and peasants for the practical achievement of socialism.

Therefore, he proclaimed, "Bolshevism can serve as a model of tactics for all" proletarians in the whole world. In 1920, he presented the same point even more strongly:

> At the present moment of history the situation is precisely such that the Russian model reveals to *all* countries something . . . of their near and inevitable future.

This was the presumption underlying Lenin's relations with foreign socialists.

The Communist outreach into Europe was matched by "capitalist" intervention in the Russian civil war by France, England, the United

States, and Japan. Their motives for this venture were exceedingly complex. Starting with a desire to maintain the second front and to forestall German capture of Allied war material stored in Russia or a German thrust toward India, the three Western powers began to support any anti-Bolshevik force willing to continue the war. From this intermediary position they drifted, with varying degrees of conviction, into an openly anti-Communist policy. Needless to say, neither Western statesmen nor their constituents possessed much understanding of the conditions of Russia nor of the necessities prompting its internal evolution. All they saw was a regime that proclaimed domestic policies outrageous to their sensibilities, flouted the decencies of international discourse, and fostered universal revolution. The Allied leaders faced troubles enough at the end of the war. The seemingly unlimited ambitions of the Communists to create further chaos only inspired deep revulsion.

In addition, the interventionist powers were guided by specific interests: France by its extensive investments in Russia, Britain by its political position in the Near and Middle East, Japan by its desire for a bridgehead on the Asian mainland. Only the American government, benefiting from past isolation, maintained a relatively impartial policy. Its intervention in European Russia was prompted by a need for cooperation with England and France; in Siberia it was to check the Japanese appetite. It was no wonder that those governments with concrete stakes in Russia should carve out, on paper, prospective spheres of influence and operations and exact from the White regimes humiliating pledges of future concessions in return for their aid. Like the treaty of Brest-Litovsk, these agreements testified anew to the weakness of Russia.

Measured in terms of the Allies' recent war effort, the extent of Western intervention in Russia was ludicrously small. Yet in terms of the tiny weights needed to tip the scales of the civil war, of the traditional and well-nigh irrational Russian fear of Western invasion, or of Bolshevik desperation, foreign intervention loomed large. The presence of Western troops and, more significantly, the grant of food and war material to the anti-Bolshevik forces did have its effect. Otherwise Denikin would never have come so close to Moscow. Nor would Trotsky have been forced to cancel the military aid to Béla Kun. British and French assistance to the Poles, furthermore, did stop the Communist advance at the gates of Warsaw and permit the subsequent Polish penetration into Byelorussia. Without British and German aid, finally, neither Finland nor the Baltic states would have been able to gain independence.

The advantages in this far-flung battle, however, did not all lie with the West. The Communists also scored some successes. They achieved the withdrawal of the French occupation forces from Odessa by thor-

oughly contaminating them with their propaganda. Through the sympa-
thies that they had aroused among British workers, they stopped Lloyd
George from sending more war material to Poland. And in a thousand
other ways they profited from the universal war weariness. Interventionist sentiment, found particularly among conservatives, was defeated at
the source of public opinion. And, last but not least, the Communists
had the advantage of the unspeakable messiness of Russian civil war
politics, which quickly frustrated all who were venturesome enough to
meddle in it, Czechs, Frenchmen, Englishmen, and Americans.

Yet in the end, the revolutionary potential proved far less effective
than Lenin had anticipated. In its periphery, the cyclone merely produced a mild disturbance. No red flag flew from Buckingham Palace or
in the Champs Élysées, no socialist revolution took place in Central
Europe where the chances had seemed so propitious. Nationalism rather
than socialism and communism attracted the uprooted intellectuals. The
bulk of the German proletariat was committed to the continuity of the
state organization, which rescued employment, social security, and all
the other benefits of order from the defeat; it turned a cold shoulder to
Lenin's overtures and, under Social Democratic leadership, became one
of the pillars of the Weimar Republic. In Austria, the moderate socialists, likewise, retained the leadership of the workers and played a prominent part in the early years of the new republic. In Hungary, Béla Kun's
regime, unpopular even with the workers, was suppressed without much
trouble, and Hungarian communism ceased to exist until the end of
World War II. Throughout Eastern Europe, nationalism proved an effective rampart against communism. The Communists, to be sure, succeeded in gradually transforming the extreme groups among the
European socialists into pliant and dependable Communist parties; but
in the end they could not prevent a new era of "capitalist consolidation."
Lenin's hopes for a revolution among the colonial peoples went likewise
unfulfilled. Except for a few skirmishes, the masses of Asia were not
ready to leap to arms. It was not so easy, after all, to build a counterpower to European imperialism. Lack of response, however, did not stop
Lenin from casting the Communist bread on the colonial waters—for a
profitable return, perhaps, in future years.

IV

By the end of 1920, the Soviet experiment of matching the revolutionary
weapons of foreign policy against Western arms and influence had run
its course. A realistic equilibrium had been struck. Soviet Russia had

lost Finland, the Baltic littoral, Poland, parts of Byelorussia, and Bessarabia. Yet it had retained the Ukraine and preserved intact the Middle Eastern borders of the empire (except for small losses to Turkey) and, after the Japanese withdrawal in 1922, its Far Eastern boundaries as well. And thanks to the Communist International, it was still a force to be reckoned with.

Most important of all, however, the Communists were entrenched as masters of Russia. They had decisively won out over their domestic enemies, for many reasons. They had preserved control of the areas of their main strength, Great Russia and its industrial centers; they had also held on to their following in the Ukrainian heavy industries and in the Urals. They had retained the advantages of interior communications while their enemies, who could never coordinate their sallies, had to strike from the periphery. As heirs of the tsars, they had represented the integrity and continuity of the Russian state, claiming the loyalty of all patriots. They had shown superior leadership, too, and the ability to rally the fanaticism that upholds men under extreme strain. In addition they had excelled in organizational skill. The Red Army had emerged as a modestly respectable fighting force, superior to that of the Whites in the decisive engagements of the war. The Communists had even managed, by desperate measures that played havoc with all planning, to preserve a minimum of industrial production, to prevent mass starvation, and actually to dignify their economic improvisations by the term "war communism."

Under these conditions, the outcome of the civil war proved only that the political balance emerging from the fall of the monarchy was basically sound. The moderate groups were all but extinct; the dictatorship of the right had no chance. The political ineptitude of the old Russia dogged the anti-Bolshevik forces at every step. The Whites, who continuously quarreled among themselves, could draw no mass support. They could never clear themselves of the suspicion that they yearned to turn the clock back or that they conspired with the foreigners (despite the fact that in their negotiations with the Allies they had obstinately tried to safeguard Russia's sovereignty). Faced with the stark choice between White and Red, the bulk of the population inclined toward the Red, the harshness of Soviet rule notwithstanding. And the many local nests of resistance were too anarchic and weak to offer a real threat. Once the Whites were defeated, the Greens were quickly snuffed out.

After three years of incredible violence (described in Gorky's essay, "On the Russian Peasantry," and Sholokhov's novel, *The Don Flows Home to the Sea*), the Bolsheviks managed to survive as the sole rulers of

Russia. But they had saved little else. The country, which had lived so long on the accumulated capital of the prewar period—how fat the old leanness now appeared!—had reached the point of utter exhaustion. The biggest cities had lost almost half of their population, as city folk with relatives in the country had drifted back to the source of food (which showed again how closely the urban masses were still related to the village). Industrial production, likewise, had catastrophically declined. In 1920, large-scale industry produced only 14 percent of its prewar total. Steel production, which in 1918 was down to 10 percent of its 1913 level, sank to an all-time low of 5 percent in 1921. The harvest did not shrink quite so drastically but fell off enough to cause a searing famine in southeastern and eastern Russia during 1921–1922. So desperate were the conditions in the striken regions that the Communists were forced into the humiliation of admitting Herbert Hoover's American relief organization, which, estimatedly, saved 10 million lives.

Two events in 1921 brought home to Lenin the true state of affairs. The first was the collapse of a renewed effort of the German Communists to seize power in Germany, which proved to him that no outside support could be expected; the second, a series of strikes by Petrograd workers culminating in an uprising of the Baltic fleet at the Kronstadt naval base in March. It was an alarming moment when their erstwhile shock troops turned against the Communists and pointedly demanded Soviet but not Communist democracy. It also pointed to the danger of another peasant revolution. The Kronstadt uprising was put down with sickening terror, but it convinced Lenin that the time had come for a strategic retreat. After so many years of war, revolution, and civil war he had to give the peasants—and all inhabitants of Soviet Russia—a chance to catch their breath and to recuperate by their traditional remedies, with a minimum of government interference. Lenin stated in March 1921:

> Our poverty and ruin are so great that we cannot at one stroke restore
> large-scale factory state socialist production. This requires that we
> accumulate large stocks of grains and fuels in the big industrial cen-
> ters, replace worn-out machines with new ones, and so on. Experience
> has convinced us that this cannot be done at one stroke.

Thus began a new phase of Soviet rule, based on a New Economic Policy (NEP) which gave its name to the entire era from 1921 to 1928. It was designed to let the peasants sell most of their grain for whatever price it would fetch and thus stimulate the production of consumer goods in general through the incentives of the open market, as under capitalism. Private trade was thus allowed to revive, as was, under certain safeguards, the hiring of labor by private enterprise. Large-scale industry remained under state control, but even here capitalist accounting methods were introduced. Lenin was no longer trying to achieve socialism in a hurry. The timetable had to be revised to suit a country whose population consisted largely of peasants. Instead of taking the phantom Bolshevik express, Soviet Russia had to travel for a stretch by the old fourth-class carriages. Said Lenin:

> Our aim . . . is to prove to the peasant by deeds that we are beginning with what is intelligible, familiar, and immediately accessible to him in spite of his poverty, and not with something remote and fantastic from the peasant's point of view; we must prove that we can help him. . . . Either we prove that or he will send us to the devil. That is absolutely inevitable.
>
> Link up with the peasant masses, with the rank-and-file toiling peasants, and begin to move forward immeasurably, infinitely more slowly than we expected, but in such a way that the entire mass will actually move forward with us. If we do that we shall in time get an acceleration of this movement such as we cannot dream of now.

The partnership of the proletariat with the peasant masses was one of the key slogans of the new era, hailed as a great Communist accomplishment. Yet making the pace of Soviet development dependent on the peasants' lethargy constituted a tremendous retreat from the original impatience—a "peasant Brest-Litovsk" not easily tolerated by the party stalwarts.

The NEP also brought a considerable relaxation in other respects. The terror came to an end: freedom of self-expression was partially restored; life in Russia returned to a semblance of normalcy, which swept to the surface much of the scum of revolution and civil war but also allowed some quiet mending of the damage. In foreign affairs, the shift coincided with the resumption of peaceful foreign relations. Soviet Russia was forced to coexist with "capitalism." It had to establish diplomatic relations with its neighbors and, if possible, also with the Great Powers. Even if full diplomatic recognition by France, England, and the United States was as yet impossible, efforts were made to resume foreign trade and obtain foreign credit for rebuilding Russia's economy. Capitalist assistance was again solicited, although with greater caution than under Witte. Thus the blockade of Soviet Russia was ended. Soon a trickle of foreign visitors arrived to assess the changes that had occurred and the price that had been paid.

What an incredible test of endurance these years had been for the peoples of Russia! In retrospect, the trials of the war and the year 1917 paled as compared with the agonies of the civil war. No other people in these years had been so tortured at the outer limits of endurance as the inhabitants of the Russian Empire. Yet amidst the filth, the disease, the hunger, the fear, and the insane slaughter one could also sense a wild exhilaration. There was one boon in anarchy: the freedom to live and die for once by one's deepest convictions, without shame or compromise. And to some of the best minds, the shambles revealed a glimpse of vital human depths which normalcy had always hidden. Pasternak has written of these days in his deeply moving novel, *Dr. Zhivago:*

> Everything established, settled, and everything to do with home and order and the common ground has crumbled into dust and been swept away in the general upheaval and reorganization of the whole of society. The whole human way of life has been destroyed and ruined. All that is left is the bare, shivering human soul, stripped to the last shred, the naked force of the human psyche, for which nothing has changed because it was always cold and shivering and reaching out to its nearest neighbor, as cold and lonely as itself.

These were the moments of insight to be remembered through the barren, gray years to come. They provided the subject matter of the best Soviet literature.

Thus, after reaching cyclone strength, the great flood tide of spontaneity in Russian life subsided. The survivors, bone tired and chastened by the recent orgy of violence, slowly shuffled back to their traditional routine of making a living, under a regime that despite incredible exertions had lost little of its revolutionary vitality.

NINE

The Bases of Soviet Strength, 1921–1924

I

The events which had taught Lenin that a socialist economy could be achieved only through a number of transition stages, while slowing down the advance toward that goal, did not touch the core of the Communist myth. The only adjustment required by the tactical retreat concerned the timetable of the dialectic process. The delay, however, was easily justified by the "world historical" magnitude of the Bolshevik Revolution; heaven could not be stormed overnight. The New Economic Policy, therefore, entailed no relaxation of the inherent drive of communism. Too much was still to be done toward consolidating the dictatorship in the vast territories of Eurasia, too many foundations still to be laid before the inevitable resumption of "socialist reconstruction." Despite the exhaustion of Russia, the early years of the NEP were crowded with administrative and political innovation continuing and completing the transformation begun in 1917.

One of the major problems still facing the Soviet regime was the relationship of the non-Russian minorities to the new Soviet power. The elemental tide of revolutionary spontaneity had given new prominence to the ethnic variety within their Eurasian empire. Every minority group had felt encouraged to stress its identity and to cultivate its peculiarities. Before the November Revolution, the Bolsheviks, forever in search of revolutionary allies, had boosted this tendency by their slogan of national self-determination. Yet behind this facile phrase lay hidden many mental reservations, the result of a long search for the proper place of nationalism in the Marxist creed. Marx had taught his followers to consider nationalism a bourgeois phenomenon doomed to disappear in the global melting pot of the future. He and Engels, "Red Prussians" both, had always assumed that the lesser peoples would be duly absorbed by the greater ones, and that, as in business so in government, strict centralization would prevail as the supreme guarantee of rational efficiency; federalism was anathema to them. These assumptions of Marxism did not, however, easily fit the political realities of the Russian Empire, or of many areas in the world where nationalism obviously was still on the rise, often as a revolutionary force. It was Lenin who, after many doctrinal disputes, devised the Bolshevik formula for yoking the revolutionary potential of nationalism to Marxist socialism. He argued that the promise of self-determination would rally the suppressed nationalities to the revolutionary cause and the revolution in turn would hasten the disappearance of nationalism. Having a choice between fragmenting society into many small national units or consolidating it into ever larger supranational blocks, the victorious proletariat of all countries would wisely opt for the latter.

When the Bolsheviks came to power, they formally recognized the importance of the nationality question by creating a People's Commissariat for Nationalities, with Stalin as its chief. Yet as they put Lenin's formula to the test, they met with the most unwelcome results. The advanced non-Russian nationalities along the western border made use of self-determination in order to escape from Bolshevik control, while the many lesser ones, which could not secede because they were surrounded by Russians or incapable of statehood, pressed for federal autonomy as promised in the Social Revolutionary program. Finland, in one of the first Bolshevik decrees, was granted full independence. Yet almost at once Finnish secession was contested by an uprising of Finnish Communists who, under orders from Petrograd, clamored for unification with Soviet Russia. A civil war ensued in which the Finns managed, with German help, to ward off the threat. The Lithuanians, Latvians, and Estonians set up their own states that lasted until 1939, drawing on British as well as German support. Lacking such allies, the other nationalities had to submit. After many struggles that made a farce of self-determination, the Communists reinforced native Communist elements, which sometimes were minute indeed, with units of the Red Army or Russian settlers, and thus secured adherence to the proletarian cause.

Aware of the strength of nationalism, however, the Communists made two essential concessions that hardly accorded with their Marxist inheritance. They granted cultural autonomy to their subject nationalities and adopted an element of federalism in the formal structure of their state.

Granting cultural autonomy to the non-Russian nationalities under their control implied an acceptance of local custom and language as the medium of social action. Henceforth, each national group conducted its affairs in its own vernacular and in terms of its own national tradition (purged of "feudal" or "capitalist" traits). The Ukrainians, for instance, were allowed to cultivate the Ukrainian language as their official language, which the tsars had never permitted. The most widely hailed products of Soviet nationality policy were the newly devised alphabets for peoples who had never before enjoyed a written language. Yet the new script was also the chief vehicle of Communist propaganda and of the advanced urban-industrial civilization for which Soviet communism stood in the eyes of its underdeveloped subjects. It helped to subvert the native civilization, while ostensibly safeguarding it. Modernization in turn inevitably entailed Russification.

Thus the nationality problem, particularly in the Asian territories of Soviet Russia, became fused with the larger problem of extending modern civilization into backward areas. In central Asia and parts of Siberia, the Communists were creating the same tensions against which they were railing in their relation with the "imperialist" powers. The native nationalism that refused to wither away was often merely an instinctive reaction against the Soviet Russian subversion of the native heritage. The only remedy against such subversion would have been, as a perceptive spokesman of Soviet Moslems, Sultan-Galiev, once wrote, "the dictatorship of the colonies and semi-colonies over the metropoles," which was like asking that water run uphill. The grant of cultural autonomy, in short, did not solve the nationality problem. It did not satisfy the more primitive nationalities, because it did not prevent the gradual dissolution of their native culture. And in the case of the more advanced ones, like the Ukrainians, it was found wanting because it was not accompanied by appropriate political opportunities.

The concession of federalism was designed, to be sure, to meet that objection. Yet federalism remained merely a matter of form. The nature of Soviet federalism was foreshadowed in the first Soviet constitution of 1918, which organized the ethnic minorities encased in the Russian heartland as autonomous Soviet socialist regions or republics, allowed to conduct their own affairs (under proper supervision). In the aftermath of the civil war, the border nationalities which had meanwhile tasted genuine independence were granted privileges, above all in the right of secession (a fine case of window dressing). But the essentials of the Communist dictatorship such as armed power, foreign policy, communications, economic planning, and the political police remained under the control of Moscow in form as well as in substance.

Late in 1923, the basic guidelines of Soviet federalism were laid down in the new constitution of the Union of the Soviet Socialist Republics

(USSR) then composed of the Russian republic Byelorussia, the Ukraine, and the Transcaucasian Federation. Before the decade had ended, these four were joined by the Uzbek and Turkman republics (in 1924) and the Tajik republic (in 1929). Under this constitution, the pattern of Soviet government outlined in 1918 was extended to the entire country, except that the All-Russian Congress of Soviets now became the All-Union Congress of Soviets. Soviet federalism, however, was but a façade for a rigidly centralized regime controlled by the Communist party. In the ranks of the party, not even a trace of federalism was tolerated. The party remained the same "Russian Communist Party (Bolshevik)" for all the territories of the Soviet Union regardless of the national origin of its members. Thus did the prerevolutionary heritage of Russian hegemony persist under the new regime. The preeminence of the Communist party, incidentally, was not even mentioned in the new constitution.

Whether the non-Russian nationalities improved their lot under Soviet rule is debatable. They escaped the worst of Russification, as there lingered in party circles enough suspicion of "Great Russian chauvinism" to curb the former excesses. But like all other Soviet subjects, they fell under the ever stricter political supervision of masters who, like the tsars, spoke Russian and tended to hasten the process of integration artificially. Neither cultural autonomy nor federalism offered any protection against the rising Soviet totalitarianism. In the Communist treatment of the nationality question, one can again trace the paradox of the Bolshevik Revolution. The Communists encouraged spontaneity only to take away its substance in the name of a higher social order which pretended to grant all that had been originally desired (and more). In reality it merely turned out to be a more efficient version of Russian domination.

II

Another major problem brought under control in these years was the relationship between party and state. As Kerensky had already observed, the soviets were not suited to be organs of government. The Communists proved the point, even though they built an imposing structure of government on them. It was, however, no easy task to reduce to docility the original soviet spontaneity which had helped the Bolsheviks into power. It meant ousting all unruly and hostile elements, eliminating Menshevik and Social Revolutionary competitors, and introducing efficient Communist leadership among the remaining members.

In the taming of soviet spontaneity, the assertion of central administrative control played a significant part. The Council of People's Commissars issued decrees to all lower soviets which it considered binding upon them, regardless of whether or not they met with local approval. In this respect, too, the years following the civil war completed and regularized the process of uncompromising centralization begun after the seizure of power. In theory, to be sure, a balance was preserved. The soviets, instead of expressing the will of people and guiding the government, became, in Stalin's phrase, mere transmission belts of the party's will from the center of power to the periphery. In return they were expected to transmit essential information on the state of mind among the masses. But the Communist leaders, while sensitive to public opinion in order to mold it effectively, would never defer to it. All other public bodies permitted to the toilers, such as the trade unions or the cooperatives, were likewise considered as transmission belts. In this manner, the executive at the center was closely linked with the masses in a relationship that stunted genuine participation among the population but integrated it into the state. The Soviet peoples, in short, were treated like children still to be educated into a superior Soviet socialist citizenry.

The initiative in this grandiose process of social engineering and its constant supervision of every aspect of Soviet life inevitably rested with the Communist party. The proper relationship between party and state, however, was not easily defined. If the party was to lead, it had to assume administrative responsibility. Yet if it became encumbered with administrative routine, it lost the freedom necessary for effective leadership and became merged with the state. The official rule, laid down in 1919 and subsequently carried into effect as far as possible, stated that the Communist party was to lead the activities of the soviets but not to replace them. But where under any given circumstances did the dividing line between leadership and administration run?

Inevitably the party took precedence over the state. From the start, the important issues of Soviet policy were always considered first in the inner councils of the party; for the party, as the self-appointed vanguard of the proletariat, was the core of the Soviet dictatorship. After the end of the civil war it, too, passed through a process of adjustment and consolidation. With their keen sense for the necessities of power, Lenin and his closest advisers tried to preserve and improve its original character as a militant revolutionary elite. Their success was perhaps the most remarkable feat of Communist rule in this period. The internal cohesion which had always remained imperfect, even while the party was small and persecuted, was still more difficult to accomplish as its membership more than trebled with success, rising from 200,000 to over 700,000 between 1917 and 1921. The Bolshevik triumph, one can imagine, attracted many undesirable and self-seeking elements. In order to guard the party against any weakening of its revolutionary fiber, the top leaders instituted in 1921 a thorough cleansing of the rank and file, a purge directed, as Lenin put it, against all "rascal bureaucrats, dishonest or wavering Communists and . . . Mensheviks who have repainted their façade, but who have remained Mensheviks at heart." In this manner, party membership was again reduced to half a million.

At the same time the party imposed the strictest control over the admission of new cadre. Former members of the privileged classes, of course, need not apply at all. Peasants were likewise distrusted. Workers stood the best chances, but even they had to prove their mettle before being accepted. Only the most energetic and dedicated men and women could live up to the party's stern code of conduct. The duties of a Communist (as laid down in 1919) stated that the individual had:

> (a) to observe strict Party discipline, to take an active part in the political life of the Party and of the country, and to carry out in practice the policy of the Party and the decisions of the Party organs;

> (b) to work untiringly to raise his ideological equipment, to master the principles of Marxism-Leninism and the important political and organizational decisions of the Party and to explain these to the non-Party masses;

> (c) as a member of the ruling Party in the Soviet state, to set an example in the observance of labor and state discipline, to master the techniques of his work and continually raise his production and work qualifications.

Thanks to the party leaders' drive, these duties were never allowed to become a dead letter. A party member must always be a paragon, both as an agitator and on the job.

The considerable enlargement of party membership called for a corresponding adjustment in the decision-making process. The Central Committee, which formerly had been the control center of the party, soon proved too large and cumbersome. Its function was taken over by a small committee, the Political Bureau (Politburo), officially sanctioned in March 1919. It was charged with making "decisions on questions not permitting any delay" and consisted of only five regular members. It sat almost uninterruptedly during the critical days of the civil war and even thereafter; to Communists, politics were as continuous as time itself. The party program of 1919 echoed Lenin's earlier directives:

> The party finds itself in a situation in which the strictest centralism
> and the severest discipline are absolute necessities. All decisions of
> the higher instance are absolutely binding on the lower ones. Every
> decision must first of all be carried out, and only later can it be
> appealed to the proper party organ. In this sense the party must pos-
> sess in the present epoch virtually a military discipline.

Thus the party, like the machinery of state, was welded into a tight
apparatus of sociopolitical control. And the ideal party functionary
became an *apparatchik*, an unthinking, docile cog in the political
machine.

The chief obstacle to party unity, however, did not lie in numbers or
the laxity of party discipline in the lower echelons but in the factionalism
that rent the party from top to bottom at the most crucial moments. We
have already seen how the treaty of Brest-Litovsk provoked bitter dissen-
sion. Later, in the civil war, the question of the proper position of the
trade unions in a workers' state aroused another internal tempest. Controversies were inevitable, given the dilemmas of fitting a utopian myth
into the harsh realities of Russian conditions. Most frequently the split
occurred between idealists who let themselves be carried too far ahead
by their lofty visions and realists who were guided by the necessities of
the moment. Whatever the merits of each point of view, the party could
not afford divisive debates between them, particularly when it was
engaged, under the New Economic Policy, in a political retreat. The
same party congress that endorsed NEP therefore adopted a resolution
designed to end all factional strife. It permitted the Central Committee to
expel, by a two-thirds vote, any factious members from the party. This
spelled the end of "party democracy," that is, of an open debate on current issues within the party ranks. The importance of this decision
was not lost on the more perceptive members. As Karl Radek, an
articulate Communist prominent in Comintern affairs, observed, "This
[rule] may be turned against us, yet it is less dangerous than any wavering as at present."

In the following year, the party leadership went even one step further.
It set the secret police, hitherto only used against the enemies of the
regime, to spy on the troublemakers within the party. It is well to remember, however, that these measures were accepted with noticeable unanimity. Like Radek, most Communists realized the seriousness of their
party's situation—which showed that the new rules represented an
inherent logic of principles to which all Communists were committed.
After 1922, in short, the party command had accomplished the seemingly impossible. For the first time in its history, it possessed the disci-

plinary powers needed to run the party like an army. It was paradoxical that Lenin, whose vision of a monolithic party was becoming reality at last, fell sick in the early summer of 1922 and was forced to withdraw from active leadership. The benefits of these changes accrued only to his successor.

When Lenin died in January 1924, the Communist party was in a stronger position than ever. The strategic retreat of the New Economic Policy, to be sure, still continued. Just then it seemed particularly precipitous, as the peasants were encouraged to produce more foodstuffs by such arch-capitalist slogans as "get rich." Yet on all the other political fronts a steady advance had taken place. In state and society, the party was the undisputed master.

In the essentials of modernization, the Communist party continued where Witte had left off at the beginning of the century. In its first six years in power, it had proved that it could master the condition of Russia better than the tsars (although in practice it never half lived up to the perfection of its theory).

III

In the first place, the Communists had introduced a superior form of leadership. Unlike the tsar, who jealously guarded his solitary prerogatives, the Communists possessed a many-headed center of leadership. In the Central Committee (and later the Politburo), Lenin, Trotsky, Stalin, and other leading Bolsheviks—each one a human dynamo in his own right—decided the chief questions of policy conjointly. The Communist party never quite abandoned the ideal of a collegial, cooperative brain center which could concentrate so much more ability and vitality than had been possible under a single autocrat.

The Communist leaders, furthermore, were people of proven leadership, and had earned their positions the hard way; all were passionately committed to the new style of mass politics. In time of crisis they could go into the provinces and rally an army, save a city from the Whites, or solve any other tough political problem that had arisen. They also had at their disposal a reasonably effective machinery of administration, linking them with the population at large through the party, the soviets, the trade unions, and other transmission belts. Never had the tsars been blessed with such a devoted corps of agents. The party members gave zest to implementing government policy at every point of contact with the population. The party, furthermore, was imbued with a keen ambition to rescue Russia from its weakness through a policy of rapid economic development. It was prepared to indoctrinate the entire population with its guiding myth as a necessary precondition of that advance and to battle, if need be, the ingrained popular resistance to drastic change.

The Revolution, moreover, had prepared, at a frightful price, the groundwork for industrialization by drastically simplifying the social structure of Russia. The regime recognized only the toiling masses. The toilers, furthermore, were singularly defenseless against the all-powerful state. Under the New Economic Policy, to be sure, the peasants by the nature of their work still enjoyed a considerable measure of independence; so did the workers under the protection of the trade unions, whose autonomy had been conceded as a result of embittered controversy within the party. Yet the universal obligation to work was an integral part of the Soviet system. And the conditions of employment for all men and women were determined, in the last analysis, by the state, which thus could draw on the physical energies of its subjects to an unprecedented degree. How much of the social energy released by the Revolution was channeled into the Soviet system and how much was wasted remained, of course, an open question.

Nothing in the past, at any rate, could compare with the Communists' propaganda effort to mobilize that social energy. So geared to propaganda was the entire party that in these early years it never created a separate propaganda agency. All its members and affiliated organs, all the media of mass communications, diffused the Marxist-Leninist creed among the population as the basis of a common Soviet socialist "consciousness." In its endeavor to form the proper attitudes, it took full advantage of Russia's new isolation from Western Europe. No longer was "Europe"—now derided as "capitalist" and "decadent"—allowed to influence Russian life at will by the uncontrolled influx of goods and ideas. The party barred, as best it could, all harmful foreign influences and thereby diminished or concealed the traditional subversion from without that had eaten away the authority of previous governments. Not only was true comparison with the conditions of the West made difficult (or downright impossible), but also Soviet citizens were actually made to feel superior in the fake comparison undertaken by the party. The following assertion, taken from the introduction to the Constitution of 1923, was typical of this effort:

> There in the camp of capitalism we find national animosities and inequalities, colonial slavery and chauvinism, national oppression and pogroms, imperialist brutality and wars.

> Here in the camp of socialism there is mutual confidence and peace, national freedom and equality, and the fraternal collaboration of nations peacefully dwelling side by side.

More commonly, Soviet propaganda sounded a much harsher and cruder note. There was hardly a distortion or outright lie to which the regime would not stoop in order to discredit "capitalism." Half a year after his return from New York (where he had lived from January to March 1917), Trotsky, for instance, spoke to the Petrograd Soviet of food riots in New York "such as we ourselves have never seen here." Such falsification, partly deliberate, partly—at least in the early years—the result of overenthusiasm and chiliastic expectation, became standard grist in the Soviet publicity mills.

By such desperate—and despicable—means Soviet Russia was now held up as the most advanced society in the world, marching toward socialism, while the "capitalist" world was falling further behind. Increasingly Soviet artists and intellectuals were ordered to create a full-blown autochthonous culture, superior to "capitalist" civilization, on the basis of a Russified Marxism. Thus the Bolsheviks tried to foster the necessary built-in arrogance of superiority which more than any other force cements the loyalty indispensable for modern government. In this new and artificially heightened isolation the Communists could more confidently pursue their social experiment of rapid modernization.

IV

Yet while the new setting provided many of the conditions necessary for making Western technology take root and advance in the Russian environment, it introduced some obstacles of its own. However appropriate as an ideology for the early stages of industrialization, and however superior to the spirit of the tsarist regime, Marxism-Leninism was no suitable creed for the later phases of modernization when Soviet Russia competed with the older industrial countries. It harmonized with modern industrialism as poorly as hammer and sickle with the assembly line (which Henry Ford had perfected even before the Communists came to power). Although easing the transition to industrialism, the Marxist-Leninist myth, operating with economic concepts suitable to the early nineteenth century, saddled Soviet Russia with antiquated tools of social and economic analysis. The handicap was to tell more strongly as time went by, and particularly when the myth was foisted on the natural sciences.

The greatest—and most tragic—flaw in the Communist dictatorship, however, was the suppression of freedom. At the root of all innovations of the Communist regime, as we have noticed, lay the same paradox: In the name of spontaneity, spontaneity was suppressed. The social energies released by a revolution of liberation and consistently invoked by party propaganda as the mainspring of Soviet life were always in danger of being stifled by the strict controls imposed by the party on every sphere of life. It was spontaneity that accounted for the amazing vitality of Western civilization. Yet the free flow of the same creative energy among the Russian people, having proved uncooperative or even anarchic, was increasingly hemmed in and frustrated in the name of the common good. And worse, as the party would never admit this fact, it was forced to cloak its controls in terms of a fake spontaneity. In the process, it tended to pervert by an infusion of crass political expediency every honest, idealist, straightforward human impulse into a rigid, mechanical act of duty. Deceit and falseness thus crept into every nook and cranny of the Soviet system and killed the natural grace and wholesomeness that spring from spontaneity. True creativity was driven back into the furthest recesses of the mind, leading a starved existence in an "inner emigration" deeper than Siberian exile. And yet, what else could the Communists have done so long as spontaneity continued to spell anarchy, and anarchy collective weakness? An honest admission of the deceit was impossible, for it would have toppled the elaborate façade of superiority and even scrapped the myth, spreading confusion, disillusionment, and all the ills of renewed subservience to foreign models.

V

The internal reorganization of Russia was only one part of the Communist design—increasingly the weightier one; the other part was world revolution. Domestic and foreign policy were of the same mold, shaped by the same myth. In foreign affairs the myth carried over into peacetime the brutal absolutes of the war. "Capitalism" (the West) and "socialism" (Soviet Russia), so the myth read, were locked in a mortal combat in which capitalism was ready to go to any lengths of ruthlessness and trickery, and socialism could take no chances. There could be no alliances, no peace, no good faith. At best, there might be temporary ties based on fleeting expediency and at worst the most grueling war, fought by any suitable weapons. In this manner, the myth ruled out Soviet participation in the League of Nations or any other activity of the international community as reestablished after the war. (Only in 1934, when circumstances made membership advisable, did the Soviet Union join the League—to be booted out again after its attack on Finland in 1939.) The party stalwarts, too, scrupulously avoided personal contact with the representatives of the Western bourgeoisie, employing men of lesser standing as go-betweens. In short, Soviet Russia stood apart in deep spiritual isolation.

Thus did the myth infuse the long-festering resentments of the Russian revolutionary intelligentsia into the conduct of international relations. Between the lines of their notes, memoranda, and protests to the Western powers one could perceive their sense of inferiority, their vulnerability, their fear of being taken advantage of by the craftier and more experienced Western diplomats. In their dealings with them, suspicion alternated with flashes of ambition. How they yearned to turn the tables for once and treat the "capitalists" as they themselves had felt treated for so long! It was indicative of their pride that they never measured themselves but against the most powerful countries, Great Britain at the start and later the United States. The acute uneasiness of their position also produced a heightened craving for independence and self-sufficiency, an air of secretiveness and xenophobia, a self-esteem all too easily offended. They were not, after all, equals in the grand competition of global politics, whatever the pretense of superiority in their myth.

The heightened sensitivity of the Soviet leaders gave Communist doctrine a better appreciation of the varieties of power at work in the global world than could be found in liberal political theory. The Communists knew in their bones that in the relation between states that are not equally matched every form of contact is apt to carry political connotations. It was not only diplomacy, economic pressure, the threat (or force) of arms that constituted effective power. The ubiquitous Western cultural influences that had pervaded Tsarist Russia and now again knocked at the gates of Soviet Russia contained the ability to change the direction of Russian development. The West, in short, possessed invisible resources of power that Russia signally lacked but which, in the global competition, were crucial. Why should not Russia exude as much of this form of power as the West and become a model in its own right, both for its own protection and for the assertion of its existence in the world, defensively and offensively?

There was another factor of power that the Communists felt more keenly than Western statesmen: the stability and cohesion of the body politic. Relatively well-integrated societies like those of England, France, and the United States, which could afford to grant their citizens full civic freedom without impairing their power in the world, possessed a natural advantage over those that, like Soviet Russia, could enforce the proper social discipline only by compulsion. Invulnerable to invidious comparison, they did not need to channel a significant part of their resources into the maintenance of internal security and control.

Seen from this angle, the inequality between the Soviet Union and the "capitalist" West amounted to much more than Russia's notorious deficiency in the traditional resources of power. In trying to understand Soviet foreign policy, one must keep in mind these invisible forms of power which have shaped so much of recent world history and yet have remained unperceived by those whom they benefited the most. Much of Communist foreign policy was designed to counteract or offset these invisible weapons.

In the first place, the Communists held up their Soviet system as a countermodel, which, in the realm of theory at least, was not a particularly difficult achievement. From the start, they had always incorporated the extreme visions of peace and social harmony into their myth as the highest human goals. There still remained the discrepancy between the myth and Soviet realities. But that could be covered up by secrecy or explained away by a variety of clever arguments, all embroidering the contention that the Soviet Union, regardless of its present appearance, had already attained a higher stage of dialectical development than the "capitalist" countries. Given the phenomenal will to believe in utopia so widespread in Europe during the interwar years, the Communists succeeded amazingly well in presenting their countermodel as a living reality.

In the second place, they were masters of what one might call "deliberate countersubversion," that is, of aggravating by the skills of agitation all the cleavages found in "capitalist" society. The freedom of the "capitalist" system indeed provided them with ample opportunity for such attack. They need but cull from the free press of the West or from its literature the evidence of human imperfection in order to furnish themselves with unlimited political ammunition against "capitalism." With such help, the local Communist parties, increasingly under direct orders from the Comintern headquarters in Moscow, cleverly exploited the frustrations of "people living together in one place, without friendship or common understanding, and without capacity, when the test came, to pull together for survival"—a condition, unfortunately, not infrequent in many parts of Europe. Rubbing salt into the social wounds of the "capitalist" countries, sabotaging the process of justice or of government, and tearing at the bonds of community where they were weakest was gain enough for the Soviet leaders even if these activities no longer held out a prospect of genuine revolution. By half-truths and lies they tried to discredit the capitalist system and thereby raise the appeal and the power of Soviet Russia. By contrast, the Western countries possessed no equal weapons capable of piercing the monolithic crust of the Soviet regime, for, as we have seen, the unchecked subversion by the Western model was now ended. Hampered by the fullness of publicity and the complexities of parliamentary procedure, the Western democracies found themselves at a disadvantage—much overrated, to be sure—in their day-by-day dealings with the Communist dictatorship. Faint-hearted Westerners even began to suspect that the competition between a viable free society and a dictatorship might be won by the latter. Thus did the Bolsheviks achieve one of their most significant victories.

Non-Communists, too, were drawn into the service of Soviet Russia. When the chances of revolution subsided, the Communist parties abroad were instructed to cooperate with all people of goodwill, in other socialist parties, in the trade unions, or in "front" organizations especially created for the purpose. Thus the Soviet leaders tapped, for their own carefully disguised aims, the reservoirs of social idealism contained in liberal democracy. In this part of their agitation, they displayed an astounding energy and psychological insight. They enlisted considerable support, collected large funds, and unearthed hidden resentments and weaknesses in individuals that could be turned to good use in building up an underground network for revolutionary action or espionage. They operated at a depth in society and in the individual mind to which liberal-democratic politicians never stooped. Not all such work, however, was successful. Some of the leading Communists of Western Europe left the cause in militant disillusionment (at some risk to their lives). But they were replaced without too much difficulty by new recruits seeking personal fulfillment in the Communist myth. For a small group of European (and American) intellectuals and workers, Soviet Russia indeed became the model of the good society.

While experimenting with these new instruments of foreign relations, the Communist regime did not fail to make the most of the traditional tools of diplomacy. Under the condition of "capitalist encirclement," Soviet Russia was one state among others. It had to play its part in the traditional manner, if only to call attention to its accomplishments, draw assistance from naïve profit-seeking capitalists, and exploit the rivalries within the "capitalist" camp. After 1921, Lenin eagerly worked for the diplomatic recognition of the Soviet Union by the "capitalist" governments and for the reestablishment of commercial relations with them, which, as we have seen, accorded well with the principles of the New Economic Policy. It was also natural that, on this level of its foreign relations, Soviet Russia should openly side with Germany, another outcast in the international community, against the Western Allies. This it did in the famous Rapallo treaty of 1922, which led even to a secret military liaison with the German army. Yet the following year, the Soviet leaders had no scruples about again inciting the German Communist party to overthrow its government, the ally of the Soviet Union. The duplicity of simultaneously conducting foreign relations on the two mutually exclusive levels of diplomacy and of revolution caused Soviet diplomacy some sharp setbacks. Yet these reverses never annulled the advantages derived from the combination.

Outside Europe, Soviet foreign policy in this period was primarily concerned with the possibilities of revolution in Asia. Here it dealt with simpler societies possessing neither powerful capitalists nor a well-organized proletariat. The revolutionary forces were nationalist rather than socialist in outlook. Turkey and Iran, for instance, were ruled after the war by nationalist movements with an anti-Western edge. They fitted, however loosely, into Lenin's grand design. Yet Soviet support for these movements did not rule out a bid for retaining, in the name of anti-imperialism, the privileges that Tsarist Russia had once enjoyed. In the eyes of the Asian masses Soviet Russia posed as liberator and a model for emancipation from colonialism. It even dangled before them the possibility of skipping the capitalist phase altogether and advancing directly into socialism—with Soviet help. In order to spread this gospel, the Communists spent considerable sums in drawing young Asians to Moscow for study and indoctrination.

The Soviet example found its most ardent response among young Chinese intellectuals at the University of Beijing, the promoters of the Fourth of May Movement, who were deeply aroused by the Japanese expansion into their country. In 1921 they founded the Chinese Communist party (at a girls school in Shanghai) and, amidst the usual disputes and with direct Soviet prompting, slowly made it into a minor political force in the seaboard cities. From Moscow's perspective, however, the Chinese nationalist movement, the Guomindang, was of still greater significance. In the mid-1920s its leaders, Sun Yat-sen and, after his death, Chiang Kai-shek, were advised by a famous Russian agent, Michael Borodin. Soon, however, it became apparent that Soviet encouragement of anti-Western national movements in Asia did not add up to world revolution. The nationalists resented being used as Soviet tools and before long made their peace with the West. Even where the local Communists survived such a debacle, as in China, they were reduced to impotence for many years. In the long run, too, they found it difficult (or impossible) to carry the Soviet prototype into their almost exclusively agrarian societies. Mao Zedong signified the Soviet model, adapting it to Chinese conditions.

Whether in Europe or Asia, the Soviet regime was, in short, far less successful than at home. Lenin's expectations of world revolution had not been fulfilled. Yet despite this failure—and despite the appalling lack of the hard assets of power—Soviet foreign policy had achieved a remarkable feat. It had succeeded in keeping an exceedingly weak Soviet Russia in the global forefront. The specter of world revolution was stalking the globe. As long as communism did not have to meet the test of war, its potency was roughly equal to what it was thought to be. Indeed, the greater the fear of communism the greater was its power. That was no mean triumph.

Yet the effectiveness of global communism, in the last analysis, depended on the strength of the revolutionary movement and on the acuteness of social and political disintegration in Europe and Asia. In a period of "capitalist consolidation," when the wounds of the war were healing and the basic cohesion of the Western democracies was reasserting itself; when vigorous anti-Communist dictatorships appeared where—according to their theory—the Communists should have prevailed; when, furthermore, the national liberation movements in Asia turned pro-Western and conservative, the potency of the novel instruments of foreign policy waned. Against the threat of war, Soviet Russia needed the traditional tools of war, a strong, well-armed home base and an industrial society to support it. This, in 1924, was still a distant goal. At the time of Lenin's death, Soviet Russia had not much advanced, in terms of military and industrial power, beyond the point where Tsarist Russia had ignominiously left off. But the day of the decisive attack on the trammels of weakness was rapidly approaching.

TEN

The Stalin Revolution, 1924–1930

I

Two traits stood out in the history of Russian communism as shaped by Lenin. The first was the boundless will to advance the country (not as an accidental base of world revolution but as Russia—Holy Russia) to a position of global preeminence, particularly in terms of industrial strength, the basis of modern civilization. Soviet socialism was the guarantee that this goal could be reached. The other trait was a fanatical reliance on organization, "our fighting method," as Lenin had called it in 1918. There were times, of course, when dire necessity, such as the ruin at the end of the civil war, set a limit to what organization could do. Yet the very retreat of NEP led to a reaffirmation of this principle, as the tightening of party and state apparatus indicated. He, then, who could give vigor to these Leninist traits and advance them with the same monstrous impatience that Lenin had shown almost to the end of his career would be his true heir. In these essentials, Stalin was indeed the perfect Leninist by more than his own, all too brazenly proclaimed judgment. His rise to power did not mark, therefore, a Thermidorian reaction, but rather a Fructidorian one, the high summer of fruition for the most dynamic and emotion-charged element of Bolshevism. But there also entered an element of cold-blooded soberness and retrogression, resulting from his coming to grips with his country's backwardness.

Joseph Vissarionovich Djugashvili, known in the revolutionary underground as the Man of Steel or Stalin, did not possess the residual sensitivity of the Russian intelligentsia, the ear for the music of humaneness that Lenin had retained, however unwillingly. He came from the toughest ethnic stock in the empire, the Georgian mountaineers, who had feuded for centuries with each other and their neighbors. He was further hardened by his rise from a lowly station and by his subsequent career as a professional revolutionary. While Lenin had lived abroad in relative ease, Stalin had worked and suffered for the cause inside Russia. The exiles' mastery of Marxist theory and their cultural refinement were out of his reach. But he possessed an advantage over them by representing the agitators and organizers without whom they were impotent. To all appearances, he was a humble man who put the party before personality and honored Lenin with a steadfast loyalty; he was always calm and dependable. At the time of the Bolshevik Revolution, he did not match Trotsky's brilliance but he was an indispensable member of the Bolshevik high command. As such, he received an important assignment in the new Soviet government as People's Commissar for Nationalities. Subsequently he also headed the Workers' and Peasants' Inspection, an agency that was to realize Lenin's dream of checking the abuses of bureaucracy by letting the toilers, even the housewives, take turns at public administration.

Yet his chief service always lay within the inner circles of the party. Here he proved without peers. He was appointed to the Politburo and the Orgburo (bureau of party organization) when they were first constituted; he continued to serve on them even after he was named secretary general. Thus he combined more vital functions in his own person than any other party official, including Lenin himself. He was a model chairman, tending to keep himself in the background and getting things done, with a monumental capacity for work. Although Stalin quarreled bitterly with Trotsky during the civil war, his appointment to so many posts caused no controversy within the party; no one else seemed so well suited to perform the unwanted drudgery of party administration. It was he, then, who made the party into the model monolith by supervising the entire membership, appointing reliable men to key positions in the lower echelons, and keeping them alert and docile. And it was he who laid down the basic rules of power adjustment within this ever-growing leviathan which Kremlinologists have ever since watched as the key to Soviet policies.

What he lacked were the very qualities in which the former exiles excelled. He was not much of a writer or speaker. His rhetoric was stodgy, repetitious, interspersed with simple questions to which, catechism-like, he gave simple answers, only occasionally lighted up by trivial jokes or a touch of folklore. Yet his style, while devoid of flare, was not ineffectual; like all the trappings of the Stalin regime as they evolved over the years, it catered to an audience of naïve, slow-witted, overworked, and bewildered people who retained a fairy-tale wonder for the demigods who shaped their destinies.

His style as an administrator was also several degrees too rough, even for Lenin. But it was not Lenin who had to cope with the stubborn realities of the new Soviet Empire. A monolithic party composed of former revolutionaries who, like most Russians, lacked the capacity of spontaneous mutual accommodation, was indeed no "girls dormitory"; it required drastic methods of compulsion. And what was true of the party was even more true of the country as a whole. All the devils of disunity and division in the empire that had plagued the tsars also beset the Soviet regime. Stalin had no respect for mass participation in public administration. What counted in his eyes was masterminding the minute and unending details of control, observing the drift of power at the articulation points of organization, and being willing to go to any lengths of ruthlessness for the sake of success. Against the Whites or the Georgian Mensheviks (as, later, against his opponents within the party and potential enemies throughout the body politic), Stalin showed the extremes to which he might go. His harshness in imposing Bolshevik rule on his native Georgia shocked even Lenin, who during the last months of his life became rather critical of the secretary general's crudities. Yet were ruthlessness and terror not part of the Leninist tradition, the price that the Russian revolutionaries had always been willing to pay for their ideals?

It was proof of Stalin's ability as an administrator that his hold over the party was discovered only when it could no longer be effectively challenged. In order to secure the succession, he merely needed to prove that he possessed the required support among the membership (which he largely controlled) and then invoke party discipline against all dissenters. In this contest he drew on all the advantages of his cold-blooded endurance and superior craftiness in a game where everybody played for the highest stakes. Politics for Stalin was a round-the-clock, year-in, year-out watch on the quarterdeck. Those who could not stand the strain counted themselves out.

There is no need here to relate the sordid tale of deceit, lies, defamation, threats, punishment, recantation, surrender, self-doubt, self-torture, and police torture that sum up the struggle for Lenin's succession. But who among Stalin's rivals possessed the qualities necessary for carrying the Leninist heritage to its logical conclusion in a Soviet Russia? Trotsky, who possessed the strongest claim, was no statesman capable of sustaining the continuous burden of supreme responsibility. He did not even seem to comprehend the fact that effective leadership called for meticulous, large-scale, and unrelenting organization. Besides, he showed an amazing lack of nerve at the time of Lenin's death. Instead of brushing aside Stalin's objections and rushing at once to Moscow, he idled away his time at a southern spa where he had gone in order to cure an "indisposition." The other contenders counted even less. Zinoviev was a coward, Bukharin too soft. The rest did not really possess the proper qualifications for leadership. And since there was no settled machinery of succession, every one of these men, had *he* risen to the top, would have had to eliminate his rivals by some form of wolfishness. A militant Communist party required a single head. No collegium could maintain in the long run the dynamic drive of the Communist myth. Thus Stalin emerged as the first complete heir of the imperial autocrat. Under the prevailing conditions, Russian society did not manage to produce a better dictator. The blame, if blame there must be, falls on the country and on circumstances rather than on one man.

Stalin completed the fatal progress toward dictatorship inherent in Lenin's concept of the Bolshevik party. Before the Revolution, the organization of the party had already taken the place of the party itself. Afterward the Central Committee—and later the Politburo—took the place of the organization, and finally, under Stalin, the dictator took the place of the Central Committee and even the Politburo. At the same time, Stalin became the charismatic "leader" and the all-wise "father" of the Soviet peoples, providing in these comforting symbols a better emotional resting place for his subjects' worries than the tsars had ever furnished.

II

After Lenin's death, another strong man was needed. However completely the party now controlled the country, its future course was shrouded in doubts. Lenin had faded from leadership without indicating a successor or even leaving a clear-cut legacy. On the one hand, his followers remembered the Bolshevik militancy of his prime; on the other, they were bound by the hesitation and caution of his last years. His directives for NEP were unprecedently tame. They emphasized the need to appease the peasants and to make Soviet progress dependent on their willingness to change. He had also left open the basic question of whether Soviet Russia could, within the foreseeable future, move into full socialism. It had been generally assumed that a predominantly agrarian society like Russia's could be propelled into socialism only with the help of a socialist West (or a least a socialist Germany). Now that revolution in Europe was ruled out, was the Soviet regime merely to mark time?

Against these undercurrents of doubt and amidst the din of the struggle for the succession, Stalin sponsored, in an uncertain and fumbling way, a note of optimism which resumed the earlier buoyancy of Bolshevism. At the fourteenth party congress in December 1925, a historic resolution was passed which again set the sights far ahead. The party pledged itself to carry on economic construction with the intention of

> transforming the USSR from a country importing machines and equipment into one producing machines and equipment, so that the USSR under the conditions of capitalist encirclement cannot be made into an economic adjunct of world capitalism, but will represent an independent economic unit built in the socialist manner and capable . . . of serving as a powerful means of revolutionizing the workers of all countries and the suppressed peoples of the colonies and semi-colonies.

Subsequently the resolution states the theoretical premise for the projected advance, saying that "Russia possesses all that is necessary for the construction of a socialist society." This was Stalin's famous doctrine of "Socialism in One Country," which taught that Soviet Russia could confidently go ahead by itself on the road to socialism.

In the following year (1926), another party gathering pointed even more emphatically toward industrialization as the fulfillment of Soviet ambition:

> The biggest historical task set before the dictatorship of the proletariat, the creation of socialist society, demands the concentration of all forces of the party, the government, and the working class on the problems of economic policy.

The goals of that policy were now set sky high. Nothing less than "overtaking and surpassing the level of industrial production in the leading capitalist countries in a relatively short span of time" would do.

Yet how were these ambitions to be put into practice? Party economists were sharply divided over the proper course of Soviet economic development. One group, led by N. Bukharin, proceeded from Lenin's directives for NEP. It wanted to give the peasants, particularly the kulaks, still more freedom. It resumed, as it were, Stolypin's policy. Only when a strong and prosperous rural base had been established, so ran the argument, could—and should—industry grow. Yet this approach, echoing the criticism levied against the Witte system, endangered the monolithic nature of the Soviet dictatorship. A house divided between a free peasantry and a regimented urban working class could not long survive; granting freedom to the peasants would push the regime back toward liberal democracy. And what, meanwhile, would become of Soviet Russia's security in a hostile, "capitalist" world?

The other group, led by Trotsky and E. Preobrazhensky, started like Witte from the need for rapid industrial growth. If agriculture was to produce more, it had to be supplied with more and better industrial goods. Yet this was bound to become more difficult as the existing industrial equipment, inherited from tsarist days, began to wear out. Under these conditions, even maintaining the current level of industrial production (which had steadily risen after 1921 without, however, regaining prewar levels) would be impossible, let alone advancing to socialist plenty. The escape from this difficulty, so the group argued, lay in deliberate industrial expansion. Unfortunately, this policy cost the country dearly. In the absence of foreign capital, the huge capital outlays could be obtained only by further lowering the standard of living, by "primitive socialist accumulation," as Preobrazhensky indiscreetly put it. That, from a political point of view, seemed suicidal. Had not the Soviet regime promised a higher income to the toilers of Russia? This school of thought thus ran into the same predicament that had forced Witte's dismissal from the Ministry of Finance. The Russian people would not tolerate any further sacrifices. In short, whichever direction economic analysis took, it ended in a cul-de-sac.

By 1928, when Stalin's power over the party was at last firmly entrenched, the problem of Soviet economic development could no longer be disregarded. While his own authority was limited and the experts had disagreed, he had straddled the fence, urging rapid industrialization yet also inclining toward Bukharin's side, not wishing to antagonize the peasantry. By 1928, however, Bukharin's policy had proved a fiasco. Were the peasants to slow down the economic advance to which the party had repeatedly pledged itself ever since 1925, and was the entire regime to bog down in the peasant sloth? Furthermore, the loss of political momentum that accompanied the struggle over the succession was already spreading corruption in party circles.

III

At this point, during as grave a crisis as faced Soviet Russia after the civil war, Stalin returned to the full fury of Leninism. Not possessing Lenin's ability to dramatize the new phase of Soviet policy with subtle theoretical premises, he changed course clumsily and crudely, relying more on will and brute force than on technical finesse. Yet the change contained all the ingredients of a major turning point. The first thing Stalin did was to paint the international scene, just then brightened by the "spirit of Locarno" and the Kellogg-Briand pact, in dark and ominous colors—with some justification. He remembered the collapse of Russian power at the end of World War I; he dreaded a repetition; his country was as ill-equipped for survival as in 1914.

His pessimism was justified. After the outbreak of the Great Depression in the next year, the international scene changed for the worse. In the wake of the depression, the flimsy precautions of collective security crumbled and most of the new democratic regimes established after the war perished, if they had not already done so. The trend toward dictatorship was running strong in the 1920s, as events in Italy, Spain, Portugal, Poland, and Lithuania had shown; now it accelerated. The entire Western tradition of promoting public welfare by private initiative seemed wrecked, as unemployment and poverty suddenly descended on millions of unsuspecting peoples.

Out of these unprecedented calamities emerged the aggressive forces responsible for World War II. In 1931 they led to Japan's invasion of Manchuria; in 1933 they brought to power a German totalitarian movement not without parallels to Soviet communism, despite its diametrically opposed ideology. Hitler's National Socialism, too, was a product of the imperialist age. It thought in terms of global power—not of a class, to be sure, but of nationality and its supposed essence, race—and it throbbed with a national pride made fanatical by the recent defeat of Germany. It, too, was geared to the age of psychopolitics, with techniques of appeal and agitation often copied from Marxist experience. At the same time it aroused more spontaneous mass support than communism enjoyed in Russia.

It might be argued that the Great Depression offered Stalin unrivaled opportunities for revolutionary agitation abroad. The final crisis of "capitalism" seemed imminent; communism gained new disciples everywhere. Yet weighing the solid advantages of a strong Soviet base against the uncertainties of world revolution, Stalin had long decided that the strength of Soviet Russia must have precedence. Like Witte he dreaded the weakness of Russia, and like him he realized that concentration on industrial development at home ruled out costly foreign adventures. Indeed, the immediate effect of Stalin's first Five Year Plan was a distinct weakening of Soviet strength. Thus, despite the new fierceness of Soviet revolutionary propaganda—foreign Communists were ordered to turn against the moderate socialists (now branded as "social fascists"), which signally aided Hitler's rise to power—Soviet foreign policy on all levels bore an essentially defensive character. (There is even evidence to suggest that Stalin welcomed Hitler's victory as a guarantee of sharpened division within the capitalist camp.) Lenin's vision of a revolutionary counterpower to the "imperialist" West was not forgotten, but it was giving way to the Stalinist conviction that world revolution stood a better chance if it possessed an impregnable base in the Soviet Union. Thus Soviet Russia's self-interest moved steadily into the foreground as the drive for industrialization got into high gear and the age-old ambitions of Russian pride were mobilized to support it.

In 1928, Stalin pledged the Communist party "to be responsible for the escape from backwardness." In the following year, digging even deeper into the recesses of Russian ambition, he boasted:

> We are going full steam ahead toward socialism through industrialization, leaving our century-old "racial" background behind. We are becoming a land of metals, a land of automobiles, a land of tractors, and when we set the USSR on an automobile and the *muzhik* on a tractor, let the noble capitalists, so proud of their "civilization," attempt to catch up. We shall see then which countries can be labeled as backward and which as advanced.

Finally, in 1931, when the Stalinist revolution was at its height, he summed up the humiliations of centuries in a famous speech in which Leninist socialism was revealed as an updated version of Russian nationalism—both Lenin and Stalin were Russian patriots in Marxist disguise:

> One feature of the history of old Russia was the continual beatings she suffered for falling behind, for her backwardness. She was beaten by the Mongol Khans. She was beaten by the Turkish beys. She was beaten by the Swedish feudal lords. She was beaten by the Polish and Lithuanian gentry. She was beaten by the French and British capitalists. She was beaten by the Japanese barons. All beat her—for backwardness, for military backwardness, for cultural backwardness, for political backwardness, for industrial backwardness, for agricultural backwardness. She was beaten because to beat her was profitable and went unpunished. . . . In the past we had no fatherland and could have none, Now, however, that we have overthrown capitalism and the workers wield power in our country, we have a fatherland and shall defend its independence. Do you want our Socialist fatherland to be beaten and to lose its independence? If you do not want that, then you must abolish its backwardness and develop a really Bolshevik pace in

the establishment of its Socialist economy. . . . We are fifty or a hundred years behind the advanced countries. We must make good this lag in ten years. Either we accomplish this or we will be crushed.

The dire choice between advance or extinction, familiar in imperialist rhetoric from Disraeli to Hitler, was, in the light of Russia's bare survival in World War I, of crucial significance to the Soviet leaders. It hounded the Soviet citizens as they tried to fulfill their production quotas under the preposterous, inhuman experiment of rapid industrialization known as the first Five Year Plan.

IV

That plan set forth the Marxist terms of rational economic control which the party had already proclaimed as its ideal in 1919, the goals of industrial production to be reached within a five-year period (starting in 1928). As the official text stated:

It is a plan for the radical reconstruction of the productive foundations of our country. . . . Our country makes the unprecedented experiment of tremendous capital construction carried out at the expense of current consumption, at the price of a harsh regime of economy and by sacrificing the satisfactions of today's needs in the name of great historical aims.

The plan was no beggar's gamble to patch his economic garment from the insufficient scraps of cloth available, but a dictator's command that a gala uniform be provided at any cost and on the double. The goals were exceedingly specific. From 1928 to 1933, gross industrial output was to increase 235.9 percent, that of the heavy industries alone by 279.2 percent. Production costs were decreed to fall by 35 percent, prices by 24 percent, and labor productivity to rise by 110 percent, thus allowing internal savings to finance part of the expansion.

The decimal-point precision of the plan was, to be sure, mere show. Its directives were shot through with a thousand inconsistencies, bottlenecks, and other flaws. Underneath the impressive façade it was never more than a loosely meshed set of goals that bore scant relation to economic reality. One grave miscalculation, for instance, was made in regard to foreign trade, through which vital industrial equipment was to be procured. Despite the Communist claim to understand the laws of history, the Great Depression had not been foreseen. As it ran its course, it knocked out the carefully planned export-import schedules and upset everything geared to them. Before the five years were out, the plan had to be terminated, to be followed by further and somewhat more refined Five Year Plans. Yet whatever the appalling waste and human sacrifice that accompanied the first Five Year Plan, a determined start toward the distant goals had been made.

The industrial plan, however, was only half of the economic offensive. The other half was the compulsory collectivization of agriculture. If the industrial drive was to succeed, agricultural production could not be left to the discretion of recalcitrant peasants. They too had to be subjugated to state control. This, of course, had been the Communists' ambition from the start. In 1917, they had let the land pass into peasant hands only because the Revolution needed peasant support. Yet in their minds they had always subscribed to the Marxist conviction that effective agriculture was possible only in large, mechanized units resembling factories. For that reason, the Communists had tried to save the large estates and the model farms of Tsarist Russia from the peasants' land hunger and transform them into state farms. They had also experimented with various forms of collective farming, without arousing much interest in the countryside. Under the NEP, these experiments subsided as peasant agriculture reverted to the prewar pattern of small-scale farming. Unfortunately, because of the absence of large estates producing for the market, less grain was delivered to the urban consumers than before the war, a fact that neatly confirmed the Marxist analysis. Considering the peasants' limited resources and their innate conservatism (their "petty-bourgeois natures," as the Communists put it), there could be little hope of any basic improvement. Obviously, peasants left to their own devices were bound to keep Russian agriculture backward, a drag on economic progress.

Economic and political necessity thus drove Stalin to seek a better method of controlling Soviet agriculture. The instrument chosen for this purpose was the collective farm, a compromise between private farming and the farm-factory. It consolidated many small household plots into large units suitable for mechanized equipment, combined the herds and draft animals, and pooled the equipment needed to operate the new holding. Machinery, however, was handled separately by the Machine Tractor Stations, which served a number of collective farms. The peasant, now raised to the dignity of a "collective farmer," merely retained his hut, a small plot of land to go with it, and a few animals for his private needs.

In theory the collective farm was run democratically, through an elected leadership. In reality the chairman was appointed by the local party secretary, and the guiding decisions on production were determined by the national plan. The collective farmers could do as they pleased on their private plots—from them they have provisioned much of the urban population to this day—but the collective had to deliver to the state its planned products according to schedule, regardless of the vagaries of the harvest. While the collective farm was not quite as effectively controlled as a factory, a long stride toward that goal had been made.

The transition from private to collective farming was pushed forward with utter recklessness in 1929 and early 1930. For the countryside, it meant a far more brutal upheaval than any previous agrarian measure since the imposition of serfdom. Word went out that the kulaks, that is, the most successful peasants under the NEP and all other recalcitrant peasants who sided with them, were to be "liquidated as a class." What household did not feel resentful at having to surrender its land, livestock, and costly implements! The more it possessed, the more it fought against collectivization. Thus millions of families who resisted it were uprooted and separated: The men were sent to forced labor in the new industrial centers and the wastelands; the women and children were left behind to shift for themselves. Thousands of peasants were killed on the spot in pitched battles that recalled the atrocities of the civil war. Famine broke out in the wake of collectivization: In the Ukraine millions died of starvation—a form of punishment for the Ukrainians' attempt to break away from Russia after World War I. The loss of livestock and draft animals was so severe as to offset for decades the gains of control achieved by collectivization.

V

The years of the first Five Year Plan and of collectivization were indeed bleak ones, a new Iron Age visiting untold hardship and sacrifice on a population that had barely recovered from the civil war. Yet the appalling suffering that had been dreaded by both Bukharinites and Trotskyites in the controversy over Soviet economic development produced no insurrection, no revolution. How, one cannot help wondering, did Stalin produce such a political miracle? The answer points to the heart of the Stalin revolution. While the economic transformation was underway, Stalin developed to their fullest potential the controls that the Bolshevik Revolution had prepared. For the first time, the political and social framework was ready to permit the concentration on economic development which the party for so long had had to postpone. And it was ready also to absorb the shock of the sudden, enforced transition into an industrial society without visible damage to the regime.

Political leadership, as we have seen, was now centralized as never before. It was agreed, furthermore, on the need for hurried industrialization. The will of the party also permeated the machinery of the state, and the state controlled the energies of its subjects to an unprecedented degree. Private initiative, for all practical purposes, was eliminated. The party, through the state, took charge of all public affairs. The state was the only employer; all independent sources of income were wiped out. Even the peasants (except for their garden plots) were now subject to state supervision. There could arise no tensions between different social groups, no class struggle in the traditional sense. The relations between the various categories of state employees were regulated according to state necessity, not by their independent social bargaining power.

The Stalinist revolution also transformed the role of the trade unions, which had hitherto still enjoyed a measure of autonomy as spokesmen for the industrial workers. They were now made into agencies of production, transmission belts of the economic plan, on the theory that the workers in a workers' state needed no protection against themselves. Even social security and housing, administered by the trade unions, were used to enforce labor discipline and to increase production. The change, however, was not without some gains to the workers. The trade unions took charge of all the problems facing a new labor force all too suddenly shifted from fields to factory. The newcomers no longer had to cope with the harassment of adjustment unaided, as under the tsars.

Another radical change was the abandonment of the original Bolshevik egalitarianism. Wages were now graded according to a man's output and his contribution to the plan's success: "from each according to his ability, to each according to his deserts," as the new slogan, derived from Marx himself, proclaimed. Thus originated a slight differentiation in income levels that never approached the divergence between rich and poor in the "capitalist" countries. But in the awards of nonmonetary incentives, medals, titles, and other insignia of honor, it surpassed them, reverting again to the carefully graded hierarchy of tsarist officialdom. These incentives were part of "socialist competition," a device designed to offset the lethargy resulting from the replacement of private initiative by state directives.

Now that the individual's energies were enlisted in state activity as never before, the individual's conduct also came under close state scrutiny. Stalin carried to an extreme Lenin's earlier call for proletarian self-control for the sake of greater productivity. Social discipline, still lax after the Revolution, was greatly tightened. Mme. Kollontai's libertinism was outlawed, the legal bonds of marriage were again strengthened, divorce made difficult, abortion prohibited. Sex was banished from sight and mind to a degree incomprehensible in the West. Parents' authority over their children was likewise reinstated, as was the teachers' power over their pupils. Students were now drilled in their subjects as in the old days. And the old days of Russia, denigrated as "capitalist" or "feudal" in the first exuberance of the Revolution, were reincorporated into the Soviet tradition as part of a great national heritage. The official new Soviet patriotism indeed drew heavily on Russian national pride, at times boosting it by claiming many great inventions of modern technology as Russian discoveries. Stalin even arranged a truce with the church. While fitfully promoting antireligious propaganda, the party now permitted at least a bare minimum of religious worship, provided that it did not compete with the party's claim over its subjects' "consciousness."

The Stalinist revolution indeed paid the closest possible attention to the "consciousness" of the Soviet peoples. It wanted to form "the whole man," knowing that this could be done only through the control of his mind. Everything shaping that vital center was scrupulously controlled—art, literature, music, journalism, aesthetics, philosophy, historical writing, even scientific research. The poets were bidden by Stalin to become "engineers of the soul." In all these fields, the party closely prescribed the canons of proletarian rectitude. In the arts, the guiding formula was "socialist realism," a style presumably set by Maxim Gorky, yet in its righteous and roseate simplicity more expressive of petty-bourgeois Philistinism. In all these efforts, the chief responsibility for developing the proper consciousness was laid on the individual, who could be punished if he or she continued to harbor "capitalist" or "anti-Soviet" views. This was no laughable pretension. The party was astonishingly resourceful in devising a great variety of pressures on individuals to mend their consciousness.

The avowed purpose of these efforts was the creation of a "new Soviet man," the type of citizen required for successful industrialization. Scrutiny of the individual's attributes reveals a blend of Bolshevik militancy and Victorian respectability, a disciplined, clean-living, neat, cooperative, patriotic citizen, thinking as much of the public good as of personal advancement, and an intransigent Leninist. Unfortunately, this paragon was never a creature of flesh and blood but an abstraction foisted on an unresponsive people and therefore basically hollow. Men and women had to strive exceedingly hard—too hard for happiness—to live up to that ideal. This strained fanatical Stalinist Russia was decked out deceitfully as the highway to socialist utopia and the embodiment of the will of the toilers, making a mockery of what most socialists had expected of the Communist ideal—all in a desperate effort to escape from the vulnerabilities of backwardness.

Inevitably, the disillusionment was turned against Stalin who, as a man of action, was not given to elaborate theoretical justifications which might have absolved him. Yet was the disillusionment not also the fault of those who, as in the old days, wanted the benefits of a modern industrial society without being willing to pay the inevitable price under their country's disheartening adversities? The social discipline of the advanced countries, instilled over centuries of often none-too-gentle coaxing, could not be matched by the peoples of Eurasia, not even under the most drastic compulsions.

By the early 1930s the process of revolution begun around the turn of the century had come to an end; a reasonably stable form of government had emerged. By the letter as well as the spirit of their political system (though not by the bonds of spontaneity) the government and the people were now in alignment, the people integrated into the state and both government and people set to work with breathtaking single-mindedness on the tasks of economic modernization. On this harsh Stalinist foundation Soviet Russia proceeded, with some adjustments, for the next half-century.

Stalinism: From the 1930s to 1985

I

It is difficult to remain impartial when looking back from the collapse of the Soviet Union to the brutal days of Stalin. But in order to assess Gorbachev's failure and explore the prospects for his country's future, we need to take an objective look at Stalinism, the starting point for Gorbachev's reforms and their unexpected consequences.

It may be best to consider Stalinism as a crude political experiment of vast dimensions, conducted at a time of acute danger, for assuring the Russian Empire's political survival. Designed in Marxist-Leninist ignorance of cultural dynamics and guided by a ruthless dictator with the help of unprepared and bewildered human tools, the experiment had a breathtakingly grandiose goal. It aimed at changing as rapidly as possible the recalcitrant masses of the largest country in the world into citizens capable of competing with the peoples of the West who set the pace of power politics and progress worldwide. It was an unprecedentedly rash venture, facing frightful obstacles.

In the first place, Stalin's alarmist grasp of his country's precarious position in the world lay beyond his subjects' comprehension. The run of the people—and even most intellectuals—were incapable of rising above their narrow horizons (often so rich in human depth); they would never understand that the drastic recasting of their customary ways was in their own interest. Yet, viewed objectively, they had no choice. If they wanted to overcome their country's vulnerability in the precarious postwar years, improve their standards of living, let alone feel free, they first had to achieve the necessary preconditions, above all the external security and pervasive civic cooperation that undergird a modern country's strength. These factors were taken for granted in the West but did not exist in Russian historical experience.

Second, the experiment, conceived by a small elite, demanded a working relationship with the masses. In that sense it was "democratic," despite the fact that it had to be highly authoritarian—"democracy" was part of the Soviet vision: Eventually the proletariat would assume control as the authoritarian state withered away. But Marxist scientific materialism offered no advice on how to manage a peaceful transformation of vast human multitudes set in ways utterly different from Western civic tradition into modern citizens. The goal of that transformation was equality with the West; the West provided the inescapable model. But how could it be matched on a mass basis—democratically—with the resources, human and material, available in Stalin's Eurasia? The complexity of large-scale cultural transformation, a problem also in Gorbachev's times as at present, is hardly recognized by social scientists, let alone by the popular mind.

The essence of the Western model lies in the ceaseless industrial advance promoted by individual self-interest subconsciously socialized into collective cooperation in all aspects of life—never perfectly, but reasonably effective for all purposes of statecraft. Under Stalinism that invisible totality of spontaneous social interaction, the product of centuries of Western historical evolution, was to be reproduced artificially in the shortest possible time by the Communist party. The effort was hailed as the triumph of rational control over human destiny. The result was Soviet totalitarianism.

In the absence of effective private enterprise it created a centrally planned economy promoting rapid industrialization combined with collectivized agriculture. In addition it designed social, political, intellectual, and emotional controls guiding all aspects of life from the cradle to the grave, trying to create a new sense of civic efficiency, a new consciousness holding state and society together with an almost Puritan discipline. For a suitable ideological framework Soviet intellectuals devised an integrated worldview based on official Marxism-Leninism. However repulsive to Western sensibilities, Stalinist totalitarianism represented an impressive, if highly experimental and imperfect, collective achievement accomplished by fallible human beings trapped in the brutishness of a backward society.

Transforming people's motivation against the grain of their cultural conditioning certainly was a most difficult task. Rational argument obviously was insufficient among people helplessly suspended between the high-pitched party line and down-to-earth everyday reality. Ceaseless propaganda, deception, threats, secret surveillance, and punishment for noncooperation had to train obedience. Like a tyrannical father breaking the will of a recalcitrant child, Stalin's terror beat the masses into submission. All traditional rules of moral decency were suspended in the grand experiment designed to create the preconditions for civilized life.

Special attention had to be paid to the ever present danger of subversive comparison with Western (or "capitalist") society, a danger made more acute by physical hardship and moral qualms about Stalin's terror. Soviet totalitarianism therefore isolated the people from foreign contact, systematically cultivating an elemental fear of foreigners. Only in deep seclusion could the claim of Soviet superiority provide the pride needed to spur the supreme effort at cultural transformation. Woe to the Stalinist system if that unnatural isolation broke down! At the top of the government, however, Stalin paid close attention to world affairs, which strengthened his fear-ridden determination to build up Soviet power as fast as possible. And his spies, expertly trained since the days of the revolutionary underground, provided him with valuable secret information from abroad—thereby antagonizing the Western public already alarmed by the news of his terror and Lenin's earlier call for world revolution.

The human price of the Stalinist experiment as it unfolded in the 1930s was indeed appalling. Millions of people were killed in the collectivization drive and in the Gulag prison camps, valuable human resources destroyed and material assets wasted. In addition, the moral damage, though less visible at the time, was extensive. People were torn between the private morality as traditionally practiced in their village communities and the expediency-based morality of a superior socialist society as defined by the party. Which way were they going to turn? The Communist vision offered many attractions to ambitious young peasants, opportunities for responsible work in a society that proudly claimed to stand as a model for the world. Yet the flagrant disregard of human dignity and life—or of political reality—undercut the party's efforts to create a cohesive political community. Marxist materialism offered little satisfaction to the Russian soul; the Stalinist system lacked an enduring spiritual base. And enforced conformity to an untried ideologically imposed way of life tended to kill spontaneous creativity.

Yet what else would one expect in a precipitous experiment guided in unparalleled raw times by the shallow insights of Marxism-Leninism and conducted with the help of such unqualified human beings? The experiment was engineered by Stalin, a domineering but deeply insecure product of the revolutionary underground during the late tsarist regime further calloused by revolution and civil war. And as for Stalin's henchmen, it is well to remember Alexander Solzhenitsyn's testimony: The "wolftribe" of torturers was composed of ordinary people charged with carrying out the experiment's sordid details. The wolfish people were trained in inhumanity by their poverty, the war, the revolution, and the civil war. Russian novelists' accounts of those times bear witness to their beastly inhumanity.

Under these conditions (perhaps insufficiently appreciated by the present generation of Russian intellectuals) the Stalinist experiment proceeded. It was marred by egregious mistakes in domestic and foreign policy inevitable in an unprecedented gamble and conducted by an extraordinary yet still fallible leader, who was assisted by multitudes of other frail human beings. Yet, despite huge human calamities and endless material waste, it also mobilized some deep-seated traditions in rallying selfless devotion and heroic sacrifice on the battlefronts of industrial construction. Such dedication resulted in some overall improvement in living conditions by the late 1930s.

By 1945 the experiment had achieved its supreme goal: The Soviet Union survived Hitler's invasion in 1941, a far bigger threat than the German advance in World War I. At the end of World War II Red Army tanks were superior to their German counterparts. Whatever the senseless atrocities of Stalin's rule in the 1930s, consider the barbaric inhumanities that Hitler planned to inflict on "the Russian desert." On October 17, 1941, he, an even more monstrous product of World War I, outlined his thoughts about the future of Russia under German rule: "We'll let [the Russian towns] fall to pieces . . . no remorse on that subject. . . . We are absolutely without obligation as far as these people are concerned. . . . There is only one duty: to Germanize this country . . . and to look upon the natives as Redskins." Better a homegrown tyrant ignorantly and brutishly dedicated to save his country from extinction than a foreign tyrant cold-bloodedly determined to enslave the natives! Better to survive at present whatever the price for later generations, than to provide for a potentially better but irretrievably lost future!

The Great Fatherland War, which for a time put Russian patriotism ahead of Marxism-Leninism, topped the heroic exertions, sacrifices, and horrors of the 1930s with four years of brutal fighting. It cost about 30 million lives and ruined industry and agriculture in the western parts of the country. What other peoples had suffered so much in so short a time? Yet victory in that ruthless carnage did not soften Stalin's craving for protection against both subversion by Western superiority and foreign conquest. Extending Soviet territorial control to the heart of Germany,

Stalin turned Eastern Europe into a Soviet buffer zone against future aggression from the West. While the war-torn parts of the country were rebuilt with impressive speed, his scientists matched the American production of atomic bombs, and his engineers laid the groundwork for the first space flight. The stage was set for the cold war between the Soviet Union and the United States allied with the countries of Western Europe.

At a time when Stalin is furiously condemned it may be well to remember his accomplishments, which enhanced his country's security and eased the tasks of his successors. He had launched the crippled victim of World War I on the road to superpower status and worldwide significance. In the postwar era of decolonization the Soviet Union became a model for ambitious state-builders in Asia and Africa who, like him, wanted to liberate their peoples from humiliation by the imperialists. It was not surprising that in the tightly closed world of Soviet life Stalin became, at least for a time, a source of collective pride, a sacred icon giving a positive meaning to heart-rending human suffering. Only people who have lived through those years of agony have a right to moral judgment over the conduct of their fellow sufferers. In 1953, at his funeral in Moscow, mourners were crushed to death in the tear-stained crowd.

Viewed in perspective, Stalin stands out as a landmark in the most monstrous years of the twentieth century. Next to Mao Zedong no other man in that age has wielded such unrestrained control over so many subjects during such protracted times of over-rapid change at home and abroad. Inevitably the pervasive insecurity reaching into his innermost self heightened his craving for self-assertion and personal power to the extremes of vindictive ruthlessness. Yet for a mortal engaged in the high wire act of self-made caesars, he carried his responsibilities with impressive command over detail. His omnipotence, to be sure, remained a propaganda façade; his influence over the course of events was more limited than advertised in his public image. In any case, he should be judged not by the criteria that have grown out of the secure and relatively well-ordered societies of Western Europe and the United States but by the cataclysmic conditions torturing his country during his formative years.

But what would happen when economic development reached a level of complexity that central planning could never match? Even more basically, what of the Stalinist system as a whole when the new external security achieved by Stalin permitted a gradual relaxation of the Stalinist controls and opened the country to Western values derived from far happier historical circumstances?

II

Stalin's successors continued the problematical experiment of trying to transform the peoples of Soviet Eurasia into citizens capable of outperforming their Western prototypes. Firm believers in the correctness of their Marxist-Leninist vision of history, they recognized the continuing weaknesses of their country. Yet they benefited from its new external security, which allowed them to retreat from Stalin's inhuman expediency. Stalin had prepared the way for gradual de-Stalinization.

Nikita Khrushchev, an impetuously energetic patriot of peasant origin who rose to power without embittered controversy, was eager to bring the government closer to the people. He changed the official label of the Soviet state from the "dictatorship of the proletariat" into "the state of all the people," renewing the promise of democracy. Sensitive to the human damage caused by Stalin's terror, he virtually dismantled the apparatus of mass terror. The "thaw" in Stalinist oppression brought a touch of openness into Soviet life, for the first time permitting eye-opening accounts of Stalin's Gulag. Privileged Russians were allowed a glimpse of the West; Khrushchev himself visited the United States, in line with his advice (of 1956) that "we must study the capitalist economy attentively . . . study the best that the capitalist countries' science and technology have to offer in order to use the achievements of world technological progress in the interests of socialism."

He also worked toward consolidating the Soviet security in the cold war by proclaiming "peaceful coexistence" with the United States. At the same time he cultivated the popularity of the Soviet model among the newly decolonized countries of Asia and Africa. In these years the Soviet Union fully emerged as a superpower, rivaling, at least superficially, the United States.

Always exuding confidence, Khrushchev even came to grips with Stalin's atrocities, the heaviest burden of the Stalinist heritage. In a secret speech (soon known worldwide) at the end of the 1956 party congress he ripped the propaganda façade from Stalin's image, revealing the dictator's ferocious cruelties to a shocked audience. A foretaste of Gorbachev's *glasnost*, this speech, so damaging to the Soviet reputation abroad and arousing the first domestic doubts about the Stalinist experiment, was delivered by the head of the Communist party eager to strengthen the party's credibility. Within two Eastern European satellite countries his speech set off anti-Soviet agitation. In Poland Khrushchev arranged a compromise with reformers representing the Polish workers. In Hungary, however, he bloodily suppressed, Stalin style, a national uprising that attempted to remove the country from Soviet domination.

The following year (1957) Khrushchev had cause for special confidence: the launching of *Sputnik*, the first artificial earth-circling satellite, and the American dismay over this Soviet triumph. This "majestic event in the epoch of building communism," followed by further first-time space exploits, boosted his Soviet utopianism sky high. Disregarding his earlier admiration for American science and technology he boasted to an American audience: "We will bury you." In 1959 he sponsored a seven-year economic plan designed for "the historic task of surpassing the most highly developed of the capitalist countries."

The East seemed to be overtaking the West when in 1961 Yuri Gagarin circled the earth in the Soviet space capsule *Vostok* (the East). In 1962 Khrushchev even claimed that "Soviet society is the most highly educated society in the world," predicting that by 1970 the Soviet Union would surpass "the strongest and richest capitalist country, the U.S.A. in per capita production." Carried away by his naïve vision of "scientific" socialism, he put all his cards on impressive industrial and technological advance, blind to the human and ecological consequences in the future. What counted was matching right away the pride underlying the Western sense of progress—let the Soviet people be prompted by a similar pride: "Consciousness of the grandeur of the tasks we pursue is multiplying the efforts of the Soviet people tenfold, causing them to be more exacting of themselves and more intolerant of shortcomings, stagnation, and inertia."

Since, unfortunately, that consciousness was missing, he continued to bombard his people with stern admonitions. "We must strive to accelerate technical progress. . . . We must advance along the entire front of cultural and social development." What was wanted, according to a detailed catechism in the party program that alluded to all the shortcomings of the Soviet people, was

> conscientious labor for the good of society—he who does not work, neither shall he eat; concern on the part of everyone for the preservation and growth of public wealth; a high sense of public duty, intolerance of actions harmful to the public interest; collectivism and comradely mutual assistance—one for all and all for one: humane relations and mutual respect between individuals—man is to man a friend, comrade and brother; honesty and truthfulness, moral purity, modesty and guilelessness in social and private life; mutual respect in the family, and concern for the raising of children; an uncompromising attitude to injustice, parasitism, dishonesty, and careerism.

These exhortations (still valid today) proved that the party was now diluting its Stalinism with moral preaching. But would such moralizing not discredit party practice?

Trapped between wildly unrealistic hopes and harsh realities, Khrushchev eventually became a liability to his more sober-minded advisers. In 1964 his colleagues in the Politburo ousted him for his "harebrained schemes" (one of them his failed attempt in 1962 to place Soviet nuclear missiles in Cuba). He retired in peace, taping his memoirs for publication abroad.

III

Fear of increased subversion by Western influence ended the "thaw" and stopped economic reforms. The threatening openness of the expanding globalism put a premium on stability as well as on technical competence in the Soviet leadership. These qualities were supplied by Khrushchev's successors, Alexei Kosygin, a modest, incorruptible technocrat, and Leonid Brezhnev, an administrator with impressive achievements in early Five Year Plans, the war, and the development of the Soviet space center in Kazakhstan. They worked together as a team, although Brezhnev soon overshadowed his colleague, shaping the character of the next 18 years. Both stressed scientific management and pragmatism, further downgrading Stalinist harshness while trying to advance the Stalinist experiment along its ideological guidelines. As Brezhnev observed in 1976: "Capitalism is a society without a future"; socialism was "the most dynamic force in the world." He could cite encouraging evidence, indicating yet greater external security for his country.

By the mid-1970s the Soviet Union had achieved a rough balance in nuclear weapons with the United States, a country weakened by its unsuccessful war in Vietnam and therefore ready for better relations with its archenemy; in 1973 President Nixon, in an unprecedented visit, had gone to Moscow. In 1975 the Helsinki agreements had legalized Soviet domination of Eastern Europe, signifying a further relaxation of the cold war. At Helsinki the Soviet Union had even blandly agreed to open its borders to cultural exchanges and respect human rights—promises it could not possibly keep. Had not Brezhnev shown his true colors in 1968, when he used military force to crush a reform movement in Czechoslovakia designed to produce "socialism with a human face"? But he avoided bloodshed, unlike Khrushchev in Hungary 12 years earlier.

In any case, the country dared to open its windows to the outside world more than before, assessing through its diplomats and foreign-policy experts the new globalism emanating foremost from the United States. Party members were allowed to travel abroad; Mikhail

Gorbachev, then a provincial official, freely toured France in 1966 and Italy in the following year, accompanied by his wife. In need of access to Western technology, to foreign grain in case of domestic crop failures, and to markets for Soviet oil, the Brezhnev government cautiously tied the Soviet economy to the world market. Eager to win Western goodwill, it even allowed a trickle of Jewish emigration.

At the same time a new sense of satisfaction emerged at home. The Soviet Union was the largest producer in the world of electricity, coal, oil, steel, and cement. Living conditions had markedly improved for the rapidly growing population (approaching 286 million in the 1980s, slightly more than half of them ethnic Russians). Education had produced both widespread literacy and outstanding scientists; health services had sharply reduced mortality rates; a predominantly rural society had been widely urbanized. The Stalinist command economy was slightly relaxed in the spirit of the New Economic Policy as practiced in the 1920s. Stability and economic security prevailed; the common people had enough to eat; all could now talk more freely with each other. Pruned of its grossest inhumanities, the Stalinist experiment was succeeding, at least when viewed from within Soviet perspectives. Outspoken dissent was kept under control; the most threatening critics (like Solzhenitsyn) were exiled abroad. The Soviet leadership relaxed; Brezhnev certainly deserved a restful conclusion to his strenuous career. And the Soviet peoples enjoyed a civilizing moment of calm after decades of dehumanizing change.

But, as it turned out, the seeming success of the Soviet experiment in the mid-1970s created the crisis that led to its downfall. The new confidence and relative well-being undermined the selfless dedication that once had sparked the undeniable progress. After 60 years of unparalleled deprivation and excruciating effort, moral and physical exhaustion crept into the system. Corruption reached even into the Brezhnev family. Drunkenness, slackness at work, and political lassitude—old habits reinforced by the passivity resulting from automatic obedience to harsh commands—began to pervade Soviet society. As Brezhnev himself observed, there was too much "money-grubbing, hooliganism, private ownership tendencies, red tape, and indifference." An unofficial "second economy"—the black market—flourished, as did an informal uncontrolled public opinion; people now whispered that Marxism-Leninism "tastes like stale bread." Not surprisingly, the superficial smugness of the Brezhnev era led from stagnation to economic decline, a development especially distressing to loyal communists who dared to look abroad.

The new outreach to the world encouraged invidious comparison. Any realistic assessment of Western capitalism was bound to show up the bottomless weaknesses of Soviet socialism and even discredit the entire experiment of compulsory reculturation; socialism, after all, was not the most dynamic force in the world. In 1978 the top Soviet diplomat, Under Secretary General of the United Nations Arkady Shevchenko, dramatically defected; he had come to look at his country through Western eyes. How were responsible Soviet leaders to react in the face of that relentless threat to their creed, their form of government, and the loyalty of their peoples? How were they going to cope with the escalating costs of the arms race which hurt the rising expectations of Soviet consumers? These questions became acute after Brezhnev, long incapacitated by illness, died in 1982.

Brezhnev's two short-lived successors were both old men. The first, Yuri Andropov, was inclined toward reform but too ill for decisive action. The second, Konstantin Chernenko, was a devoted Brezhnevite. Both stood by Brezhnev's decision, optimistically taken in 1979, to invade Afghanistan for the purpose of propping up a pro-Soviet regime. But both warned that developed socialism as promised by Lenin was a long way off.

Meanwhile a new generation of intellectuals more tuned to the world made its influence felt in society and the party. Looking around the world, they openly admitted their country's increasing backwardness. Their opportunity struck when in 1985 the competing factions in the Politburo elected Mikhail Sergeyevich Gorbachev secretary general of the Communist party. With his rise to leadership over half a century of Stalinism came to an end. A new era began in the Soviet Union, its effects felt far beyond the Soviet borders.

Gorbachev: From High Hopes to the Bitter End

I

Born in 1931, Mikhail Sergeyevich Gorbachev was a privileged product of the Stalinist experiment, growing up among collective farmers in the out-of-the-way Stavropol area north of the Caucasus. A grandfather was sent for a time to the Gulag; the Germans briefly and relatively peacefully occupied Stavropol. Protected by his family, he himself escaped physical and psychological harm. A promising and ambitious student, he went to Moscow University in 1950, studying law and reading Western political theory; before graduating he married a bright fellow student, Raisa Maximovna, who ever thereafter worked with his as his teammate. Back in Stavropol he became a hard-working successful party official in charge of agriculture, eventually rising to the position of local party secretary. Markedly ambitious yet never arrogant, he cleverly adjusted to the politics of the times, praising in turn Stalin, Khrushchev, and Brezhnev, keeping his own critical judgment while advancing his political career.

His unusual qualities aroused the interest of high party officials, who called him to Moscow in 1978 as a secretary of the Central Committee, a vantage point providing him with vital opportunities. In 1983 he spent some time in Canada, briefed about world conditions by the Soviet ambassador, Alexandr Yakovlev, who for a time became his closest adviser. In December of the following year he visited England, where Margaret Thatcher described him as "a man I could do business with." Gorbachev entered the political stage as a civilized Russian Communist

in stark contrast by temperament and political style to Stalin, a beneficiary of his system yet also, in greatly changed times, its gravedigger.

Assessing his country's condition as the newly appointed general secretary of the Communist party, he privately agreed that "everything is
rotten through and through." Or, as he publicly explained more forcefully in 1991, the country was "in danger of ending up on the sidelines of
historical progress, not only in technological respects but also in the
social area"; it was "rolling toward ruin." What had become of Soviet
Socialist superiority?

II

An objective look around the world in 1985 would indeed indicate a
remarkable advance in "historical progress," inexplicable by Marxist-
Leninist theory. Compared with the tensions leading up to World War I
and the furies released by that war, which had shaped Lenin's and
Stalin's brutal policies, the decades after World War II witnessed a
major leap toward international cooperation. The North Atlantic Treaty
Organization allied Western Europe with North America; the United
Nations extended its agencies around the world; in the Far East Japan
rose to economic prominence, leading the "Little Dragons" of the Pacific
rim. These developments built a non-Communist globalism responsible
for an unprecedented improvement in material well-being. In the field of
technology, computerization and telecommunications were daily producing new triumphs, refining industrial productivity and advancing worldwide interdependence. The prosperity of Western Europe, North
America, and the leading countries of East Asia, based essentially on
free enterprise, was impressing people around the world. Despite defeat
in Vietnam, the economic, political, and cultural influence of the United
States had grown to new heights, radiating, with the new intensity of
modern communications, its ideals of freedom, democracy, and human
rights (all assisted by affluence) deep into the Soviet Union.

Yet the new era had brought one crucial benefit to the Soviet Union.
Its rise to superpower status and the balance of nuclear weapons—all
premised on Stalin's policies—provided his country with unprecedented
external security. This fact eliminated the major cause of the defensive
ferocity built into the Soviet system; the threat of foreign conquest was
gone. Gorbachev's reforms would have been unthinkable without this
major turn in his country's fortunes. But, alas, "historical progress" perpetuated the old insecurity in a new form.

"We are not encircled by superior armies," he said in 1986, "but by superior economies." The declining Soviet economy could not meet both the rising costs of the nuclear arms race escalated by President Reagan's denunciation of the Soviet Union as "the evil empire" and the rising expectations of Soviet consumers no longer isolated from the world; the Soviet people's poverty stood out even more alarmingly. While more secure, the country had become more vulnerable in the merciless power politics of invidious comparison. "Superior economies" and "historical progress" generally undermined the loyalty of its peoples to the Communist ideal, or to any regime that could not live up to its promise of a better life. Here lay a source of endless misery.

What remedies then did Gorbachev, a devoted Soviet patriot prompted by "historical progress" in the world, offer his beleaguered country?

III

Like all ambitious political leaders in the twentieth century, he framed his vision in global terms. He saw "a new world civilization developing since 1945" dedicated to peace and the improvement of the human condition everywhere with due care for the natural environment. In a characteristically non-Marxist formula called "New Thinking," Gorbachev linked his country's self-interest to the fear of nuclear holocaust widespread in the West. He frankly admitted, "We need normal international relations for our internal progress. . . . We want a world free of war, without arms races, nuclear weapons and violence."

Trying to restore his country's fading prestige with a new universal mission, Gorbachev worked heroically for peace. He needed to win international goodwill as the crucial precondition for recasting the Soviet system. Promoting "the deideologicalization" of international relations, he announced that "we do not claim to teach others"; the Soviet Union was no longer exporting revolution. Communist planning likewise had lost its appeal in most Third World countries. Down came the pretentious Soviet model for the world's future. Down came also Soviet territorial power, as Gorbachev recalled the Soviet army from Afghanistan and, more dramatically, in 1989 permitted the peaceful anti-Communist revolutions of Eastern Europe. In the following year he even agreed to the reunification of Germany, thereby strengthening NATO. All along he agitated for curtailing the arms race, especially in regard to nuclear weapons, taking the initiative in reducing the Soviet armed forces.

What breathtaking moves! For the sake of promoting internal progress and earning foreign goodwill Gorbachev took an initiative for unilateral political and psychological disarmament utterly without parallel in history. Abandoning not only Stalin's postwar expansion into Central Europe but also Lenin's advocacy of world revolution, he virtually gave up both the tsarist and Soviet claims to indigenous superiority that had long served as defense against subversive foreign influence. Picking up a phrase from de Gaulle, he humbly talked of integrating his country into "a common European home reaching from the Urals to the Atlantic" (disregarding the Asian half of his country). In the same spirit he welcomed the "unprecedented richness of foreign contacts," which provided an opportunity "to know and understand the world better and to construct our policy accordingly"—at the price of profound cultural disorientation among his people.

For better or worse, the country had never been so wide open to the Western impact; indeed, it had never so drastically surrendered its cultural sovereignty. By its huge size and its nuclear arsenal, it still commanded respect in the world, one reason why hardened anti-Communists remained unconvinced of Gorbachev's peaceful intentions. But realists in Europe and North America heaved a sigh of relief. To judge by his actions and statements, the Soviet Union had repudiated its ambition as a superpower. The 70-year-long, world-spanning ideological and political competition between Soviet communism and Western capitalism had ended in a resounding Western victory. Not surprisingly, the head of the Soviet Communist party was suddenly the most popular figure in capitalist countries. In December 1990 "Gorby" (as he was affectionately nicknamed in the West) was awarded the Nobel Peace Prize.

IV

At home meanwhile he directed the risky experiment of *perestroika* (restructuring). The essence of *perestroika*, restated over time with increasing urgency through the new medium of television, was simple. It started from the recognition, plainly expressed in February 1986, that "sluggishness, ossification in the forms and methods of management" had led to decreased dynamism at work and to rigid bureaucratism. As a result, the Soviet system "lagged behind the demands of the times . . . the political economy of socialism is stuck with outdated concepts and . . . no longer in tune with the dialectics of life." In order to reverse that fatal trend and realign the Soviet Union with "historical progress," "a genuine revolutionary transformation" of society, however difficult, had to be undertaken. Thus in high hopes began the reforms that ended in the collapse of the Soviet Union.

The reforms were to stimulate the initiative and creativity of the masses at the grassroots level. They called for no less than restructuring the people's consciousness and psychology by elevating "the individual spiritually, respecting his inner world, and giving him moral strength" and personal dignity. The "Stalinist model [was to be] replaced by a civil society of free people."

In addition, the revolutionary transformation required a new openness of public discussion called *glasnost*: "Communists always need the truth"—the truth made accessible by "a real pluralism of opinions, an open comparison of opinions and interests." But in allowing the truth to surface did Gorbachev know that he was playing with fire? Blinded by his Communist upbringing, he seemed to be unaware of the hidden resentment among the Soviet peoples that *glasnost* was bound to mobilize. He and his advisers certainly underestimated the ethnic and national rebelliousness widespread in the country.

The changes Gorbachev envisaged added up to more democracy (Soviet rather than Western bourgeois style): "Democracy is the wholesome and pure air without which the socialist social organization cannot lead a full life." Even more intensively, Gorbachev called for more socialism, a socialism cast in a highly Westernized form. "More socialism means a more dynamic pace and creative endeavor, more organization, law, and order, more scientific methods and initiative in economic management, efficiency in administration, and a better and materially richer life for the people." As he said in September 1990, *perestroika* rejected "the administrative command system that was forcibly imposed on our society. We must not draw people by force into new forms of economic life." But would the people be able to change their ways voluntarily?

Those new forms of economic life, constituting the culminating innovation of *perestroika*, were to be shaped by a socialist market economy stimulated by competition between people working together with socialist awareness in cooperatives and collective enterprises. Under the slogans of "destatization" and "demonopolization," major industries were to be given a free hand to operate in pursuit of profit, with private property playing a new but still limited role; economic incentives were to stimulate individual effort within a society dedicated to the welfare of all its members. In short, the people themselves, acting with newly revived social responsibility, had to build the foundations of an up-to-date economy that would in the foreseeable future "saturate the market with goods and services"—the brightest light in Gorbachev's promise. In his optimistic vision, the Soviet Union would soon match Western societies at their best. Reality, however, proved to be otherwise.

V

Gorbachev's reforms were hampered from the start by the inherent contradictions that had long plagued the Soviet rulers. Their Marxist ideology idealized the creativity of the proletariat, their hope for the future. Yet the Soviet system by necessity had employed compulsion and terror in order to make the working masses live up to the ideological promise. The Leninist cliché of "democratic centralism," still employed by Gorbachev, cleverly covered up the contradiction between central control and popular initiative, but offered no practical solution; Gorbachev remained trapped, often taking refuge in vague phraseology.

His positive view of the human raw material with which he had to work clashed with his realistic assessment of its true nature. He praised the creativity of the masses and their sense of social justice, arguing that "socialism is ingrained, ingrained in the people, in all of us." Given their opportunity, "the people will work things out by themselves." Yet, assessing the resistance he encountered, he also admitted that "we lack a political culture." He observed widespread "departmentalism," "parochialism," and a habit of dividing people and issues into either black or white. Obviously, Gorbachev himself wondered if the people were prepared to support, let alone lead, *perestroika*. Sometimes he reverted to the moral admonitions familiar in Soviet indoctrination, although never as preachily as in Khrushchev's times: "*Perestroika* requires greater . . . conscious discipline of citizens." Vain hopes!

The conflict between vision and reality showed up most glaringly in his early effort to suppress rampant alcoholism. In 1986 he boasted that "the working people constantly remind us of the need to intensify our efforts to combat this evil." By 1989 it was obvious that the working people had defied his curtailment of liquor production by distilling their own brew, causing a sugar shortage and inflicting embarrassing losses on the government budget (previously balanced by liquor taxes). His anti-alcohol drive was cancelled; the working people had let him down.

This setback indicated quite early the obstacles Gorbachev was to encounter in his desire to adjust his people to "historical progress" by persuading them "to work things out by themselves." Letting people learn new ways, however, required political stability over a long period of trial and error. Unfortunately such lead time did not exist. Taking advantage of their new freedom the people began to assert their traditional divisive spontaneity; the artificially imposed Communist consensus disintegrated. What Gorbachev had planned as a controlled process of modernizing the Soviet Union turned into an elemental drift toward its dissolution.

VI

The reduction of government controls and the decline in living standards combined with the massive opening of Soviet society to Western ideals and ways of life set off a flood of conflicting public responses. Among intellectuals and the younger generation around the country, freedom and democracy inspired visions of a better life; private enterprise was to revive the economy. Liberated at last, the people could join "historical progress" and escape the humiliation of living under a discredited political order. The pent-up anger turned furiously against the Soviet past, revealing its lies, inefficiencies, and brutalities against human beings and the environment. Sacred symbols of Stalinism came tumbling down; cities renamed after prominent Communists resumed their original names; the tsarist heritage was idealized.

The new mood soon raised to prominence new political leaders impatiently pressing for radical democratization and a market economy. Its spokesmen included Gavril Popov, the mayor of Moscow, and Anatoly Sobchak, the mayor of Leningrad (renamed St. Petersburg in 1991). Its most popular hero was Boris Yeltsin, a temperamental open-minded populist who knew how to tap the pro-Western sentiments among young Russians; he often contradicted Gorbachev, attacking his policies. Unfortunately the transmission of Western ideals into the Soviet Union did not guarantee their political effectiveness. The lack of practical experience combined with the brittleness of Russian spontaneity prevented the formation of an effective party organization after the democratic victories in Moscow and (what then was still) Leningrad. And in the absence of a working consensus, Yeltsin and other democratic leaders were driven, by temperament and the pressure for quick decisions, to turn authoritarian—without, however, changing their pro-democracy convictions, which were loudly cheered by the Western media.

On the opposite side of the political spectrum the Communist hardliners, afraid of losing their power and privileges, deplored Gorbachev's surrender of their country's control over Eastern Europe and cited the growing disarray in Soviet society; they dreaded the collapse of the Soviet Union. Counting on support from the armed forces, the KGB, and some layers of public opinion, they sabotaged Gorbachev's reforms, ready to stage an armed uprising when the opportunity came. Yet they lacked both effective leadership and the zest of "political progress." Communism had lost its universal appeal; Communist party membership sharply declined. In their opposition to *perestroika* the hardliners, however, could tap the newly revived anti-Western gut reaction in Russian nationalism, including its anti-Semitism. But their strongest appeal lay in the deep-seated popular desire for stability; temptation beckoned to seize power in the face of public apathy. Ordinary people were hardly ready to face the harrowing uncertainties opened up by Gorbachev's reforms.

The bulk of the Soviet masses—and the older generation foremost—felt uneasily suspended between the political extremes. Pleased to be released from official restraints, they yet lacked the self-reliance, energy, and knowledge necessary for coping with the challenges of democratic government and free enterprise. Their revived interest in religion—Raisa Gorbachev was a prominent figure at the celebration of the Russian Orthodox Church's millennial anniversary in 1988—hardly prepared them for active citizenship; the Orthodox Church has little tradition of social outreach. Resentment of money-grubbing entrepreneurs was widespread; many people still preferred the economic equality advocated by socialism. They also were suspicious of foreigners and their alien ways, with some justification. The rampant Western influence promoted sexual license, illicit drugs, and irresponsible consumerism. As social controls relaxed, crime and violence increased, stirring the wolfish underside of Soviet life. At a time when Gorbachev's reforms demanded widened perspectives and enlarged social responsibility, the daily hardship of making ends meet contracted individual awareness and deepened traditional divisiveness. Gorbachev himself commented on "a more or less pronounced discrepancy between the vital interests of society . . . and the immediate day-to-day interests of the people."

Perestroika, furthermore, accelerated the economic decline started in Brezhnev's times. The progressing cultural disorientation was accompanied by economic deterioration. The dismantling of the planned economy in favor of a market economy was a highly complex and painfully protracted task causing endless administrative and economic problems. The old officials were still in place, resisting the growth of the private sector. In order to maintain public confidence and raise incomes,

Gorbachev ordered even more money to be printed. As a result, inflation soared, productivity slumped further, goods disappeared from the stores, the black market flourished more than ever. People had to forage for themselves, as did individual enterprises, local communities, cities, and even the Union republics. The economic interdependence built up under soviet rule was endangered. Worse, *perestroika's* promise of a better life proved to be empty.

The biggest threat to the cohesion of the multinational and multiethnic Soviet Union resulted from the explosion of nationalism incited by the ideal of freedom. Freedom meant self-determination to all the non-Russian minorities in the Soviet state, which had consistently down-graded national or ethnic identity in favor of the mythical unity of the universal working class. *Perestroika* inflamed the desire for recognition and even independence, foremost in the Baltic republics led by Lithuania, and spreading to the border republics along the western and southern rim of the Soviet Union into Central Asia, whose Muslims are tied into the Islamic world. And at the center, the Russian Republic, the biggest, richest, and most populous in the Union, elected its own parliament, which in May 1990 chose Yeltsin, now a powerful rival to Gorbachev, as its president, and in June declared itself a sovereign state. Soviet constitutions had always guaranteed the sovereignty of the Union republics, but only in words; now at last it was to be made real.

Unfortunately, no cohesive national territories exist anywhere in the open spaces of Eurasia; boundaries are in dispute, ethnic enclaves dot the landscape. Encouraged by *perestroika*, ethnic and national conflict surged, leading to bloody confrontations in Kazakhstan, Azerbaijan, Armenia, and Georgia. Some observers in Moscow mockingly spoke of the "Lebanonization" of the Soviet Union; others drew parallels with the dissolution of the Russian Empire after World War I (unfairly disregarding the country's current external security). Radical democrats welcomed the extension of their ideals to all of Soviet Eurasia. But how could the divergent local interests, ancient animosities, and the imbalance in size and strength be harmonized with the need to preserve an effective center capable of ensuring the security and welfare of the entire area?

What then about Gorbachev's mission to align his country with "historical progress"?

VII

Unaware, like other communist leaders in the Soviet bloc, of the depth of public resentment, Gorbachev yet recognized the hurdles that blocked *perestroika*. His chief concern in trying to overcome them was to hold his country together by sticking to a middle ground between the political extremes. He started his reforms slowly, avoiding any sharp break with the past and willing to learn from experience. All along he was guided by a cautious pragmatism in trying to let the mass of people adjust gradually to the drastic reforms he proposed, hoping that in time a supporting consensus would energy. He wanted to promote social awareness, continuing to use for that purpose the term "socialism" as part of his rhetoric.

This policy required cunning maneuvering between the Radical Democrats and the Communist hardliners. Sensing the popular reluctance to change, he restrained the impatience of Yeltsin and his advisers, although he still needed their support. On the other hand he catered to the party *apparatchiks*, calling himself a Communist as late as 1990; he tried to transform the party into the vanguard of *perestroika*. There was no time, however, to develop a firm, consensus-based middle ground; besides, his liberalized Leninism offered no effective unifying vision offsetting the subversive comparison with Western prosperity invited by *glasnost*. In April 1989 he casually admitted that he and his advisers did not really know the country in which they lived; he certainly did not grasp the explosive social and political dynamics set off by his reforms. Under the ever heavier burden of his mission his temperament flared; his manner became more dictatorial. His privileged lifestyle separated him from the common people. His popularity steadily declined.

Meanwhile, *perestroika* proceeded, troubled along the way by terrible catastrophes like the nuclear explosion at Chernobyl in 1986 and the Armenian earthquake in 1988, and by revolting revelations of past industrial disasters. Censorship was formally ended, Solzhenitsyn's *Gulag Archipelago* published, Andrei Sakharov (a famous scientist and bitter critic of human rights violations) recalled from internal exile and raised to prominence, emigration eased, and the circle of *perestroika* supporters in the top agencies of the government enlarged. At the same time, the rigidity of central planning was tentatively loosened and support given to small-scale cooperatives on the road to a market economy. More importantly, *perestroika* was promoting political pluralism. Beginning in 1988 reasonably open local elections with competing candidates were held, followed in March 1989 by the country-wide election, under rather complicated rules favoring the Communist party, of a Congress of Peoples Deputies. This large body in due time elected a Supreme Soviet, a smaller parliament, which in March 1990 chose Gorbachev as president of the Soviet Union.

Gorbachev now held double office as General Secretary of the Communist Party and executive head of a government that was no longer an agent of the party (which had fared badly in the elections and had suffered a special blow when, in late July 1990, Yeltsin and his closest allies publicly repudiated their party membership). In September Gorbachev was voted special emergency powers—he needed unassailable personal authority above public opinion and the party's Central Committee, in order to keep a measure of control amidst the mounting threats to his leadership and to his country's unity. There was talk, however, of a directly elected presidency once the crisis had passed.

VIII

In 1991 the crisis came to a head, upsetting Gorbachev's plans. He still basked in the global limelight, affirming the Soviet presence in world politics, negotiating with the United States the reduction of strategic nuclear weapons, and now beginning to ask for Western economic support. But at home dark thunderclouds gathered over his head. Apprehensive over the drift of events, Gorbachev started the year by leaning toward the hardliners, fighting against Lithuanian independence. Alarmed, Yeltsin demanded his resignation in February. They sharply disagreed over the rights to be given to the Union republics, Yeltsin favoring full sovereignty, Gorbachev protecting the powers of the Moscow center. In March a vaguely worded union-wide referendum was held, testing, in a touch of democracy, public support for continuing the union. The results were vaguely positive, but the drift toward devolving power to the republics continued. In April Gorbachev halfheartedly shifted again to the left; he and Yeltsin joined forces, encouraged by a huge demonstration in Moscow protesting an anticipated coup by party hardliners.

Meanwhile the country's economic condition worsened, causing a dispute over emergency measures. Gorbachev rejected the radical reform plan advanced by the Yeltsin faction. But even his own more moderate proposal called for a drastic break with the centrally planned economy and a positive move toward a full market economy. The key to remedying the failing economy lay in settling the relationship between the republics and the union. How much of the all-essential economic interdependence could be preserved? Without a stable political framework holding the union together that interdependence could not be safeguarded. Western statesmen, though supportive of Gorbachev, could not guarantee economic assistance unless that problem was resolved. In July, Gorbachev, supported by hardliners he had appointed to high positions, negotiated a union treaty with the secession-minded republics, trying to strike a balance between their desire for self-rule and the need for a common center. A treaty offering a reasonable compromise was to be signed on August 20.

IX

One day before, lightning struck. The hardliners on his staff, led by his vice president, deposed Gorbachev (who was on vacation in the Crimea) and declared a state of emergency. Their coup, counting on a favorable response from a public fed up with *perestroika's* empty promises and the country's disintegration, was poorly planned and carelessly executed. The military command was divided; the armed units sent to control Moscow were swayed by the upsurge of popular resistance. While the average Muscovite remained on the sidelines, the most Westernized segments of the population, young people and intellectuals, enthusiastically rushed out to defend Yeltsin, the coup's chief target. Thanks to them, the coup failed within three days. But its major and utterly unforeseen effect was to bring Gorbachev's reforms crashing down. Yeltsin, who had shown great courage during the coup, was the chief beneficiary. His vision of freedom, democracy, and the market economy Western style was winning—with unexpected consequences.

Within a week after Gorbachev's return to Moscow the coup had turned the drift toward dissolution started by *perestroika* into a headlong stampede. Gorbachev was right when he said that he faced "a different country." His constitutional authority was abolished (he himself publicly humiliated by Yeltsin), the Congress of Peoples Deputies adjourned, the Communist party suspended, and the Soviet Union doomed, as one Union republic after another moved toward independence.

Admittedly, there remained much unfinished business. The faltering Soviet Union still claimed command over the armed forces and their nuclear weapons remained scattered in several republics (a matter of grave concern to all Western countries). It also held the key to Eurasia's economic interdependence, which was to be preserved both for the benefit of the sovereign republics and for effective business relations with the outside world. Potential foreign donors of badly wanted economic aid pointedly demanded that there be a single currency, a central bank, a common trade policy, and a collective responsibility for the large Soviet debt.

Yet whatever the pressure for preserving the essentials of unity, the centrifugal drift intensified. A hurriedly formed interim government soon disintegrated, while Gorbachev continued his mission, vainly working for an eventual confederation guaranteeing continued unity in foreign policy, military affairs, and economic management. For a while he still represented the defunct Soviet Union abroad, trying to assert its presence as an agency for peace while soliciting economic aid for a former superpower that during his term of office had dwindled into an international charity case. But he and his work were now at the mercy of the republic's inexorable rush toward self-determination.

As the Soviet Union collapsed, its member republics (none of them yet governed democratically) asserted themselves, foremost the Russian Republic under Boris Yeltsin, by far the biggest and most powerful state. Following Russia's example, Ukrainians voted for separate statehood in early December, insisting on a separate Ukrainian army. But a few days later, in another major surprise, Ukraine together with the two other Slavic republics, Russia and Belarus (the former Byelorussia), formed a *sodruzhestvo*, a friendly association of independent states centered not in Moscow but in Minsk, the capital of Belarus. Inviting other republics to membership, that new "commonwealth" declared the Soviet Union dissolved while agreeing to take over—somehow—its major functions. Yet interrepublic cooperation still faced a highly uncertain future, as the other independent republics of the former Soviet Union (except Georgia and, of course, the now independent Baltic states) joined. Nuclear weapons were put under joint control, but all other issues, including all the unfinished business accumulated after the coup, were left unresolved. At any rate, on December 24, 1991, a cold gray day, the red flag of the Soviet Union with its symbolic hammer and sickle ceased flying over the Kremlin in Moscow, replaced without fanfare by the new white, blue, and red flag of the Russian Federated Republic. Yeltsin took over virtually all of Gorbachev's functions. As the Soviet Union was formally terminated, Gorbachev's extraordinary political career came to an end, quietly, in a world he had liberated from the dread of nuclear confrontation between two superpowers.

X

Whatever the coup's objectives on August 19, 1991, it had crushed not only the plotters' hopes, but also Gorbachev's promise. Even more important, it had pushed the country to an historical turning point: The ruthless ambition of tsars and Communists to provide Eurasia with political stability, economic growth, and a leading role in world affairs had suddenly collapsed into utter humiliation—an extraordinary event in human affairs.

Liberated at last from centuries of enforced unity, Eurasia's fate now hangs in the balance. Its territories are reasonably free from threats of military aggression, but its peoples face a bottomless crisis. As Yeltsin, the president of the Russian Republic, observed on October 18, "Under current conditions, one of the fundamental obstacles in the way of Russia's emergence from crisis is the lack of governability from top to bottom throughout the state." Deprived of a stable social, economic, and political framework, his people—and especially the younger generations—lack a firm sense of direction. Torn between incompatible convictions and hopes, and vulnerable as never before to the disorienting inroads from foreign cultures, they are threatened by endless social chaos. The wolftribe described by Solzhenitsyn rears its ugly head, freed now of all ideological restraint. Conditions in the other republics of Eurasia hardly offer more encouraging prospects.

Thus yet another formidable collective experiment has started. How, under vision-shrinking material and psychological hardship, is it possible to create in the multiethnic and multinational vastness of Eurasia a political and economic order capable of lifting its peoples out of their demeaning backwardness? (That backwardness, it is now admitted, has been aggravated over half a century by the Stalinist urge to manifest the superiority of Soviet Socialism at the expense of civil refinement and environmental protection.) What formerly had been attempted in relative isolation by compulsion and terror is now to be achieved by voluntary cooperation in an open and ever more competitive world. The unifying ideology of Marxism-Leninism has been defeated, replaced by the universal appeal of freedom, democracy, and national self-determination. Will these ideals bring peaceful cooperation in interdependence, or more misery, violence, authoritarianism, and even civil war? Comparing the hugeness of the task with the available human resources and the drift toward civic disintegration, one can understand both the gloom prevailing among Russian intellectuals in the aftermath of the coup and the worldwide apprehension over the collapse of the world's largest state.

T H I R T E E N

Summarizing
Reflections

I

Understanding the harrowing efforts of modern state building in the lands of the former Russian and Soviet Empire requires a broad-based comparative grasp of the long-range cultural dynamics at work in the West and the Eurasian East. These efforts were unprecedented experiments prompted by a portentous question: How, in the ever more intense worldwide competition for wealth and power, was it possible in the vast open lands of Eurasia to build a state capable of standing up to the countries of Western Europe and North America which set the model of progress? There existed no prior experience in history for such ambitious attempts to remold the social and political character of the human multitudes in the largest country in the world. Always in a hurry to overcome their country's inferiority, well-intentioned but ignorant and exceptionally vulnerable leaders had to improvise methods and policies for matching the standards set by alien models with the limited human and material resources at their disposal. Striving for independence, they were forever condemned to copy foreign ways.

Western Europe had set the model for the tsars since the early eighteenth century. At the beginning of the twentieth century Sergei Witte had pleaded for rapid industrialization: "international competition does not wait. . . . Our economic backwardness may lead to political and cultural backwardness as well." The backwardness revealed by the country's collapse at the end of World War I prompted Lenin's utopian ambition to surpass and overtake the victorious capitalist countries, among whom the United States took an ever more prominent role. In 1931 Stalin drove home Witte's point more drastically: "We are fifty or a hundred years behind the advanced countries. We must make good this distance in ten years. Either we do it or we shall be crushed." Ten years later Hitler invaded his country determined to crush it; thanks to Stalin (whatever his massive errors) and the heroism of his peoples he was thwarted.

Twenty-one years later (in 1962) Khrushchev overconfidently predicted that the Soviet Union would overtake the United States economically in ten years. But by 1985 Gorbachev realized that his country had fallen far behind; the foreign challenge was stronger than ever. In 1991 his short-lived experiment of aligning his country with "historical progress" had failed. Even worse: The Western ideals of freedom and democracy had destroyed the bonds holding the state of the tsars and the Soviets together. In the power politics of envious comparison—a force more potent than nuclear weapons—Western culture generalized as "historical progress" had triumphed.

Admittedly, the experiments had produced some positive results. Industrialization under the last tsar had advanced considerably—but had proved insufficient in World War I. The achievements of Soviet socialism, the dominant experiment, were more impressive. The Soviet Union had inspired ambitious leaders in the Third World; it had raised the level of education and public health; it had trained prominent scientists and developed the country's resources; it had sent the first man into space; it had posed for a time as a superpower—at the price of suppressing popular creativity. Yet by comparison with the advanced countries around the world, the traditional inferiority had not been overcome. Stalin's brutish experiment of planned imitation has been discredited; so has Gorbachev's civilized experiment of guided de-Stalinization. And the current experiment of state building in Eurasia, it is safe to say, will pass through lengthy and painful trials and errors before it can deliver the minimal comforts of the Brezhnev years. Why did the well-intentioned experiments of the past fail so miserably? Why are there such grim prospects for the experiment currently underway?

II

The answer, suggested throughout this essay, lies in the impossibility of transferring cultural achievements, especially human attitudes, values, and institutions, from one country (or group of closely related countries) to other, unprepared, countries. However attractive, Western ways do not fit into the Eurasian setting where their invisible foundations do not exist. The Stalinists tried to match Western power through the non-Western methods of compulsion. The current generation of pro-Western Russians strives to implement freedom and democracy, unable to muster the moral and social discipline that make these ideals work constructively. More broadly, Eurasians eager to modernize themselves copy the consumerist surface of Western life, ignorant of the hidden underpinnings that have shaped the Western ascendancy. If we are to achieve better insight into the impact of Western achievements on Eurasia, we have to probe into that elusive dimension of human activity and do so comparatively, looking at the privileged West and disadvantaged Eurasia from a transcendent common perspective.

Western culture extending from Western Europe to North America is the historical product of a unique cultural hothouse thanks to many favorable circumstances beyond human control. In western Europe geography provided easy communications in fertile lands. It favored close human interaction in small communities competing intensely for superiority in all aspects of life, yet united by common religious values that promoted a tight civic discipline. Ethnic diversity interacted with cultural and political unity within a well-balanced state system called, in the nineteenth century, the Concert of Europe. Competition, sweeping across the Atlantic to the opportunity-laden United States, spurred economic and technological progress based on individual enterprise endowed with a sense of social responsibility; capitalism had socialism built into its system. Vision-expanding good times, extensive individual responsibility, and social awareness made democracy possible. Democratic government combined with advanced technology in turn provided unprecedented strength in the bloody conflicts of international relations.

Western society, furthermore, was never threatened by foreign domination, never overshadowed by a superior alien model. Its peoples were free to refine their skills on their own. Competing with each other, they developed a creativity-promoting sense of confidence in their capacities: Who in the world could stand up against them? Admittedly, the heated competition was laced with much inhumanity. But increasing material security combined with the spiritual values of the Judeo-Christian tradition gradually promoted a remarkable respect for human life and dignity (now subject to profound challenges in our overpopulated, multicultural world).

The invisible, tight, and humane collectivism of Western society has enlarged the scope of human cooperation phenomenally. Individual survival and opportunity now depend on an endless chain of services provided by society. In this setting of civic interdependence individualism and individual freedom are premised on voluntary submission to the rules that make possible such extensive life-supporting dependence. Thanks to long conditioning, that submission has been built into the socialization process for the run of citizens, never perfectly, but sufficiently, so as to make society function in reasonable consensus. Countries that successfully follow the ideals of freedom and democracy benefit from the social discipline and wide-ranging human awareness anchored in the human subconscious. Elsewhere—as in Eurasia—these ideals lead to discord and anarchy, which in the past have been overcome by the artificial unity achieved by authoritarian command delivering the goods and services expected in modern society.

By contrast with the uniquely favored peoples of Western Europe and the settlers of North America, circumstances beyond human control have burdened Eurasia's inhabitants with endless hardships. Compared with the Western cultural hothouse, Eurasia is a frigid landmass. Warmed in the northwest by contact with Europe, it turns colder further east and southwest. In the chilling Eurasian politics of "conquer or be conquered," the Moscow-based Russians had gradually expanded their domination over the adjacent non-Russian peoples, including the Muslims of Central Asia; they turned Eurasia into the Russian Empire. Yet long distances, ethnic and religious diversity, poverty, and innumerable obstacles to communication prevented stimulating interaction and the rise of a viable polity. Under these adversities indigenous human creativity had been impressive. But for the run of people, energy was concentrated on physical survival; life always was cheap. Within a loose awareness of ethnic identity, human relations remained limited to family and village; no country-wide civic-mindedness emerged.

In this setting government was an oppressive alien force ruling the country, for 200 years after Peter the Great, from its extreme northwest corner. The tsars' efforts to Europeanize their state proceeded far over the heads of the common people. While posing as a major power in the European state system, the Russian Empire never enjoyed the Western freedom of cultural sovereignty. For the sake of keeping up with its Western rivals it was always driven to Westernize its peoples, enforcing alien ways on rebellious subjects—Soviet totalitarianism had its origins in tsarist times. Under these conditions ordinary people thought of freedom as an escape from an enforced citizenship that had no roots in local life.

At the same time an important minority of privileged and educated Russians was tuned to a different meaning of freedom, the civic freedom propagated by the French Revolution and subsequently embedded in the aims of both liberal and socialist democracy. Pitting a Western ideal against the government's efforts to hold the country together by compulsion, Western freedom was a relentlessly subversive force, causing political violence unknown in the West. The yearning for freedom toppled the tsarist regime in 1917, starting a more radical experiment of state building inspired by the vision of Marxist socialism. But, as this essay has shown, that experiment too was doomed to failure both by its ideology and by the adversities built into Eurasia.

III

What then, in the light of the cultural determinism here outlined, would be an enlightened prescription for state building in Eurasia? The most sensible answer to this question was suggested in 1951 by George Kennan, perhaps the wisest among American experts:

> Give them time; let them be Russians; let them work out their internal problems in their own manner. The ways by which people advance toward dignity and enlightenment in government are things that constitute the deepest and most intimate processes of national life. There is nothing less understandable to foreigners, nothing in which foreign influence can do less good.

What Kennan wrote applies now not only to the Russians but to all the peoples of Eurasia. Let all of them analyze their conditions with an honest nonideological realism and then work out, by trial and error, their own solutions to state building, in external security and reasonably free from the pressure of alien models. Let us Westerners help by scaling down the heightened expectations that we often so arrogantly promote among the Eurasian peoples; our own ways cannot be easily adapted to the adversities of Eurasia. Let us give material aid in a form suited to their circumstances and in a manner that does not diminish the self-confidence of the indigenous population. Let us contribute to their security from external attack and reduce worldwide the weapons of war. In addition, we should help repair, as part of the global concern for the environment, the ecological damage of their past ill-considered schemes of economic development. Equally important, let us stress, more consistently than under Stalin and Khrushchev, the Puritan qualities (including individual discipline) necessary for an effective society. Inevitably, Eurasia's future is set into uncertainties of the global context. Changing circumstances may reduce the magnetism of the Western model and thereby ease the indigenous feeling of backwardness. Leaving the peoples of Eurasia to their own creative initiative in linking their destiny to their common conditions will, it is hoped, lead to some form of effective cooperation among them in line with Gorbachev's work and vision. The peoples inhabiting the vast open spaces of Eurasia can prosper only if they recognize their interdependence; but interdependence can function only by agreement matching common responsibilities with freedom for local initiative. Human abilities and natural resources are sufficiently available. What the Russians and other Eurasian peoples lack is a unifying vision encouraging capacious perspectives, hard work, and the social skills of large-scale voluntary cooperation. Nurturing among them these advanced capacities means building a new political culture, which will take a long passage through harrowing experiences.

To end this essay with a moral plea: Let the privileged Westerners rise to a compassionate understanding of the human adversities caused in Eurasia by climate, geography, and history—by factors beyond human control. Let them treat with sympathy all experimental efforts to cope with these adversities. In this manner they will not only promote respect in the Eurasian lands for human rights and individual freedom, but also contribute to building common ground for peaceful cooperation in our globally interdependent world.

SUGGESTIONS FOR FURTHER READING

In case this essay should tempt readers into further study, the following books, chosen from a vast array of historical analyses and human recollections, may be of special interest. For perspectives on the twentieth century generally, one might consult P. Johnson, *Modern Times* (1983), P. Kennedy, *The Rise and Fall of the Great Powers* (1987), or my *The World Revolution of Westernization* (1987). The background of Russian history is well presented in J. H. Billington, *The Icon and the Axe* (1966) and N. A. Riasanovsky, *A History of Russia* (4th ed., 1992). As for the last decades of Tsarist Russia, *The Memoirs of Count Witte* (1921) is an interesting source; P. Miliukov's *Russia and Its Crisis* (1906) reflects the views of a historian who has lived through those years. H. Troyat examines *Daily Life in Russia under the Last Tsar* (1961), while T. G. Stavrou's *Russia under the Last Tsar* (1969) sums up major controversies that have arisen over the viability of the tsarist regime in the age of industrialism and mass politics. H. Rogger's *Russia in the Age of Modernization and Revolution, 1881–1917* (1983) presents a more recent survey of those seminal years. Two foreign diplomats present at the collapse of the tsarist regime have left their eyewitness accounts: M. Paléolgoue, *An Ambassador's Memoirs* (1924–1925), and his British colleague G. Buchanan, *My Mission to Russia* (1923).

As for the revolutionaries who toppled the tsarist regime, J. H. Billington's *Fire in the Minds of Men: Origins of the Revolutionary Faith* (1980) provides fascinating insights into their motivation. Lenin, of course, stands in the center of attention, and his writings are available in many English editions, of which R. C. Tucker's *The Lenin Anthology* (1975) is one of the handiest. But Lenin's key writings are also presented in R. V. Daniels, *A Documentary History of Communism* (1984), a highly useful sourcebook on communism generally. Lenin's life and work have been subject to innumerable studies. D. Treadgold's *Lenin and his Rivals; the Struggle for Russia's Future, 1898–1906* (1955) analyzes an early phase. For a complete account students might look at A. Ulam's *The Bolsheviks* (1965) or R. Conquest's *Lenin* (1972), or for a variety of interpretations in S. Page, ed., *Lenin, Dedicated Marxist or Revolutionary Pragmatist* (1977). Nina Tumarkin has traced Lenin's influence after his death in her book *Lenin Lives: The Lenin Cult in Soviet Russia* (1983). Trotsky, too, has received ample attention, foremost in I. Deutscher's three volumes: *The Prophet Armed: Trotsky 1879–1921* (1954); *The Prophet Unarmed: Trotsky 1921–1929* (1959); and *The Prophet Outcast: Trotsky 1929–1940* (1963). S. F. Cohen's *Bukharin and the Bolshevik Revolution, 1888–1938* (1980) deals with yet another important revolutionary. Further accounts of these revolutionaries are found in the innumerable works dealing with the Bolshevik Revolution.

For that crucial subject readers might first consult Trotksy's *History of the Russian Revolution* (1932), before looking at J. L. Keep's *The Russian Revolution: A Study in Mass Mobilization* (1976), or L. Shapiro's *The Russian Revolution of 1917* (1984); R. Medvedev's *The October Revolution* (1979) presents a contrasting interpretation by a Soviet dissident. A ground-floor closeup on 1917 is available in D. Mandel's two volumes, *Petrograd Workers* (1983–1984). Accounts by contemporary Russian observers are also worthy of attention: the liberal A. M. Kerensky's *Russia and History's Turning Point* (1965) and the anti-Bolshevik revolutionary N. Sukhanov's *The Russian Revolution of 1917* (1962). In this context George Kennan's essay, *Russia and The West under Lenin and Stalin* (1961), still deserves mention. For the human aspects of the revolution we need to go to the literary works: A. Tolstoy's *Road to Calvary* (1946), M. Sholokhov's *And Quiet Flows the Don* (1934) and *The Don Flows Home to the Sea* (1940), Maxim Gorky's *Untimely Thoughts; Essays on Revolution, Culture, and the Bolsheviks, 1917–1918* (1968), and above all B. Pasternak's *Doctor Zhivago* (1958).

As for Stalin, I would suggest R. C. Tucker's two volumes, *Stalin as Revolutionary, 1879–1929* (1973) and *Stalin in Power: The Revolution from Above 1929–1941* (1990), with a look at D. Volkogonov's *Stalin: Triumph and Tragedy* (1991). R. W. Davies, *The Industrialization of Soviet Russia* (1982, 1989) and Moshé Lewin, *Russian Peasants and Soviet Power; A Study of Collectivization* (1968) deal with the two most crucial aspects of the Stalin revolution. Lewin's book might be read alongside R. Conquest's heart-rending *The Harvest of Sorrow: Soviet Collectivization and the Terror-Famine* (1986). R. Medvedev's volumes *Let History Judge: The Origins and Consequences of Stalinism* (rev. ed., 1989), *On Stalin and Stalinism* (1979), and *All Stalin's Men* (1983) are also worth consulting, as is, for a whiff of Stalinism, the once official *History of the Communist Party of the Soviet Union; Short Course* (1939). Some human aspects of the early years of Stalin's dictatorship are well traced in A. Rybakov's novel *Children of the Arbat* (1988), while A. Solzhenitsyn has heroically recorded the suffering caused by Stalin's terror, first in *One Day in the Life of Ivan Denisovich* (1963), then in *Cancer Ward* (1968), and finally *The Gulag Archipelago* (1974–1976). The Soviet Union during World War II has been described in two volumes by J. Erickson, *The Road to Stalingrad: Stalin's War with Germany* (1984) and *The Road to Berlin* (1983); the battle of Stalingrad by V. Grossman in his novel *Life and Fate* (1985); and the siege of Leningrad by H. E. Salisbury, *The 900 Days: The Siege of Leningrad* (1969).

Among Stalin's heirs, Khrushchev comes to life in his autobiographical *Khrushchev Remembers: The Last Testament* (1974) and *Khrushchev Remembers: The Glasnost Tapes* (1990), while Brezhnev is dealt with more briefly in P. Murphy, *Brezhnev, Soviet Politician* (1980). Historical accounts linking Stalin and his successors include A. Nove, *Stalin and After* (1975) and S. Cohen et al., eds., *The Soviet Union Since Stalin* (1980). Tariq Ali has edited the most inclusive approach, *The Stalinist Legacy; Its Impact on Twentieth Century World Politics* (1984).

And now Gorbachev in his own words, *Perestroika: New Thinking for Our Country and the World* (1987), followed by a spate of Western analyses, such as Hedrick Smith's *The New Russians* (1990); D. Doder and L. Branson, *Gorbachev: Heretic in the Kremlin* (1990); M. Lewin, *The Gorbachev Phenomenon* (1991); and S. White, *Gorbachev in Power* (1991). M. Goldman analyzed the subject in *What Went Wrong with Perestroika* (1991). H. Goscila and B. Lindsay have edited *An Anthology of Russian Literature under Gorbachev* (1990), while J. Eisen compiled *The Glasnost Reader* (1990).

A few surveys and books on special topics may help to round out a reader's grasp of Soviet realities, for example, B. Kerblay, *Modern Soviet Society*, which begins with an excellent characterization of Eurasia's geographic conditions (a subject too often overlooked). V. Shlapenstokh has probed into *The Private Life of the Soviet People* (1989); A. Jones, W. D. Connor, and D. E. Powell have examined *Soviet Social Problems* (1991). Nationality problems are explored in H. R. Huttenbach, ed., *Soviet Nationality Policies; Ruling Ethnic Groups in the USSR* (1990), while T. Mamonova discusses the role of women in *Russian Women's Studies; Essays on Sexism in Soviet Culture* (1989). The painful vulnerability of a vital minority is explored in two books: L. Kochan, *The Jews in Soviet Russisince 1917* (1978), and B. Pinkus, *The Jews of the Soviet Union* (1984). And finally, for a taste of Russian literature, it is worth dipping into *The Portable Twentieth Century Russian Reader*, edited by C. Brown (1985).

Periodicals. The most direct access to Soviet reality is provided by the weekly *Current Digest of the Post-Soviet Press.* Relevant articles and book reviews are found in the *Slavic Review* and the *Russian Review. Problems of Communism* and *The USSR Today* also offer useful information. The *New York Review of Books* frequently carries articles and reviews of books that may help readers follow the bewildering course of events, as does *Current History.*

INDEX